Raspberry Pi Cookbook for Python Programmers

Over 50 easy-to-comprehend tailor-made recipes to get the most out of the Raspberry Pi and unleash its huge potential using Python

Tim Cox

PUBLISHING

BIRMINGHAM - MUMBAI

Raspberry Pi Cookbook for Python Programmers

First published: April 2014

Production Reference: 2230414

Published by Packt Publishing Ltd.
Livery Place
35 Livery Street
Birmingham B3 2PB, UK.

ISBN 978-1-84969-662-3

www.packtpub.com

Cover Image by Darren Brindley (darrenbrindleyphotography@gmail.com)

Credits

Author
Tim Cox

Reviewers
Colin Deady

Ian McAlpine

Acquisition Editors
Pramila Balan

Luke Presland

Rebecca Pedley

Content Development Editor
Arvind Koul

Technical Editors
Shubhangi H. Dhamgaye

Novina Kewalramani

Rohit Kumar Singh

Pratish Soman

Copy Editors
Janbal Dharmaraj

Insiya Morbiwala

Aditya Nair

Karuna Narayanan

Project Coordinator
Wendell Palmer

Proofreaders
Simran Bhogal

Kirsty Cox

Maria Gould

Ameesha Green

Paul Hindle

Indexer
Tejal Soni

Graphics
Ronak Dhruv

Yuvraj Mannari

Abhinash Sahu

Production Coordinator
Aparna Bhagat

Cover Work
Aparna Bhagat

About the Author

Tim Cox lives in England with his wife and two young daughters and works as a software engineer. His passion for programming can be traced back to one Christmas in the mid 1980s when he received a Sinclair Spectrum 48k+ home computer (a joint present with his two elder brothers). By typing out and modifying BASIC programs, while dreaming about building robots, an interest in computers and electronics was sparked, which has never faded. This interest saw him through university, where he earned a BEng in Electronics and Electrical Engineering, and into a career in developing embedded software for a wide range of applications, for automotive, aerospace, and the oil industry, among others.

Keen to support the vision behind the Raspberry Pi, reignite engineering in schools, and encourage a new generation of engineers, Tim co-founded the MagPi magazine. Thanks to the dedication and time of the volunteers who contribute to it every month, it continues to have monthly issues and attract an ever-increasing number of readers (and writers) worldwide. Through his site `PiHardware.com`, Tim produces electronic kits and helps people learn about the Raspberry Pi and hardware interfacing; each of them is supported with detailed instructions and tutorials to help novices build the knowledge and skills for their projects.

This is Tim's first ever book; it mirrors his own experience of discovering the Raspberry Pi and showcasing its fantastic abilities.

Writing a book about the Raspberry Pi wouldn't have been possible without the creation itself, so thanks to the Raspberry Pi foundation for their hard work (and good humor) in making it a huge success. The Raspberry Pi community consists of an excellent group of exceptionally helpful people from all over the world, and it has been a pleasure to be involved with it from the start. In particular, I would like to thank The MagPi team that has supported me by reviewing the chapters and helping me achieve the best possible standard. Also thanks to the Pi3D team who worked hard to get their library running with Python 3 for the book.

Thanks to my family, particularly my wife Kirsty, who has supported me every step of the way and daily suffered my obsession with the Raspberry Pi. The excitement my daughters, Phoebe and Amelia, have as they discover new things inspires me to share and teach as much as I can.

About the Reviewers

Colin Deady started his career in IT in the late 1990s when he discovered software testing. By now he had already fallen in love with computers, thanks to his parents buying him and his brother ZX81 and ZX Spectrum+ home computers in the 1980s. He graduated to the Amiga 1200 in the early 1990s and spent countless hours learning the insides of the operating system. Now with 14 years' experience in testing, he works as a test manager with an emphasis on test automation and extolls the virtues of Agile using Kanban and behavior-driven development to great effect. (Test early, test often; fix early, fix often.)

In his spare time, Colin is part of the editorial team for The MagPi (www.themagpi.com), a community-written magazine for the Raspberry Pi. With several published articles and having reviewed and edited many more, he has built up extensive knowledge of this tiny platform. He can also be found jointly running The MagPi stand at regular Bristol DigiMakers events in the UK, demonstrating projects such as a remote control robot arm, a roverbot, and LED display boards, all of which he has programmed in Python.

He currently runs a blog related to the Raspberry Pi at www.rasptut.co.uk.

Ian McAlpine was first introduced to computers with his school's Research Machines RML-380Z and his Physics teacher's Compukit UK101 microcomputer. This was followed by a Sinclair ZX81 home computer and then a BBC Micro Model A microcomputer, which he still has to this day. His interest in computers resulted in him acquiring an MEng in Electronic Systems Engineering from Aston University and an MSc in Information Technology from the University of Liverpool. Ian currently works as a senior product owner at SAP Canada.

Being introduced to the Raspberry Pi not only rekindled his desire to "tinker", but also provided him with an opportunity to give back to the community. Consequently, Ian is a very active member of the editorial team for The MagPi, a monthly magazine for the Raspberry Pi, which you can read online or download for free from www.themagpi.com.

I would like to thank my darling wife, Louise, and my awesome kids, Emily and Molly, for their patience and support.

www.PacktPub.com

Support files, eBooks, discount offers and more

You might want to visit www.PacktPub.com for support files and downloads related to your book.

Did you know that Packt offers eBook versions of every book published, with PDF and ePub files available? You can upgrade to the eBook version at www.PacktPub.com and as a print book customer, you are entitled to a discount on the eBook copy. Get in touch with us at service@packtpub.com for more details.

At www.PacktPub.com, you can also read a collection of free technical articles, sign up for a range of free newsletters and receive exclusive discounts and offers on Packt books and eBooks.

 PACKTLiB™

http://PacktLib.PacktPub.com

Do you need instant solutions to your IT questions? PacktLib is Packt's online digital book library. Here, you can access, read and search across Packt's entire library of books.

Why Subscribe?

- ▶ Fully searchable across every book published by Packt
- ▶ Copy and paste, print and bookmark content
- ▶ On demand and accessible via web browser

Free Access for Packt account holders

If you have an account with Packt at www.PacktPub.com, you can use this to access PacktLib today and view nine entirely free books. Simply use your login credentials for immediate access.

Table of Contents

Preface

Since the release of the Raspberry Pi computer in February 2012, hundreds of thousands of people have been introduced to a new way of computing. Modern home computers, tablets, and phones are typically focused on providing content to the user to consume, either as a passive viewer or through basic interaction via games and activities.

However, the Raspberry Pi turns this concept on its head. The idea is that the user provides the input and the imagination, and the Raspberry Pi becomes an extension of their creativity. The Raspberry Pi provides a simple, low-cost platform that you can use to experiment with and play with your own ideas. It won't feed you information; it will let you discover it firsthand.

This book takes everything I have found exciting and interesting with the Raspberry Pi and puts it in an easy-to-follow format.

I hope that people will read this book and start their own Raspberry Pi journey; it has so much to offer, and the book is aimed squarely at showing off what *you* can achieve with it.

Like any good cookbook, the pages should be worn and used, and it should be something that is always being pulled off the shelf to refer to. I hope it will become your own, personal, go-to reference.

What this book covers

Chapter 1, Getting Started with a Raspberry Pi Computer, introduces the Raspberry Pi and explores the various ways that it can be set up and used, including how it can be used on a network and connected to remotely with another computer.

Chapter 2, Starting with Python Strings, Files, and Menus, guides us on how to take our first steps using Python 3, start with the basics, manipulate text, use files, and create menus to run our programs.

Chapter 3, Using Python for Automation and Productivity, explains the use of graphical user interfaces to create our own applications and utilities.

Chapter 4, Creating Games and Graphics, explains how to create a drawing application and graphical games using the Tkinter Canvas.

Chapter 5, Creating 3D Graphics, discusses how we can use the hidden power of the Raspberry Pi's graphical processing unit to learn about 3D graphics and landscapes and produce our very own 3D maze for exploration.

Chapter 6, Using Python to Drive Hardware, establishes the fact that to experience the Raspberry Pi at its best, we really have to use it with our own electronics. It discusses how to create circuits with LEDs and switches, and use them to indicate the system status and provide control. Finally, it shows us how to create our own game controller and light display.

Chapter 7, Sense and Display Real-world Data, explains the use of an analog-to-digital convertor to provide sensor readings to the Raspberry Pi. We discover how to store and graph the data in real time as well as display it on an LCD text display. Finally, we transfer the data to the Internet, which will allow us to view and share the captured data anywhere in the world.

Chapter 8, Creating Projects with the Raspberry Pi Camera Module, teaches us how to use the Raspberry Pi camera module, creating our own applications to produce time-lapse videos, stop-frame animations, and a bedtime book reader controlled with QR codes.

Chapter 9, Building Robots, takes you through building two different types of robots (a Rover-Pi and a Pi-Bug). We look at motor and servo control, using sensors, and adding a compass sensor for navigation.

Chapter 10, Interfacing with Technology, teaches us how to use the Raspberry Pi to trigger remote mains sockets, with which we can control household appliances. We learn how to communicate with the Raspberry Pi over a serial interface and use a smartphone to control everything using Bluetooth. Finally, we look at creating our own applications to control USB devices.

Appendix, Hardware and Software List, provides us with the full list of the hardware components and modules used in the book, along with suitable places to purchase them from. A full list of the software used is also provided, along with links to documentation.

What you need for this book

This book focuses on using the Raspberry Pi with Python 3; therefore, a basic Raspberry Pi setup is required. Chapters 1 to 5 of this book make use of the Raspberry Pi only; no additional hardware is required beyond a standard setup.

The standard setup will consist of the Raspberry Pi (Model A or Model B); an SD card installed with Raspbian; suitable micro USB power supply; and an HDMI-compatible screen, keyboard, and mouse. You will also be required to download and install various software packages; therefore, the Raspberry Pi should have a working Internet connection.

Chapter 1, Getting Started with a Raspberry Pi Computer, also describes how to use the screen/keyboard/mouse of a laptop or another computer to access the Raspberry Pi (you just need a network cable and power).

Chapter 6, Using Python to Drive Hardware, and *Chapter 7, Sense and Display Real-world Data*, show how electronic components can be connected to the Raspberry Pi's interfaces. These components will be needed in order to complete these chapters.

Chapter 8, Creating Projects with the Raspberry Pi Camera Module, requires the Raspberry Pi camera module for each of the projects (although a compatible USB webcam could be substituted by adjusting the code).

Chapter 9, Building Robots, uses a range of hardware and electronics to build your own robots. You can either use your own parts or a suitable kit for this.

Chapter 10, Interfacing with Technology, shows how additional hardware can be connected to the interfaces of the Raspberry Pi using various modules and kits.

A full list of the hardware used (and the possible places to purchase it from) has been provided in the *Appendix, Hardware and Software List*.

Who this book is for

This book is intended for anyone who wants to make the most of the Raspberry Pi experience. The book gradually introduces Python, starting with the basics and moving towards more advanced topics, such as using 3D graphics and interfacing with hardware.

Although you do not need to be familiar with Python, the Raspberry Pi, or electronics, this book touches on a wide range of topics. Ideally, you should give each chapter a try, see what you enjoy, and use that as a starting point to discover and learn more.

Each example in the book consists of full setup instructions, complete code listings, and a walk-through of what you did and why. This will allow you to get results quickly, and most importantly, understand how you achieved them.

All the examples are written using Python 3, with clear and detailed explanations of how everything works so that you can adapt and use all the information in your own projects.

As you progress through the book, it will explain how to structure and develop your code efficiently, building on the various techniques that can be applied as you progress. By the end, you will have a toolset of skills that you can apply on whatever your imagination inspires you to do.

Safety and using electronics

This book encourages you to experiment and connect your own circuits to the general-purpose input/output Raspberry Pi GPIO pins. This is an excellent way to learn about electronics and software at the same time. However, it is important to remember that the GPIO pins are unprotected, and if wired incorrectly, can easily be damaged or even cause the Raspberry Pi to stop working altogether. Therefore, care should be taken to correctly follow the instructions and wiring diagrams and check everything carefully before switching the Raspberry Pi on.

All the circuits, modules, and components described in this book are intended as demonstration examples only. They have not been tested for extended use and should not be left unattended or should not be used in safety-critical applications without adequate safeguards in place. Remember that all electronics must undergo rigorous safety testing to ensure that in the event of failure, there will be no risk of harm to people or property.

You should never attempt to modify or alter devices that are connected to mains electricity without proper training, and you must never directly connect any homemade devices to the mains supply.

Conventions

In this book, you will find a number of styles of text that distinguish between different kinds of information. Here are some examples of these styles, and an explanation of their meaning.

Code words in text, database table names, folder names, filenames, file extensions, pathnames, dummy URLs, user input, and Twitter handles are shown as follows: "On a freshly formatted or new SD card, copy the contents of the NOOBS_vX.zip file."

A block of code is set as follows:

```
network={
  ssid="theSSID"
  key_mgmt=NONE
}
```

Any command-line input or output is written as follows:

```
sudo mount -t vfat /dev/mmcblk0p1 ~/recovery
```

New terms and **important words** are shown in bold. Words that you see on the screen, in menus or dialog boxes for example, appear in the text like this: "For OS X or Linux, click on **Terminal** to open a connection to the Raspberry Pi."

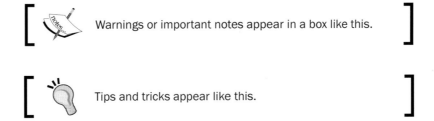

Warnings or important notes appear in a box like this.

Tips and tricks appear like this.

Reader feedback

Feedback from our readers is always welcome. Let us know what you think about this book—what you liked or may have disliked. Reader feedback is important for us to develop titles that you really get the most out of.

To send us general feedback, simply send an e-mail to feedback@packtpub.com, and mention the book title via the subject of your message.

If there is a topic that you have expertise in and you are interested in either writing or contributing to a book, see our author guide on www.packtpub.com/authors.

Customer support

Now that you are the proud owner of a Packt book, we have a number of things to help you to get the most from your purchase.

Downloading the example code

You can download the example code files for all Packt books you have purchased from your account at http://www.packtpub.com. If you purchased this book elsewhere, you can visit http://www.packtpub.com/support and register to have the files e-mailed directly to you.

Downloading the color images of this book

We also provide you a PDF file that has color images of the screenshots used in this book. You can download this file from https://www.packtpub.com/sites/default/files/downloads/6623OT_ColorGraphics.pdf.

Errata

Although we have taken every care to ensure the accuracy of our content, mistakes do happen. If you find a mistake in one of our books—maybe a mistake in the text or the code—we would be grateful if you would report this to us. By doing so, you can save other readers from frustration and help us improve subsequent versions of this book. If you find any errata, please report them by visiting `http://www.packtpub.com/submit-errata`, selecting your book, clicking on the **errata submission form** link, and entering the details of your errata. Once your errata are verified, your submission will be accepted and the errata will be uploaded on our website, or added to any list of existing errata, under the Errata section of that title. Any existing errata can be viewed by selecting your title from `http://www.packtpub.com/support`.

Piracy

Piracy of copyright material on the Internet is an ongoing problem across all media. At Packt, we take the protection of our copyright and licenses very seriously. If you come across any illegal copies of our works, in any form, on the Internet, please provide us with the location address or website name immediately so that we can pursue a remedy.

Please contact us at `copyright@packtpub.com` with a link to the suspected pirated material.

We appreciate your help in protecting our authors, and our ability to bring you valuable content.

Questions

You can contact us at `questions@packtpub.com` if you are having a problem with any aspect of the book, and we will do our best to address it.

1
Getting Started with a Raspberry Pi Computer

In this chapter, we will cover the following topics:

- ▶ Connecting the Raspberry Pi
- ▶ Using NOOBS to set up your Raspberry Pi SD card
- ▶ Networking and connecting your Raspberry Pi to the Internet via the LAN connector
- ▶ Configuring your network manually
- ▶ Networking directly to a laptop or computer
- ▶ Networking and connecting your Raspberry Pi to the Internet via a USB Wi-Fi dongle
- ▶ Connecting to the Internet through a proxy server
- ▶ Connecting remotely to the Raspberry Pi over the network using VNC
- ▶ Connecting remotely to the Raspberry Pi over the network using SSH (and X11 Forwarding)
- ▶ Sharing the home folder of the Raspberry Pi with SMB
- ▶ Keeping the Raspberry Pi up to date

Introduction

This chapter introduces the Raspberry Pi and the process to set it up for the first time. We will connect the Raspberry Pi to a suitable display, power, and peripherals. We shall install an operating system on an SD card. This is required for the system to boot. Next, we will ensure that we can connect successfully to the Internet through a local network.

Finally, we will make use of the network to provide ways to remotely connect to and/or control the Raspberry Pi from other computers and devices as well as to ensure that the system is kept up to date.

Once you have completed the steps within this chapter, your Raspberry Pi will be ready for you to use for programming. If you already have your Raspberry Pi set up and running, ensure that you take a look through the following sections as there are many helpful tips.

Introducing the Raspberry Pi

The Raspberry Pi is a single-board computer created by the **Raspberry Pi Foundation**, a charity formed with the primary purpose of reintroducing low-level computer skills to children in the UK. The aim was to rekindle the microcomputer revolution from the 1980s, which produced a whole generation of skilled programmers.

Even before the computer was released at the end of February 2012, it was clear that the Raspberry Pi had gained a huge following worldwide and has now sold over 2 million units. The following image represents a Raspberry Pi Model B:

A Raspberry Pi Model B (revision 2.0)

What is with the name?

The name, Raspberry Pi, was the combination of the desire to create an alternative fruit-based computer (such as Apple, BlackBerry, and Apricot) and a nod to the original concept of a simple computer that can be programmed using **Python** (shortened to **Pi**).

Within this book, we will take this little computer, find out how to set it up, and then explore its capabilities chapter by chapter using the Python programming language.

Why Python?

It is often asked, "Why has Python been selected as the language to use on the Raspberry Pi?". The fact is that Python is just one of the many programming languages that can be used on the Raspberry Pi.

There are many programming languages that you can choose, from high-level graphical block programming, such as **Scratch**, to traditional **C**, right down to **BASIC**, and even raw **Machine Code Assembler**. A good programmer often has to be code multilingual to be able to play to the strengths and weaknesses of each language in order to best meet the needs of their desired application. It is useful to understand how different languages (and programming techniques) try to overcome the challenge of converting "what you want" into "what you get" as this is what you are trying to do as well while you program.

Python has been selected as a good place to start when learning about programming by providing a rich set of coding tools while still allowing simple programs to be written without fuss. This allows beginners to gradually be introduced to the concepts and methods on which modern programming languages are based without requiring them to know it all from the start. It is very modular with lots of additional libraries that can be imported to quickly extend the functionality. You will find that over time, this encourages you to do the same, and you will want to create your own modules that you can plug in to your own programs, thus taking your first steps into structured programming.

Like all programming languages, Python isn't perfect; things such as adding a space at the start of a line will often break your code (indents matter a lot in Python; they define how blocks of code are grouped together). Generally, Python is slow; since it is interpreted, it takes time to create a module while it is running the program. This can be a problem if you need to respond to time critical events. However, you can precompile Python or use modules written in other languages to overcome this. It hides the detail; this is both an advantage and disadvantage. It is excellent for beginners but can be difficult when you have to second-guess aspects such as data-types, but this in turn forces you to consider all the possibilities, which can be a good thing.

Python 2 and Python 3

A massive source of confusion for beginners is that there are two versions of Python on the Raspberry Pi (**Version 2.7** and **Version 3.2**), which are not compatible with one another, so code written for Python 2.7 may not run with Python 3.2 (and vice versa).

The **Python Software Foundation** is continuously working to improve and move forward with the language, which sometimes means they have to sacrifice backward compatibility in order to embrace new improvements (and importantly, remove redundant and legacy ways of doing things).

Supporting both Python 2 or Python 3

There are many tools that will ease the transition from Python 2 to Python 3, including converters such as 2to3, which will parse and update your code to use Python 3 methods. This process is not perfect, and in some cases, you'll need to manually rewrite sections and fully retest everything. You can write the code and libraries that will support both. The import __future__ statement allows you to import the friendly methods of Python 3 and run them using Python 2.7.

Which version of Python should you use?

Essentially, the selection of which version to use will depend on what you intend to do. For instance, you may require Python 2.7 libraries, which are not yet available for Python 3.2. Python 3 has been available since 2008, so these tend to be older or larger libraries that have not been translated. In many cases, there are new alternatives to legacy libraries; however, their support can vary.

In this book, we have used Python 3.2, which is also compatible with Python 3.3.

Connecting the Raspberry Pi

There are many ways to wire up the Raspberry Pi and use the various interfaces to view and control content. For typical use, most users will require power, display (with audio), and a method of input such as a keyboard and mouse. To access the Internet, refer to the *Networking and connecting your Raspberry Pi to the Internet via the LAN connector* recipe.

Getting ready

Before you can use your Raspberry Pi, you will need an SD card with an operating system installed or with the **New Out Of Box System** (**NOOBS**) on it, as discussed in the *Using NOOBS to set up your Raspberry Pi SD card* recipe.

The following section will detail the types of devices you can connect to the Raspberry Pi and importantly, how and where to plug them in.

As you will discover later, once you have your Raspberry Pi set up, you may decide to connect remotely and use it through a network link, in which case you only need power and a network connection. Refer to the following sections: *Connecting remotely to the Raspberry Pi over the network using VNC* and *Connecting remotely to the Raspberry Pi over the network using SSH (and X11 Forwarding)*.

How to do it...

The layout of the Raspberry Pi is shown in the following figure:

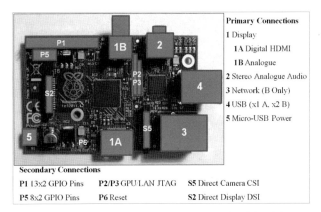

The Raspberry Pi connection layout (Model B revision 2.0)

The description of the preceding figure is explained as follows:

▶ **Display**: The Raspberry Pi supports the following three main display connections; if both HDMI and Composite video are connected, it shall default to the HDMI only.

    ❑ **HDMI**

        For best results, use a TV or monitor that has an HDMI connection, thus allowing the best resolution display (1080p) and also digital audio output. If your display has a DVI connection, you may be able to use an adapter to connect through the HDMI. There are several types of DVI connections; some support analogue (DVI-A), some digital (DVI-D), and some both (DVI-I). the Raspberry Pi is only able to provide a digital signal through the HDMI, so an HDMI to DVI-D adapter is recommended (shown with a tick mark in the following screenshot). This lacks the four extra analogue pins (shown with a cross mark in the following screenshot), thus allowing it to fit into both DVI-D and DVI-I type sockets:

HDMI to DVI connection (DVI-D adaptor)

        If you wish to use an older monitor (with a VGA connection), an additional HDMI to VGA converter is required.

❑ **Analogue**

An alternative display method is to use the analogue composite video connection (via the RCA socket); this can also be attached to an S-Video or European SCART adapter. However, the analogue video output has a maximum resolution of 640 x 480 pixels, so it is not ideal for general use.

When using the RCA connection or a DVI input, audio has to be provided separately by the analogue audio connection.

❑ **Direct Display DSI**

A touch display produced by the Raspberry Pi Foundation will connect directly into the DSI socket. This can be connected and used at the same time as the HDMI or Analogue video output to create a dual display setup.

▶ **Stereo Analogue Audio**: This provides an analogue audio output for headphones or amplified speakers. The audio can be switched between analogue (Stereo Socket) and digital (HDMI) using `amixer` or `alsamixer`.

To find out more information about a particular command in the terminal, you can use the following `man` command before the terminal reads the manual (most commands should have one):

```
man amixer
```

Some commands also support the `--help` option for more concise help, shown as follows:

```
amixer --help
```

▶ **Network (Model B Only)**: The network connection is discussed in the *Networking and connecting your Raspberry Pi to the Internet via the LAN connector* recipe later in this chapter. If we use the Model A Raspberry Pi, it is possible to add a USB network adapter to add wired or even wireless networking (refer to the *Networking and connecting your Raspberry Pi to the Internet via a USB Wi-Fi dongle* recipe).

▶ **USB (x1 Model A, x2 Model B) – Using a keyboard and mouse:**

The Raspberry Pi should work with most USB keyboards and mice available. However, you may encounter issues if your device draws more than 140mA, in which case a powered USB hub is recommended. You can also use wireless mice and keyboards, which use RF Dongles. However, additional configuration is required for items that use the Bluetooth dongles.

If there is a lack of power supplied by your power supply or the devices are drawing too much current, you may experience the keyboard keys appearing to stick, and in severe cases, corruption of the SD card.

USB power can be more of an issue with the early Model B revision 1 boards that were available prior to October 2012. They included additional **Polyfuses** on the USB output and tripped if an excess of 140mA was drawn. The Polyfuses can take several hours or days to recover completely, thus causing unpredictable behavior to remain even when the power is improved.

You can identify a revision 1 board as it lacks the two mounting holes that are present on the revision 2 board.

Debian Linux (upon which Raspbian is based) supports many common USB devices, such as flash storage drives, hard disk drives (external power may be required), cameras, printers, Bluetooth, and Wi-Fi adapters. Some devices will be detected automatically while others will require drivers to be installed.

▸ **Micro USB Power**: The Raspberry Pi requires a 5V power supply, which can comfortably supply at least 700mA (1A or more recommended) with a micro USB connection. It is possible to power the unit using portable battery packs, such as the ones suitable for powering or recharging tablets. Again, ensure that they can supply 5V at 700mA or over.

You should aim to make all other connections to the Raspberry Pi before connecting the power. However, USB devices, audio, and network may be connected and removed while it is running without problems.

There's more...

In addition to the standard primary connections you would expect to see on a computer, the Raspberry Pi also has a number of additional connections.

Secondary hardware connections

Each of the following connections provide additional interfaces for the Raspberry Pi:

▸ **P1 13 x 2 GPIO pin header**: This is the main GPIO header of the Raspberry Pi used for interfacing directly with hardware components. We use this connection in *Chapter 6, Using Python to Drive Hardware, Chapter 7, Sense and Display Real World Data, Chapter 9, Building Robots*, and *Chapter 10, Interfacing with Technology*.

▸ **P5 8 x 2 GPIO pin header**: This is present on board revision 2.0 only (no pins fitted).

▸ **P6 reset**: This is present on board revision 2.0 only (no pins fitted). A reset is triggered when P6-Pin1 (reset) and P6-Pin2 (GND) are connected together.

▸ **P5 and P6 pin header**

We use P5 and P6 in the *A controlled shutdown button* recipe in *Chapter 6, Using Python to Drive Hardware*.

- ▶ **P2/P3 GPU/LAN JTAG**: The **Joint Test Action Group** (**JTAG**) is a programming and debugging interface used to configure and test processors. A specialist JTAG device is required to use this interface.

- ▶ **S5 Direct Camera CSI**: This connection supports the Raspberry Pi Camera module (as used in *Chapter 8, Creating Projects with the Raspberry Pi Camera Module*).

- ▶ **S2 Direct Display DSI**: This connection is intended to support a display (an add-on released by the Raspberry Pi Foundation).

Using NOOBS to set up your Raspberry Pi SD card

The Raspberry Pi requires the operating system to be loaded onto an SD card before it will start up. The easiest way to set up the SD card is to use NOOBS; you may find that you can buy an SD card with NOOBS already loaded on it.

NOOBS provides an initial start menu providing options to install several of the available operating systems onto your SD card.

Getting ready

Since NOOBS creates a **RECOVERY Partition** to keep the original installation images, a 4 GB SD card or larger is recommended. You will also need an SD card reader (experience has shown that some built-in card readers can cause issues, so an external USB type reader is recommended).

If you are using an SD card that you have used previously, you may need to reformat it to remove any previous partitions and data. NOOBS expects the SD card to consist of a single FAT32 partition. If using Windows or Mac OS X, you can use SD association's formatter, as shown in the following screenshot (available at `https://www.sdcard.org/downloads/formatter_4/`):

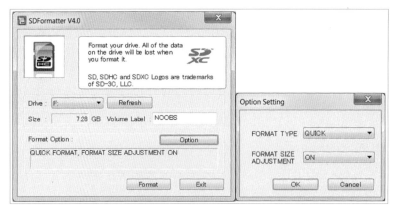

Get rid of any partitions on the SD card using SD formatter

From the **Option Setting** dialog box, set **Format Size Adjustment**. This will remove all the SD card partitions that were created previously.

If using Linux, you can use `gparted` to clear any previous partitions and reformat it as a FAT32 partition.

The full NOOBS package (typically around 1.3 GB) contains a selection of the most popular Raspberry Pi operating system's images built in. A lite version of NOOBS is also available that has no preloaded operating systems (although, a smaller initial download of 20 MB and a wired network connection on the Raspberry Pi is required to directly download the operating system you intend to use).

NOOBS is available at `http://www.raspberrypi.org/downloads` with the documentation available at `https://github.com/raspberrypi/noobs`.

How to do it...

By performing the following steps, we will prepare the SD card to run NOOBS. This will then allow us to select and install the operating system we want to use:

1. Get your SD card ready.
2. On a freshly formatted or new SD card, copy the contents of the `NOOBS_vX.zip` file. When it has finished copying, you should end up with something like the following screenshot on the SD card:

NOOBS files extracted onto the SD card

 The files may vary slightly with different versions of NOOBS, and the icons displayed may be different on your computer.

3. You can now place the card into your Raspberry Pi, connect it to a keyboard and display, and turn the power on. (refer to the *Connecting Up the Raspberry Pi* recipe for details on what you need and how to do this).

By default, NOOBS will display via the HDMI connection. If you have another type of screen (or you don't see anything), you will need to manually select the output type by pressing *1*, *2*, *3*, or *4* according to the following functions:

- ▸ Key 1 stands for the **Standard HDMI** mode (the default mode)
- ▸ Key 2 stands for the **Safe HDMI** mode (alternative HDMI settings if the output has not been detected)
- ▸ Key 3 stands for **Composite PAL** (for connections made via the RCA analogue video connection)
- ▸ Key 4 stands for **Composite NTSC** (again, for connections via the RCA connector)

This display setting will also be set for the installed operating system.

After a short while, you will see the NOOBS selection screen that lists the available distributions that have been included. There are many more distributions that are available, but these are the ones the Raspberry Pi Foundation has selected for the NOOBS system. Click on **Raspbian** as this is the operating system being used in this book.

Press *Enter* or click on **Install OS**, and confirm that we wish to overwrite all the data on the card. This will overwrite any distributions previously installed using NOOBS but will not remove the NOOBS system; you can return to it at any time by pressing *Shift* when you turn the power on.

It will take around 10 to 30 minutes to write the data to the card depending on its speed. When it completes and the **Image Applied Successfully** message appears, click on **OK** and the Raspberry Pi will start to boot into `raspi-config`.

How it works...

The purpose of writing the image file to the SD card in this manner is to ensure that the SD card is formatted with the expected filesystem partitions and files required to correctly boot the operating system.

When the Raspberry Pi powers up, it loads some special code contained within the GPU's internal memory (commonly referred to as the **binary blob** by the Raspberry Pi Foundation). The binary blob provides the instructions required to read the **BOOT Partition** on the SD card, which (in the case of a NOOBS install) will load NOOBS from the RECOVERY partition. If, at this point, *Shift* is pressed, NOOBS will load the recovery and installation menu. Otherwise, NOOBS will begin loading the OS as specified by the preferences stored in the **SETTINGS Partition**.

When loading the operating system, it will boot via the BOOT partition using the settings defined in `config.txt` and options in `cmdline.txt` to finally load to the terminal or desktop on the **root Partition**, depending on what you have set up in `raspi-config`. Refer to the following diagram:

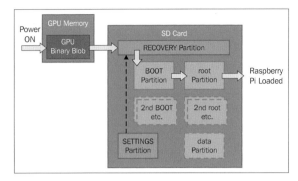

NOOBS creates several partitions on the SD card to allow installation
of multiple operating systems and to provide recovery

NOOBS allows the user to optionally install multiple operating systems on the same card and provides a boot menu to select between them (with an option to set a default value in the event of a time-out period).

You can also choose to create an optional **data Partition** that allows you to keep your datafiles separate to the operating system. This makes it easier to share files between multiple systems and allows you to keep backups of just your user data.

If you later add, remove, or reinstall an operating system, ensure that you make a copy of any files, including system settings you wish to keep first as NOOBS may overwrite everything on the SD card.

There's more...

When you power up the Raspberry Pi for the first time, it will start directly into `raspi-config` (this only occurs for the first boot of a new install), which will allow you to perform changes to your SD card and set up your general preferences. Use the `sudo raspi-config` command to run it another time. When you exit this program, it will load directly by default to the terminal interface, which is the command line of the Raspberry Pi. To start a desktop session, such as Windows or OS X, use the `startx` command, which will load the Raspbian desktop.

Changing the default user password

Ensure that you change the default password for the `pi` user account once you have logged in as the default password is well known. This is particularly important if you connect to the public networks. You can do this with the `passwd` command, as shown in the following screenshot:

```
pi@raspberrypi ~ $ passwd
Changing password for pi.
(current) UNIX password:
Enter new UNIX password:
Retype new UNIX password:
passwd: password updated successfully
```

Setting a new password for the pi user

This gives greater confidence because if you later connect to another network, only you will be able to access your files and take control of your Raspberry Pi.

Ensuring that you shut down safely

To avoid any data corruption, you must ensure that you correctly shut down the Raspberry Pi by issuing a `shutdown` command as follows:

```
sudo shutdown -h now
```

You must wait until this command completes before you remove power from the Raspberry Pi (wait for at least 10 seconds after the SD card access light has stopped flashing).

You can also restart the system with the `reboot` command as follows:

```
sudo reboot
```

Preparing an SD card manually

An alternative to using NOOBS is to manually write the operating system image to the SD card. While this was originally the only way to install the operating system, some users still prefer it. It allows the SD cards to be prepared before they are used in the Raspberry Pi. It can also provide easier access to startup and configuration files (refer to the *Networking directly to a laptop or computer* recipe), and it leaves more space available for the user (unlike NOOBS, a RECOVERY partition isn't included).

The default Raspbian image actually consists of two partitions, BOOT and SYSTEM, which will fit onto a 2 GB SD card (4 GB or more is recommended).

You need a computer running Windows/Mac OS X/Linux (although it is possible to use another Raspberry Pi to write your card, be prepared for a very long wait).

Download the latest version of the operating system you wish to use. For the purpose of this book, it is assumed you are using the latest version of Raspbian available at `http://www.raspberrypi.org/downloads`.

Perform the following steps depending on the type of computer you plan to use to write to the SD card (the `.img` file you need is usually compressed, so before you start, you will need to extract the file).

The following steps are for Windows:

1. Ensure that you have downloaded the Raspbian image, as previously detailed, and extracted it to a convenient folder to obtain a `.img` file.

2. Obtain the `Win32DiskImager.exe` file available at `http://www.sourceforge.net/projects/win32diskimager`.

3. Run `Win32DiskImager.exe` from your downloaded location.

4. Click on the folder icon and navigate to the location of the `.img` file and click on **Save**.

5. If you haven't already done so, insert your SD card into your card reader and plug it into your computer.

6. Select the **Device** drive letter that corresponds to your SD card from the small drop-down box. Ensure you double-check this is the correct device (as the program will overwrite whatever is on the device when you write the image).

 The drive letter may not be listed until you select a source image file.

7. Finally, click on the **Write** button and wait for the program to write the image to the SD card.

8. Once completed, you can exit the program. Your SD card is ready! Refer to the following screenshot:

Manually write operating system images to the SD card using Disk Imager

The following steps should work for the most common Linux distributions, such as Ubuntu and Debian:

1. Using your preferred web browser, download the Raspbian image and save it somewhere suitable.

2. Extract the file from the file manager or locate the folder in the terminal and unzip the `.img` file with the following command:

    ```
    unzip filename.zip
    ```

3. If you haven't already done so, insert your SD card into your card reader and plug it into your computer.

4. Use the `df -h` command and identify the **sdX** identifier for the SD card. Each partition will be displayed as **sdX1**, **sdX2**, and so on, where **X** will be a, b, c, d, and so on for the device ID.

5. Ensure that all the partitions on the SD card are unmounted using the `umount /dev/sdXn` command for each partition, where `sdXn` is the partition being unmounted.

6. Write the image file to the SD card with the following command:

```
sudo dd if=filename.img of=/dev/sdX bs=4M
```

7. The process will take some time to write to the SD card, returning to the terminal prompt when complete.

8. Unmount the SD card before removing it from the computer using the following command:

```
umount /dev/sdX1
```

The following steps should work for most of the versions of OS X:

1. Using your preferred web browser, download the Raspbian image and save it somewhere suitable.

2. Extract the file from the file manager or locate the folder in the terminal and unzip the `.img` file with the following command:

```
unzip filename.zip
```

3. If you haven't already done so, insert your SD card into your card reader and plug it into your computer.

4. Use the `diskutil list` command and identify the **disk#** identifier for the SD card. Each partition will be displayed as **disk#s1**, **disk#s2**, and so on, where **#** will be 1, 2, 3, 4 and so on for the device ID.

 If **rdisk#** is listed, use this for faster writing (this is a raw path and skips data buffering).

5. Ensure that the SD card is unmounted using the `unmountdisk /dev/diskX` command, where `diskX` is the device being unmounted.

6. Write the image file to the SD card with following command:

```
sudo dd if=filename.img of=/dev/diskX bs=1M
```

7. The process will take some time to write to the SD card, returning to the terminal prompt when complete.

8. Unmount the SD card before removing it from the computer using the following command:

```
unmountdisk /dev/diskX
```

Refer to the following screenshot:

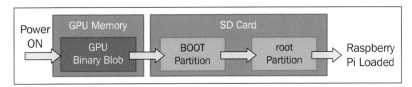

The boot process of a manually installed OS image

Expanding the system to fit in your SD card

A manually written image will be of a fixed size (usually made to fit the smallest sized SD card possible). To make full use of the SD card, you will need to expand the system partition to fill the remainder of the SD card. This can be achieved using the `raspi-config` tool.

Start the `raspi-config` tool with the following command:

```
sudo raspi-config
```

Select the menu item, `1 Expand Filesystem   Ensures that all of the SD card storage is available to the OS`, as shown in the following screenshot:.

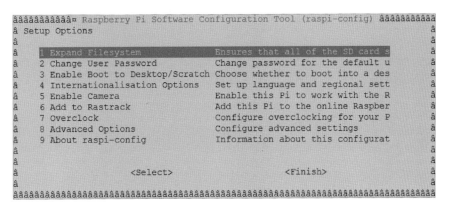

The raspi-config menu

Accessing the Data/RECOVERY/BOOT partition

Windows and Mac OS X do not support the `ext4` format, so when you read the SD card, only the **File Allocation Table** (**FAT**) partitions will be accessible. In addition, Windows only supports the first partition on an SD card, so if you've installed NOOBS, only the `RECOVERY` partition will be visible. If you've written your card manually, you will be able to access the `BOOT` partition.

The `data` partition (if you installed one via NOOBS) and the `root` partition are in `ext4` format and won't usually be visible on non-Linux systems.

 If you do need to read files from the SD card using Windows, a freeware program, **Linux Reader** (available at `www.diskinternals.com/linux-reader`) can provide a read-only access to all of the partitions on the SD card.

Access the partitions from the Raspberry Pi. To view the currently mounted partitions, use `df`, as shown in the following screenshot:

```
pi@raspberrypi ~ $ df
Filesystem      1K-blocks     Used Available Use% Mounted on
rootfs            6646112  2283852   4001608  37% /
/dev/root         6646112  2283852   4001608  37% /
devtmpfs           183312        0    183312   0% /dev
tmpfs               38316      380     37936   1% /run
tmpfs                5120        0      5120   0% /run/lock
tmpfs               76620        0     76620   0% /run/shm
/dev/mmcblk0p6      60479    19000     41479  32% /boot
```

The result of the df command

To access the `BOOT` partition from within Raspbian, use the following command:

`cd /boot/`

To access the `RECOVERY` or `data` partition, we have to mount it, by performing the following steps:

1. Determine the name of the partition as the system refers to it by listing all the partitions, even the unmounted ones. The `sudo fdisk -l` command lists the partitions, as show in the following screenshot:

```
     Device Boot      Start        End    Blocks   Id  System
/dev/mmcblk0p1         8192     240234   116021+    e  W95 FAT16 (LBA)
/dev/mmcblk0p2       245760   15212543   7483392   85  Linux extended
/dev/mmcblk0p3     15212544   15278079     32768   83  Linux
/dev/mmcblk0p5       253952    1302527    524288   83  Linux
/dev/mmcblk0p6      1310720    1433599     61440    c  W95 FAT32 (LBA)
/dev/mmcblk0p7      1441792   15212543   6885376   83  Linux
```

The partition table of a NOOBS install of Raspbian and data partition

mmcblk0p1	(vfat) RECOVERY
mmcblk0p2	(Extended partition) contains (root, data, BOOT)
mmcblk0p3	(ext4) root
mmcblk0p5	(ext4) data
mmcblk0p6	(vfat) BOOT
mmcblk0p7	(ext4) SETTINGS

If you have installed additional operating systems on the same card, the partition identifiers shown in the preceding table will be different.

2. Create a folder and set it as the mount point for the partition as follows:

   ❏ For the RECOVERY partition, use the following command:

   ```
   mkdir ~/recovery
   sudo mount -t vfat /dev/mmcblk0p1 ~/recovery
   ```

   ❏ For the data partition, use the following command:

   ```
   mkdir ~/userdata
   sudo mount -t ext4 /dev/mmcblk0p5 ~/userdata
   ```

To ensure they are mounted each time the system is started, perform the following steps:

1. Add the sudo mount commands to /etc/rc.local before exit 0. If you have a different username, you will need to change pi to match.

   ```
   sudo nano /etc/rc.local
   sudo mount -t vfat /dev/mmcbblk0p1 /home/pi/recovery
   sudo mount -t ext4 /dev/mmcbblk0p5 /home/pi/userdata
   ```

2. Save and exit by pressing *Ctrl + X, Y,* and *Enter*.

 Commands added to /etc/rc.local will be run for any user who logs onto the Raspberry Pi. If you only want the drive to be mounted for the current user, the commands can be added to .bash_profile instead.

If you have install additional operating systems on the same card, the partition identifiers shown here will be different.

Using the tools to backup your SD card in case of failure

You can use **Win32 Disk Imager** to make a full backup image of your SD card by inserting your SD card into your reader, starting the program, and creating a filename to store the image in. Simply click on the **Read** button instead to read the image from the SD card and write it to a new image file.

The dd command can similarly be used to back up the card as follows:

- ▶ For Linux, replacing sdX with your device ID, use the following command:

  ```
  sudo dd if=/dev/sdX of=image.img.gz bs=1M
  ```

- ▶ For OS X, replacing diskX with your device ID, use the following command:

  ```
  sudo dd if=/dev/diskX of=image.img.gz bs=1M
  ```

- ▶ You can also use gzip and split to compress the contents of the card and split them into multiple files if required for easy archiving as follows:

  ```
  sudo dd if=/dev/sdX bs=1M | gzip -c | split -d -b 2000m - image.img.gz
  ```

- ▶ To restore the split image, use the following command:

  ```
  sudo cat image.img.gz* | gzip -dc | dd of=/dev/sdX bs=1M
  ```

Networking and connecting your Raspberry Pi to the Internet via the LAN connector

The simplest way to connect the Raspberry Pi to the Internet is using the built-in LAN connection on the Model B. If you are using a Model A Raspberry Pi, a USB-to-LAN adapter can be used (refer to the *There's more...* section of the *Networking and connecting your Raspberry Pi to the Internet via a USB Wi-Fi dongle* recipe for details on how to configure this).

Getting ready

You will need an access to a suitable wired network, which will be connected to the Internet and a standard network cable (**Cat5e** or a similar one with a **RJ45** type connector for connecting to the Raspberry Pi).

How to do it...

Many networks connect and configure themselves automatically using **Dynamic Host Configuration Protocol** (**DHCP**), which is controlled by the router or switch. If this is the case, simply plug the network cable into a spare network port on your router or network switch (or wall network socket if applicable).

Alternatively, if a DHCP server is not available, you shall have to configure the settings manually (refer to the *There's more...* section for details).

You can confirm this is functioning successfully with the following steps:

1. Ensure that the three LEDs on the Raspberry Pi marked **FDX**, **LNK**, and **100**, light up (the 100 LED may not light up if connected to a 10 Mbps device rather than the more common 100 Mbps device), and in some cases, start to flash. This will indicate that there is a physical connection to the router and the equipment is powered and functioning.

2. Test the link to your local network using the `ping` command. First, find out the IP address of another computer on the network (or the address of your router perhaps, often `192.168.0.1` or `192.168.1.254`). Now, on the Raspberry Pi terminal, use the `ping` command (the parameter `-c 4` is used to send just four messages; otherwise, press *Ctrl + C* to stop) to ping the IP address as follows:

    ```
    ping 192.168.1.254 -c 4
    ```

3. Test the link to the Internet (this will fail if you usually connect to the Internet though a proxy server) as follows:

    ```
    ping www.raspberrypi.org -c 4
    ```

4. Finally, you can test the link back to the Raspberry Pi by discovering the IP address using `hostname -I` on the Raspberry Pi. You can then use the ping command on another computer on the network to ensure it is accessible (using the Raspberry Pi's IP address in place of `www.raspberrypi.org`). The Windows version of the `ping` command will perform five pings and stop automatically and will not need the `-c 4` option).

If the above tests fail, you will need to check your connections and then confirm the correct configuration for your network.

There's more...

If you find yourself using your Raspberry Pi regularly on the network and if you need to find out the IP address, you may find it helpful to fix the IP address to a known value by manually setting the IP address. However, remember to switch it back to use DHCP when connecting on another network.

Some routers will also have an option to set a **Static IP DHCP address**, so the same address is always given to the Raspberry Pi (how this is set will vary on the router itself).

Knowing your Raspberry Pi's IP address when it is on the network is particularly useful if you intend to use one of the remote access solutions described later on, which avoids the need for a display.

On some networks, you may be able to use the Raspberry Pi's hostname instead of its IP address (the default is `raspberrypi`), but not all networks will support this without additional software such as **Bonjour** (built in to OS X and available for Windows).

Configuring your network manually

If your network does not include a DHCP server or it is disabled (typically, these are built in to most modern ADSL/cable modems or routers), you may need to configure your network settings manually.

Getting ready

Before you start, you will need to determine the network settings for your network.

You will need to find out the following information from your router's settings or another computer connected to the network:

- **IPv4 address**: This address will need to be selected to be similar to other computers on the network (typically, the first three numbers should match, that is, `192.168.1.X` if `netmask` is `255.255.255.0`), but it should not already be used by another computer. However, avoid `x.x.x.255` as the last address since this is reserved as a broadcast address.

- **Subnet mask**: This number determines the range of addresses the computer will respond to (for a home network, it is typically `255.255.255.0`, which allows up to 254 addresses). This is also sometimes referred to as the **netmask**.

- **Default gateway address**: This address is usually your router's IP address, through which the computers connect to the Internet.

- **DNS servers**: The **DNS** server (**Domain Name Service**) converts names into IP addresses by looking them up. Usually, they will already be configured on your router, in which case you can use your router's address. Alternatively, your **Internet Service Provider** (**ISP**) may provide some addresses, or you can use Google's public DNS servers at the addresses `8.8.8.8` and `8.8.4.4`. These are also called **nameservers** in some systems.

For Windows, you can obtain this information by connecting to the Internet and running the following command:

```
ipconfig /all
```

Locate the active connection (usually called **Local Area Connection 1** or similar if you are using a wired connection or if you are using Wi-Fi, it is called wireless network connection) and find the information required as follows:

```
C:\Windows\system32\cmd.exe

Wireless LAN adapter Wireless Network Connection 2:

   Media State . . . . . . . . . . . : Media disconnected
   Connection-specific DNS Suffix  . :
   Description . . . . . . . . . . . : Microsoft Virtual WiFi Miniport Adapter
   Physical Address. . . . . . . . . : 00-19-7E-00-00-00
   DHCP Enabled. . . . . . . . . . . : Yes
   Autoconfiguration Enabled . . . . : Yes

Ethernet adapter Local Area Connection:

   Connection-specific DNS Suffix  . : home
   Description . . . . . . . . . . . : Broadcom 440x 10/100 Integrated Controlle
r
   Physical Address. . . . . . . . . : 00-1D-00-00-00-00
   DHCP Enabled. . . . . . . . . . . : Yes
   Autoconfiguration Enabled . . . . : Yes
   Link-local IPv6 Address . . . . . : fe80::f539:0000:0000:0000%12(Preferred)
   IPv4 Address. . . . . . . . . . . : 192.168.1.86(Preferred)
   Subnet Mask . . . . . . . . . . . : 255.255.255.0
   Lease Obtained. . . . . . . . . . : 24 June 2013 20:34:35
   Lease Expires . . . . . . . . . . : 25 June 2013 20:34:35
   Default Gateway . . . . . . . . . : 192.168.1.254
   DHCP Server . . . . . . . . . . . : 192.168.1.254
   DHCPv6 IAID . . . . . . . . . . . : 285220000
   DHCPv6 Client DUID. . . . . . . . : 00-01-00-01-16-C3-4A-46-00-00-00-00-00-00

   DNS Servers . . . . . . . . . . . : 192.168.1.254
                                       192.168.1.254
   Primary WINS Server . . . . . . . : 192.168.1.254
```

The ipconfig/all command shows useful information about your network settings

For Linux and Mac OS X, you can obtain the required information with the following command (note that it is `ifconfig` rather than `ipconfig`):

```
ifconfig
```

The DNS servers are called nameservers and are usually listed in the `resolv.conf` file. You can use the `less` command as follows to view its contents (press Q to quit when you have finished viewing it):

```
less /etc/resolv.conf
```

How to do it...

To set the network interface settings, edit `/etc/network/interfaces` using the following code:

```
sudo nano /etc/network/interfaces
```

Now, perform the following steps:

1. We can add the details for our particular network, the IP `address` number we want to allocate to it, the `netmask` address of the network, and the `gateway` address as follows:

   ```
   iface eth0 inet static
       address 192.168.1.10
       netmask 255.255.255.0
       gateway 192.168.1.254
   ```

2. Save and exit by pressing *Ctrl + X, Y,* and *Enter.*

3. To set the nameservers for DNS, edit `/etc/resolv.conf` using the following code:

   ```
   sudo nano /etc/resolv.conf
   ```

4. Add the addresses for your DNS servers as follows:

   ```
   nameserver 8.8.8.8

   nameserver 8.8.4.4
   ```

5. Save and exit by pressing *Ctrl + X, Y,* and *Enter.*

There's more...

You can configure the network settings by editing `cmdline.txt` in the `BOOT` partition and adding settings to the startup command line with `ip`.

The ip option takes the following form:

```
ip=client-ip:nfsserver-ip:gw-ip:netmask:hostname:device:autoconf
```

- ▸ The `client-ip` option is the IP address you want to allocate to the Raspberry Pi.
- ▸ The `gw-ip` option will set the gateway server address if you need to set it manually.
- ▸ The `netmask` option will directly set the netmask of the network.
- ▸ The `hostname` option will allow you to change the default `raspberrypi` hostname.
- ▸ The `device` option allows you to specify a default network device if more than one network device is present.
- ▸ The `autoconf` option allows the automatic configuration to be switched on or off.

Networking directly to a laptop or computer

It is possible to connect the Raspberry Pi LAN port directly to a laptop or computer using a single network cable. This will create a local network link between the computers, allowing all the things you can do if connected to a normal network without the need for a hub or router, including the connection to the Internet, if **Internet Connection Sharing** (**ICS**) is used as follows:

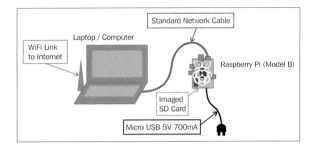

ICS allows the Raspberry Pi to connect to the Internet through another computer. However, some additional configuration is required for the computers in order to communicate across the link, as the Raspberry Pi does not automatically allocate its own IP address.

We will use the ICS to share a connection from another network link, such as a built-in Wi-Fi on a laptop. Alternatively, we can use a direct network link (refer to the *Direct network link* section under the *There's more...* section) if the Internet is not required or if the computer only has a single network adapter.

Although this setup should work for most of the computers, some setups are more difficult than the others. For additional information, see www. pihardware.com/guides/direct-network-connection.

It is likely that this functionality will be included as a part of the NOOBS/Raspbian images eventually.

Getting ready

You will need the Raspberry Pi with power and a standard network cable.

The Raspberry Pi Model B LAN chip includes **Auto-MDIX (Automatic Medium-Dependent Interface Crossover)**. Removing the need to use a special crossover cable (a special network cable wired so the transmit lines connect to receive lines for direct network links), the chip will decide and change the setup as required automatically.

It may also be helpful to have a keyboard and monitor available to perform additional testing, particularly, if this is the first time you have tried this.

To ensure that you can restore your network settings back to their original values, you should check whether it has a fixed IP address or the network is configured automatically.

To check the network settings on Windows 7 and Vista, perform the following steps:

1. Open **Network and Sharing Center** from the **Control Panel** and click on **Change adapter settings** on the left-hand side.

2. To check the network settings on Windows XP, open **Network Connections** from the **Control Panel**.

3. Find the item that relates to your wired network adapter (by default, this is usually called **Local Area Connection** as shown in the following screenshot):

Locating your wired network connection

4. Right-click on its icon and click on **Properties**. A dialog-box will appear as shown in the following screenshot:

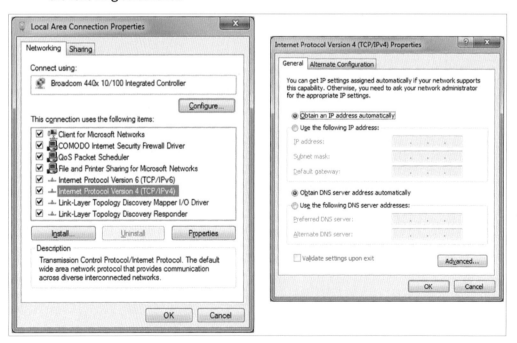

Selecting the TCP/IP properties and checking the settings

5. Select the item called **Internet Protocol (TCP/IP)** or **Internet Protocol Version 4 (TCP/IPv4)** if there are two versions (the other is Version 6), and click on the **Properties** button.

6. You can confirm if your network is set using automatic settings or by using a specific IP address (if so, take note of this address and the remaining details as you may want to revert the settings at a later point).

To check the network settings on Linux, perform the following steps:

1. Open up the **Network Settings** dialog box, and select **Configure Interface**. Refer to the following screenshot:

Linux Network Settings dialog box

2. Ensure that if any settings are manually set, you take note of them so that you can restore them later if you want.

To check the network settings on Mac OS X, perform the following steps:

1. Open **System Preferences** and click on **Networks**. You can then confirm if the IP address is allocated automatically (using DHCP) or not.

2. Ensure that if any settings are manually set you take note of them so you can restore them later if you want to. Refer to the following screenshot:

OS X Network Settings dialog box

If you just need to access or control the Raspberry Pi without an Internet connection, refer to the *Direct network link* section on the *There's more...*section.

How to do it...

First, we need to enable ICS on our network devices. In this case, we will be sharing the Internet, which is available on **Wireless Network Connection** through **Local Area Connection** to the Raspberry Pi.

For Windows, perform the following steps:

1. Return to the list of network adapters, right-click on the connection that links to the Internet (in this case, the **Wireless Network Connection** option) and click on **Properties** as shown in the following screenshot:

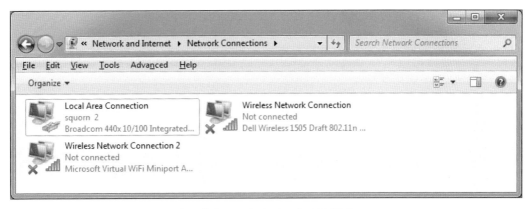

Locating your wired network connection

2. At the top of the window, select the second tab (in Windows XP, it is called **Advanced**; in Windows 7, it is called **Sharing**) as shown in the following screenshot:

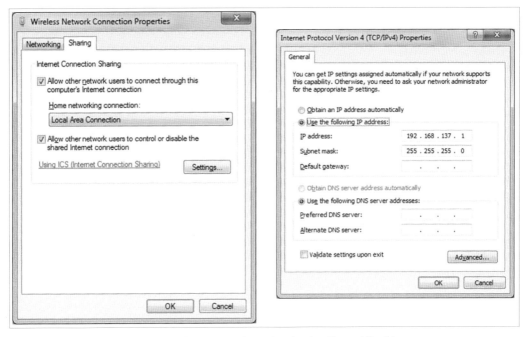

Selecting the TCP/IP properties and noting the allocated IP address

3. In the **Internet Connection Sharing** section, check the box for **Allow other network users to connect through this computer's Internet connection** and use the drop-down box to select the **Home networking connection:** option as **Local Area Connection**. Click on **OK** and confirm if you previously had a fixed IP address set for **Local Area Connection**.

4. Go back into the **Properties** dialog box of **Local Area Connection** and view the **Internet Protocol** settings as before.

5. Take note of the new IP address that has been allocated to the adapter by ICS.

For Mac OS X to enable the ICS, perform the following steps:

1. Click on **System Preferences** and click on **Sharing**.

2. Click on **Internet Sharing** and select the connection from which we want to share the Internet (in this case, it will be the Wi-Fi **AirPort**). Then select the connection that we will connect the Raspberry Pi to (in this case, **Ethernet**).

3. Take note of the new IP address that has been allocated to the adapter by ICS.

For Linux to enable the ICS, perform the following steps:

1. From the **System** menu, click on **Preferences** and then **Network Connections**. Select the connection we want to share (in this case, **Wireless**) and click on **Edit** or **Configure**. In the **IPv4 Settings** tab, change the **Method** option to **Shared to other computers**.

2. Take note of the new IP address that has been allocated to the adapter by ICS.

The IP address of the network adapter will be the **Gateway IP** address to be used on the Raspberry Pi, and we must also provide the Raspberry Pi with an IP address that matches the IP address (except the last number). For instance, if the computer's wired connection now has `192.168.137.1`, we can set the Raspberry Pi's IP address to `192.168.137.10` and set the Gateway IP to `192.168.137.1`.

Next, we will set the required settings on the Raspberry Pi. We need to edit the `cmdline.txt` file, which we can do directly on the Raspberry Pi or on the computer (this is useful if there isn't a monitor or keyboard attached to the Raspberry Pi).

To edit directly on the Raspberry Pi, perform the following steps:

1. Use the following command to edit `/boot/cmdline.txt`:

   ```
   sudo nano /boot/cmdline.txt
   ```

2. When the changes have been made, save and exit by pressing *Ctrl + X, Y,* and *Enter*.

To edit on another computer, perform the following steps:

1. Shut down the Raspberry Pi before removing the SD card.
2. Take the SD card out of the Raspberry Pi and insert into an SD card reader.

> If you have used NOOBS to set up your SD card, you will be unable to access the BOOT partition directly on a Windows computer. Windows is only able to access the first partition on the SD card (which in the case of NOOBS is the RECOVERY partition). Therefore, in order to edit the cmdline.txt file on a Windows computer, it is necessary to use a **Linux Live** CD or create a Linux Virtual Machine.
>
> If the SD card has been prepared manually (refer to the *Preparing an SD card manually* section), you will be able to access and edit it directly from Windows.
>
> Mac OS X should allow you to access both the BOOT and RECOVERY partitions.

3. Locate the SD card in the file manager, find the cmdline.txt file, and open it to edit (on Linux, it will be in the first partition; on Windows, it will be the only visible partition on the device).
4. Ensure that you safely eject the SD card, selecting the drive and ejecting or unmounting it when you have made the change.

The file will contain something similar to the following command line (all on a single line):

```
dwc_otg.lpm_enable=0 console=ttyAMA0,115200 kgdboc=ttyAMA0,115200
console=tty1 root=/dev/mmcblk0p2 rootfstype=ext4 elevator=deadline
rootwait
```

To set the Raspberry Pi's IP address (for example, 192.168.137.10) and the Gateway IP address (for example, 192.168.137.1) when it next powers up, we add the following command line to the end of the same line using ip= option:

```
dwc_otg.lpm_enable=0 console=ttyAMA0,115200 kgdboc=ttyAMA0,115200
console=tty1 root=/dev/mmcblk0p2 rootfstype=ext4 elevator=deadline
rootwait ip=192.168.137.10::192.168.137.1
```

We are now ready to test the new connection as follows:

1. Connect the network cable to the Raspberry Pi and the computer's network port, and then power up the Raspberry Pi, ensuring that you have reinserted the SD card if you previously removed it. To reboot the Raspberry Pi if you edited the file on there, use sudo reboot to restart it.

2. Allow a minute or two for the Raspberry Pi to fully power up. We can now test the connection.

3. From the connected laptop or computer, test the connection by pinging with the IP address you have set for the Raspberry Pi, for example, `192.168.137.10`, as shown in the following command (on Linux or OS X, add `-c 4` to limit to four messages or press *Ctrl* + *C* to exit):

```
ping 192.168.137.10
```

Hopefully, you will find you have a working connection and receive replies from the Raspberry Pi.

If you have a keyboard and screen connected to the Raspberry Pi, you can perform the following steps:

1. You can ping the computer in return (for example, `192.168.137.1`) from the Raspberry Pi terminal as follows:

```
ping 192.168.137.1 -c 4
```

2. You can test the link to the Internet by using `ping` to connect to a well-known website as follows, assuming you do not access the Internet through a proxy server:

```
ping www.raspberrypi.org -c 4
```

If all goes well, you will have full Internet available through your computer to the Raspberry Pi, allowing you to browse the web as well as update and install new software.

If the connection fails, perform the following steps:

1. Repeat the process, ensuring that the first three sets of numbers match with the Raspberry Pi and the network adapter IP addresses.

2. You can also check that when the Raspberry Pi powers up, the correct IP address is being set using the following command:

```
hostname -I
```

3. This should be the address that was set in the `cmdline.txt` file.

4. If not, check the file; it should not have odd characters or symbols and should contain only one line. This is particularly important if you edited the file using Windows, as Linux files use a slightly different format.

 If you end up using Windows to edit lots of files from the Raspberry Pi, it is worth installing an editor such as **Notepad++** (`http://notepad-plus-plus.org`), which supports these differences.

5. Check your firewall settings to ensure it is not blocking internal network connections.

Just remember that this address may be different on different networks and computers, so if you have problems, confirm that the IP address has not changed on the shared adapter.

How it works...

When we enable ICS on the primary computer, the operating system will automatically allocate a new IP address to the computer. Once we determine what the new IP address is, we can ensure that the Raspberry Pi is set to a compatible IP address and the primary computer IP address is used as the Gateway IP address.

Finally, we check whether the computer can communicate over the direct network link to the Raspberry Pi, back the other way, and also through to the Internet.

There's more...

If you do not require the Internet on the Raspberry Pi, or your computer only has a single network adapter, we can still connect the computers together through a direct network link. The advantage of this method is that the same IP address should work on most of the computers as long as the adapter you connect to is set to **automatic**. Refer to the following diagram:

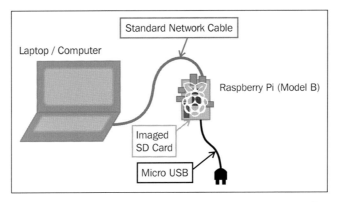

Connecting and using the Raspberry Pi with just a network cable, a standard imaged SD card, and power

Direct network link

For a network link to work between two computers, they need to be using the same address range. The allowable address range is determined by the subnet mask (for example, `255.255.0.0` or `255.255.255.0` would mean all IP addresses should be the same except for the last two or just the last number in the IP address; otherwise, they will be filtered).

To use a direct link without enabling ICS, check the IP settings of the adapter you are going to connect to and determine if it is automatically allocated or fixed to a specific IP address.

Most PCs connected directly to another computer will allocate an IP address in the range `169.254.X.X` (with a subnet mask of `255.255.0.0`). For the Raspberry Pi to be able to communicate through the direct link, it needs to have a fixed IP address in the same address range `169.254.X.X`. Again, we can set this in the `cmdline.txt` file (for example, `169.254.1.10`) as follows:

```
dwc_otg.lpm_enable=0 console=ttyAMA0,115200 kgdboc=ttyAMA0,115200
console=tty1 root=/dev/mmcblk0p2 rootfstype=ext4 elevator=deadline
rootwait ip=169.254.1.10
```

The `169.254.X.X` address is particularly useful, since this setting should work on most computers where the adapter settings are set to automatic. If you use this often, you can make a copy of `cmdline.txt` and swap them over when you wish to change the settings.

 In the later releases of the Raspberry Pi distributions, it is expected that the Raspberry Pi will detect this situation and like other computers, automatically allocate itself an IP address in the `169.254.X.X` range. This would avoid the need to change any settings, and the direct network link will be available automatically, assuming both sides are set to **automatic DHCP** settings.

If set to a fixed IP address (for example, `192.168.1.50`), simply pick one that matches except the last number and set the `ip= setting` command in `cmdline.txt` accordingly (for example, `192.168.1.10`, as shown in the following command line). This time we don't need to set the Gateway IP address:

```
dwc_otg.lpm_enable=0 console=ttyAMA0,115200 kgdboc=ttyAMA0,115200
console=tty1 root=/dev/mmcblk0p2 rootfstype=ext4 elevator=deadline
rootwait ip=192.168.1.10
```

See also

If you don't have a keyboard or screen connected to the Raspberry Pi, you can use this network link to remotely access the Raspberry Pi just as you would on a normal network (just use the new IP address you have set for the connection). Refer to the *Connecting remotely to the Raspberry Pi over the network using VNC* and *Connecting remotely to the Raspberry Pi over the network using SSH (and X11 Forwarding)* recipes.

Networking and connecting your Raspberry Pi to the Internet via a USB Wi-Fi dongle

Many home networks provide a wireless network over Wi-Fi. By adding a **USB Wi-Fi dongle** to the Raspberry Pi's USB port, it can connect to and use the Wi-Fi network.

Getting ready

You shall need to obtain a suitable USB Wi-Fi dongle; and in some cases, you may require a powered USB hub (this will depend on the hardware version of the Raspberry Pi you have and the quality of your power supply). General suitability of USB Wi-Fi dongles will vary depending on the chipset that is used inside and the level of Linux support available. You may find that some USB Wi-Fi dongles will work without installing additional drivers (in which case you can jump to configuring it for the wireless network)

A list of supported Wi-Fi adapters is available at `http://elinux.org/RPi_ VerifiedPeripherals#USB_WiFi_Adapters`.

You will need to ensure that your Wi-Fi adapter is also compatible with your intended network; for example, supporting the same types of signals **802.11bgn** and the encryptions **WEP**, **WPA**, and **WPA2** (although most networks are backward compatible).

You will also need the following details of your network:

> ▸ **Service set identifier (SSID)**: This is the name of your Wi-Fi network and should be visible if you use the following command:
>
> ```
> sudo iwlist scan | grep SSID
> ```
>
> ▸ **Encryption type and key**: This value will be **None**, **WEP**, **WPA**, or **WPA2**, and the key will be the code you normally enter when you connect your phone or laptop to the wireless network (sometimes, it is printed on the router).

You will require a working Internet connection (that is, wired Ethernet) in order to download the required drivers. Otherwise, you may be able to locate the required firmware files (they will be the `.deb` files), and copy them to the Raspberry Pi (that is, via a USB flash drive; the drive should be automatically mounted if you are running in the desktop mode). Copy the file to a suitable location and install it with the following command:

```
sudo apt-get install firmware_file.deb
```

How to do it...

This task has two stages; first, we would identify and install firmware for the Wi-Fi adapter, and then we would need to configure it for the wireless network.

We will try to identify the chipset of your Wi-Fi adapter (the part that handles the connection); this may not match the actual manufacturer of the device.

An approximate list of supported firmware can be found with the following command:

```
sudo apt-cache search wireless firmware
```

This will produce results similar to the following output (disregarding any results without `firmware` in the package title):

```
atmel-firmware - Firmware for Atmel at76c50x wireless networking chips.
firmware-atheros - Binary firmware for Atheros wireless cards
firmware-brcm80211 - Binary firmware for Broadcom 802.11 wireless cards
firmware-ipw2x00 - Binary firmware for Intel Pro Wireless 2100, 2200 and 2915
firmware-iwlwifi - Binary firmware for Intel PRO/Wireless 3945 and 802.11n cards
firmware-libertas - Binary firmware for Marvell Libertas 8xxx wireless cards
firmware-ralink - Binary firmware for Ralink wireless cards
firmware-realtek - Binary firmware for Realtek wired and wireless network adapters
libertas-firmware - Firmware for Marvell's libertas wireless chip series (dummy package)
zd1211-firmware - Firmware images for the zd1211rw wireless driver
```

To find out the chipset of your wireless adapter, plug the Wi-Fi-adapter into Raspberry Pi, and from the terminal, run the following command:

```
dmesg | grep 'Product:\|Manufacturer:'
```

This command stitches together two commands into one. First, `dmesg` displays the message buffer of the kernel (this is an internal record of system events that have occurred since power on, such as detected USB devices). You can try the command on its own to observe the complete output.

The | (pipe) sends the output to the `grep` command, `grep 'Product:\|Manuf'` checks it and only returns lines that contain `Product` or `Manuf` (so we should get a summary of any items, which are listed as `Product` and `Manufacturer`). If you don't find anything or want to see all your USB devices, try `grep 'usb'` instead.

This should return something similar to the following output (in this case, I've got a **ZyXEL** device, which has a **ZyDAS** chipset (a quick Google search reveals `zd1211-firmware` is for ZyDAS devices):

```
[    1.893367] usb usb1: Product: DWC OTG Controller
[    1.900217] usb usb1: Manufacturer: Linux 3.6.11+ dwc_otg_hcd
[    3.348259] usb 1-1.2: Product: ZyXEL G-202
[    3.355062] usb 1-1.2: Manufacturer: ZyDAS
```

Once you have identified your device and the correct firmware, you can install it, as you would for any other package available through `apt-get` (where `zd1211-firmware` can be replaced with your required firmware as) shown in the following command:

```
sudo apt-get install zd1211-firmware
```

Remove and reinsert the USB Wi-Fi dongle to allow it to be detected and the drivers loaded. We can now test if the new adapter is correctly installed with `ifconfig`. The output is shown as follows:

```
wlan0     IEEE 802.11bg  ESSID:off/any
          Mode:Managed  Access Point: Not-Associated   Tx-Power=20 dBm
          Retry  long limit:7   RTS thr:off    Fragment thr:off
          Power Management:off
```

The command will show the network adapters present on the system. For Wi-Fi, this is usually as `wlan0`, or `wlan1`, or so on if you have installed more than one. If not, double-check the selected firmware; and perhaps, try an alternative or check on the site for troubleshooting tips.

Once we have the firmware installed for the Wi-Fi adapter, we will need to configure it for the network we wish to connect. Perform the following steps:

1. We will need to add the wireless adapter to the list of network interfaces, which is set in `/etc/network/interfaces` as follows:

    ```
    sudo nano -c /etc/network/interfaces
    ```

    Using the previous `wlan#` value, add the following command:

    ```
    auto wlan0
    iface wlan0 inet dhcp
    wpa-conf /etc/wpa.conf
    ```

    When the changes have been made, save and exit by pressing *Ctrl + X, Y,* and *Enter*.

2. We will now store the Wi-Fi network settings of our network in the `wpa.conf` file (don't worry if your network doesn't use the `wpa` encryption; it is just the default name for the file) as follows:

    ```
    sudo nano -c /etc/wpa.conf
    ```

    The following information (that is, if the SSID is set as `theSSID`):

    □   If no encryption is used, use the following code:

    ```
    network={
        ssid="theSSID"
        key_mgmt=NONE
    }
    ```

    □   With the `WEP` encryption (that is, if the `WEP` key is set as `theWEPkey`), use the following code:

    ```
    network={
        ssid="theSSID"
        key_mgmt=NONE
        wep_key0="theWEPkey"
    }
    ```

    □   Or for the `WPA` or `WPA2` encryption (that is, if the `WPA` key is set as `theWPAkey`), use the following code:

    ```
    network={
        ssid="theSSID"
        key_mgmt=WPA-PSK
        psk="theWPAkey"
    }
    ```

3. You can enable the adapter with the following command (again, replace `wlan0` if required):

```
sudo ifup wlan0
```

Use the following command to list the wireless network connections:

```
iwconfig
```

You should see your wireless network connected with your SSID listed as follows:

```
wlan0     IEEE 802.11bg  ESSID:"theSSID"
          Mode:Managed  Frequency:2.442 GHz  Access Point:
          00:24:BB:FF:FF:FF
          Bit Rate=48 Mb/s   Tx-Power=20 dBm
          Retry  long limit:7   RTS thr:off   Fragment thr:off
          Power Management:off
          Link Quality=32/100  Signal level=32/100
          Rx invalid nwid:0  Rx invalid crypt:0  Rx invalid frag:0
          Tx excessive retries:0  Invalid misc:15   Missed beacon:0
```

If not, adjust your settings and use `sudo ifdown wlan0` to switch off the network interface, and then `sudo ifup wlan0` to switch it back on.

This will confirm that you have successfully connected to your Wi-Fi network.

4. Finally, we will need to check whether we have access to the Internet. Here, we have assumed that the network is automatically configured with DHCP and no proxy server is used. If not, refer to the *Connecting to the Internet through a proxy server* recipe.

Unplug the wired network cable, if still connected, and see if we can ping the Raspberry Pi website as follows:

```
ping www.raspberrypi.org
```

 If you want to quickly know the IP address currently in use by the Raspberry Pi, you can use `hostname -I` or to find out which adapter is connected to which IP address, use `ifconfig`.

There's more...

The Model A version of the Raspberry Pi does not have a built-in network port; so in order to get a network connection, a USB network adapter will have to be added (either a Wi-Fi dongle, as explained in the preceding section, or a LAN-to-USB adapter, as described in the following section.

Using USB wired network adapters

Just like the USB Wi-Fi, the adapter support will depend on the chipset used and the drivers available. Unless the device comes with the Linux drivers, you may have to search the Internet to obtain the suitable Debian Linux drivers.

If you find a suitable `.deb` file, you can install it with the following command:

```
sudo apt-get install firmware_file.deb
```

Ensure that you also check using `ifconfig`, as some devices will be supported automatically and will appear as `eth1` (or `eth0` on Model A), and be ready to use immediately.

Connecting to the Internet through a proxy server

Some networks such as workplaces or schools often require you to connect to the Internet through a proxy server.

Getting ready

You will need the address of the proxy server you are trying to connect to, including the username and password if one is required.

You should confirm that the Raspberry Pi is already connected to the network and that you can access the proxy server.

Use the `ping` command to check this as follows:

```
ping proxy.address.com -c 4
```

If this fails (you get no responses), you will need to ensure your network settings are correct before continuing.

How to do it...

Create a new file using nano as follows (if there is content in the file already, you can add the code at the end):

```
sudo nano -c ~/.bash_profile
```

To allow the basic web browsing through programs such as **midori** while using a proxy server, you can use the following script:

```
function proxyenable {
# Define proxy settings
PROXY_ADDR="proxy.address.com:port"
# Login name (leave blank if not required):
LOGIN_USER="login_name"
# Login Password (leave blank to prompt):
LOGIN_PWD=
#If login specified - check for password
if [[ -z $LOGIN_USER ]]; then
  #No login for proxy
  PROXY_FULL=$PROXY_ADDR
else
  #Login needed for proxy Prompt for password -s option hides input
  if [[ -z $LOGIN_PWD ]]; then
    read -s -p "Provide proxy password (then Enter):" LOGIN_PWD
    echo
  fi
  PROXY_FULL=$LOGIN_USER:$LOGIN_PWD@$PROXY_ADDR
fi
#Web Proxy Enable: http_proxy or HTTP_PROXY environment variables
export http_proxy="http://$PROXY_FULL/"
export HTTP_PROXY=$http_proxy
export https_proxy="https://$PROXY_FULL/"
export HTTPS_PROXY=$https_proxy
export ftp_proxy="ftp://$PROXY_FULL/"
export FTP_PROXY=$ftp_proxy
#Set proxy for apt-get
sudo cat <<EOF | sudo tee /etc/apt/apt.conf.d/80proxy > /dev/null
Acquire::http::proxy "http://$PROXY_FULL/";
Acquire::ftp::proxy "ftp://$PROXY_FULL/";
Acquire::https::proxy "https://$PROXY_FULL/";
EOF
#Remove info no longer needed from environment
unset LOGIN_USER LOGIN_PWD PROXY_ADDR PROXY_FULL
echo Proxy Enabled
}
```

```
function proxydisable {
#Disable proxy values, apt-get and git settings
unset http_proxy HTTP_PROXY https_proxy HTTPS_PROXY
unset ftp_proxy FTP_PROXY
sudo rm /etc/apt/apt.conf.d/80proxy
echo Proxy Disabled
}
```

Once done, save and exit by pressing *Ctrl + X, Y,* and *Enter.*

The script is added to the user's own `.bash_profile` file, which is run when that particular user logs in. This will ensure that the proxy settings are kept separately for each user. If you want all users to use the same settings, you can add the code to `/etc/rc.local` instead (this file must have `exit 0` at the end).

How it works...

Many programs that make use of the Internet will check for the `http_proxy` or `HTTP_PROXY` environment variables before connecting. If they are present, they will use the proxy settings to connect through. Some programs may also use the `HTTPS` and `FTP` protocols, so we can set the proxy setting for them here too.

If a username is required for the proxy server, a password will be prompted for. It is generally not recommended to store your passwords inside scripts unless you are confident no one else will have access to your device (either physically or through the Internet).

The last part allows any programs that execute using the `sudo` command to use the proxy environment variables while acting as the super user (most programs will try accessing the network using normal privileges first, even if running as a super user, so it isn't always needed).

There's more...

We also need to allow the proxy settings to be used by some programs, which use super user permissions while accessing the network (this will depend on the program; most don't need this). We need to add the commands into a file stored in `/etc/sudoers.d/` by performing the following steps:

It is important to use `visudo` here, as it ensures the permissions of the file are created correctly for the `sudoers` directory (read only by the `root` user).

1. Use the following command to open a new `sudoer` file:

   ```
   sudo visudo -f /etc/sudoers.d/proxy
   ```

2. Enter the following text in the file (on a single line):

   ```
   Defaults env_keep += "http_proxy HTTP_PROXY https_proxy HTTPS_
   PROXY ftp_proxy FTP_PROXY"
   ```

3. Once done, save and exit by pressing *Ctrl + X*, *Y*, and *Enter*; don't change the `proxy.tmp` filename (this is normal for `visudo`; it will change it to proxy when finished).

4. If prompted `What now?`, there is an error in the command. Press *X* to exit without saving and retype the command!

5. After a reboot (using `sudo reboot`), you will be able to use the following commands to enable and disable the proxy respectively:

   ```
   proxyenable
   ```

   ```
   proxydisable
   ```

Connecting remotely to the Raspberry Pi over the network using VNC

Often, it is preferable to remotely connect to and control the Raspberry Pi across the network. For instance, using a laptop or desktop computer as a screen and keyboard, or while the Raspberry Pi is connected elsewhere, perhaps even connected to some hardware to which it needs to be near.

VNC is just one way in which you can remotely connect to the Raspberry Pi. It will create a new desktop session that will be controlled and accessed remotely. The VNC session here is separate to the one that may be active on the Raspberry Pi's display.

Getting ready

Ensure that your Raspberry Pi is powered up and connected to the Internet. We will use the Internet connection to install a program using `apt-get`. This is a program that allows us to find and install applications directly from the official repositories.

How to do it...

First, we need to install the **TightVNC** server on the Raspberry Pi with the following commands. It is advisable to run an `update` command first to get the latest version of the package you want to install as follows:

```
sudo apt-get update
sudo apt-get install tightvncserver
```

Accept the prompt to install and wait until it completes. To start a session, use the following command to start a session:

```
vncserver :1
```

The first time you run this, it will ask you to enter a password (of no more than eight characters) to access the desktop (you will use this when you connect from your computer).

The following message should confirm that a new desktop session has been started:

```
New 'X' desktop is raspberrypi:1
```

If you do not already know the IP address of the Raspberry Pi, use `hostname -I` and take note of it.

Next, we need to run a VNC client, **VNC Viewer** is suitable program, which is available at `http://www.realvnc.com/` and should work on Windows, Linux, and OS X.

When you run VNC Viewer, you will be prompted for the **Server** address and **Encryption** type. Use the IP address of your Raspberry Pi with `:1`. That is, for the IP address **192.168.1.69**, use the `192.168.1.69:1` address.

You can leave the Encryption type as **Off** or **Automatic**.

Depending on your network, you may be able to use the hostname; the default is **raspberrypi**, that is `raspberrypi:1`.

You may have a warning about not having connected to the computer before or having no encryption. You should enable encryption if you are using a public network or if you are performing connections over the Internet (to stop others from being able to intercept your data).

There's more...

You can add options to the command line to specify the resolution and also the color depth of the display. The higher the resolution and color depth (can be adjusted to use 8 to 32 bits per pixel to provide low or high color detail), the more data has to be transferred through the network link. If you find the refresh rate a little slow, try reducing these numbers as follows:

```
vncserver :1 -geometry 1280x780 -depth 24
```

To allow the VNC server to start automatically when you switch on, you can add the `vncserver` command to `.bash_profile` (this is executed each time the Raspberry Pi starts).

Use the `nano` editor as follows (the `-c` option allows the line numbers to be displayed):

```
sudo nano -c ~/.bash_profile
```

Add the following line to the end of the file:

```
vncserver :1
```

The next time you power up, you should be able to remotely connect using VNC from another computer.

Connecting remotely to the Raspberry Pi over the network using SSH (and X11 Forwarding)

An **SSH** (**Secure SHell**) is often the preferred method for making remote connections, as it allows only the terminal connections and typically requires fewer resources.

An extra feature of SSH is the ability to transfer the **X11** data to an **X Windows** server running on your machine. This allows you to start programs that would normally run on the Raspberry Pi desktop and they will appear in their own Windows on the local computer as follows:

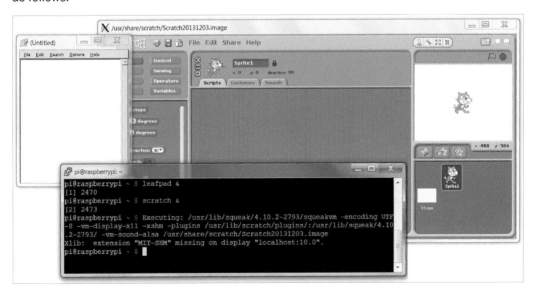

X Forwarding can be used to display applications, which are running on the Raspberry Pi, on a Windows computer.

Getting ready

If you are running the latest version of Raspbian, SSH and X11 Forwarding will be enabled by default (otherwise, double-check the settings explained in the *How it works...* section).

How to do it...

Linux and OS X have built-in support for X11 Forwarding; but if you are using Windows, you will need to install and run the X Windows server on your computer.

Download and run `xming` from the **Xming** site (`http://sourceforge.net/projects/xming/`).

Install `xming`, following the installation steps, including the installation of **PuTTY** if you don't have it already. You can also download PuTTY separately from `http://www.putty.org/`.

Next, we need to ensure the SSH program we use has X11 enabled when we connect.

For Windows, we shall use PuTTY to connect to the Raspberry Pi.

In the **PuTTY Configuration** dialog box, navigate to **Connection | SSH | X11** and tick in the checkbox for **X11 Forwarding**. If you leave the **X display location** option blank, it will assume the default `Server 0:0` as follows (you can confirm the server number by moving your mouse over the Xming icon in the system tray when it is running):

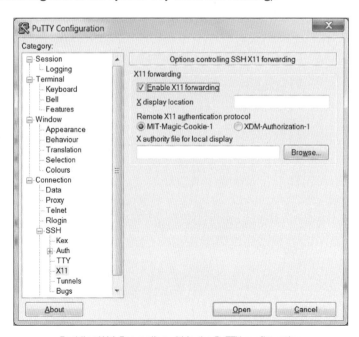

Enabling X11 Forwarding within the PuTTY configuration

Enter the IP address of the Raspberry Pi in the **Session** settings (you may also find that you can use the Raspberry Pi's hostname here instead; the default hostname is `raspberrypi`).

Save the setting using a suitable name, `RaspberryPi`, and click on **Open** to connect to your Raspberry Pi.

You are likely to see a warning message pop up stating you haven't connected to the computer before (this allows you to check you have everything right before continuing).

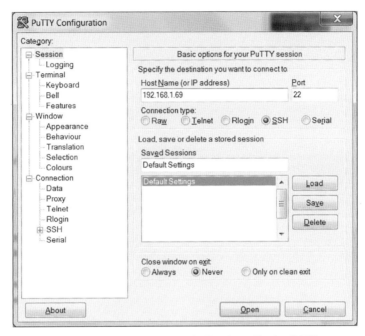

Opening an SSH connection to the Raspberry Pi using PuTTY

For OS X or Linux, click on **Terminal** to open a connection to the Raspberry Pi.

To connect with the default `pi` username, with an IP address of `192.168.1.69`, use the following command; the `-X` option enables X11 Forwarding:

```
ssh -X pi@192.168.1.69
```

All being well, you should be greeted with a prompt for your password (remember the default value for the `pi` user is `raspberry`).

Ensure that you have Xming running, bystarting the Xming program from your computer's Start menu. Then, in the terminal window, type a program that normally runs within the Raspberry Pi desktop, such as `leafpad` or `scratch`. Wait a little while and the program should appear on your computer's desktop (if you get an error, you have probably forgotten to start Xming, so run it and try again).

How it works...

X Windows and X11 is what provides the method by which the Raspberry Pi (and many other Linux-based computers) can display and control graphical Windows as part of a desktop.

For X11 Forwarding to work over a network connection, we need both SSH and X11 Forwarding enabled on the Raspberry Pi. Perform the following steps:

1. To switch on (or off) SSH, you can access `raspi config` (just type `sudo raspi-config` from the terminal) and click on **SSH** within the **Advanced Options** menu, as shown in the following screenshot (SSH is often enabled by default for most of the distributions to help allow remote connections without needing a monitor to configure it):

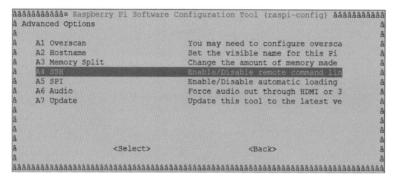

The advanced settings menu in the raspi-config tool

2. Ensure that X11 Forwarding is enabled on the Raspberry Pi (again most of the distributions now have this enabled by default).

3. Use `nano` with the following command:

```
sudo nano /etc/ssh/sshd_config
```

4. Look for a line in the `/etc/ssh/sshd_config` file, which controls X11 Forwarding and ensure that it says `yes` (with no # sign before it) as follows:

```
X11Forwarding yes
```

5. Save if required, by pressing *Ctrl + X, Y,* and *Enter* and reboot (if you need to change it) as follows:

```
sudo reboot
```

There's more...

SSH and X 11 Forwarding is a convenient way to control the Raspberry Pi remotely; we will explore some additional tips on how to use it effectively in the following sections.

Running multiple programs with X11 Forwarding

If you want to run an **X program**, but still be able to use the same terminal console for other stuff, you can run the command in the background with `&` as follows:

```
leafpad &
```

Just remember that the more programs you run, the slower everything will get. You can switch to the background program by typing `fg`, check for the background tasks with `bg`.

Running as a desktop with X11 Forwarding

You can even run a complete desktop session through X11, although it isn't particularly user-friendly and VNC will produce better results. To achieve this, you have to use `lxsession` instead of `startx` (in the way you would normally start the desktop from the terminal).

An alternative is to use `lxpanel`, which provides the program menu bar from which you can start and run programs from the menu as you would on the desktop.

Running PyGame and Tkinter with X11 Forwarding

You can get the following error (or similar) when running the **PyGame** or **Tkinter** scripts:

```
_tkinter.TclError: couldn't connect to display "localhost:10.0"
```

In this case, use the following command to fix the error:

```
sudo cp ~/.Xauthority ~root/
```

Sharing the home folder of the Raspberry Pi with SMB

When you have the Raspberry Pi connected to your network, you can access the home folder by setting up file sharing; this makes it much easier to transfer files and provides a quick and easy way to back up your data. **Server Message Block** (**SMB**) is a protocol that is compatible with Windows file sharing, OS X, and Linux.

Getting ready

Ensure that you have the Raspberry Pi powered and running with a working connection to the Internet.

You will also need another computer on the same local network to test the new share.

How to do it...

First, we need to install `samba`, a software that handles folder sharing in a format that is compatible with Windows sharing methods.

Ensure that you use `update` as follows to obtain the latest list of available packages:

```
sudo apt-get update
sudo apt-get install samba
```

The install will require around 20 MB of space and take a few minutes.

Once the install has completed, we can make a copy of the configuration file as follows to allow us to restore to defaults if needed:

```
sudo cp /etc/samba/smb.conf /etc/samba/smb.conf.backup
sudo nano /etc/samba/smb.conf
```

Scroll down and find the section named `Authentication`; change the `#    security = user` line to `security = user`.

As described in the file, this setting ensures that you have to enter your username and password for the Raspberry Pi in order to access the files (this is important for shared networks).

Find the section called `Share Definitions` and `[homes]`, and change the `read only = yes` line to the `read only = no` line.

This will allow us to view and also write files to the shared home folder. Once done, save and exit by pressing *Ctrl + X, Y,* and *Enter.*

[If you have changed the default user from `pi` to something else, substitute it in the following instructions.]

Now, we can add `pi` (the default user) to use `samba` as follows:

```
sudo pdbedit -a -u pi
```

Now, enter a password (you can use the same password as your login or select a different one, but avoid using the default Raspberry password, which would be very easy for someone to guess). Restart `samba` to use the new configuration file as follows:

```
sudo /etc/init.d/samba restart
[ ok ] Stopping Samba daemons: nmbd smbd.
[ ok ] Starting Samba daemons: nmbd smbd.
```

In order to test, you will need to know either the Raspberry Pi's hostname (the default hostname is `raspberrypi`) or its IP address. You can find both of these with the following command:

```
hostname
```

For the IP address, add `-I` as follows:

```
hostname -I
```

On another computer on the network, enter the `\\raspberrypi\pi` address in the explorer path.

Depending on your network, the computer should locate the Raspberry Pi on the network and prompt for a username and password. If it can't find the share using the hostname, you can use the IP address directly, where `192.168.1.69` should be changed to match the IP address, `\\192.168.1.69\pi`.

Keeping the Raspberry Pi up to date

The Linux image used by the Raspberry Pi is often updated to include enhancements, fixes, and improvements to the system, as well as adding support for new hardware, or changes made to the latest board. Many of the packages that you install, can be updated too.

This is particularly important if you plan on using the same system image on another Raspberry Pi board (particularly, a newer one) as older images will lack support for any wiring changes or alternative RAM chips. New firmware should work on older Raspberry Pi boards, but older firmware may not be compatible with the latest hardware.

Fortunately, you need not reflash your SD card every time there is a new release, since you can update it instead.

Getting ready

You will need to be connected to the Internet in order to update your system. It is always advisable to make a backup of your image first (and at a minimum, take a copy of your important files).

You can check your current version of firmware with the `uname -a` command as follows:

```
Linux raspberrypi 3.1.9+ #168 PREEMPT Sat Jul 14 18:56:31 BST 2012 armv6l
GNU/Linux
```

The GPU firmware can be checked using the `/opt/vc/bin/vcgencmd version` command as follows:

```
    Jul 14 2012 13:14:40
Copyright (c) 2012 Broadcom

version 325444 (release)
```

This is important if you are using an older version of firmware (pre-November 2012) on a newer board since the Model B board was only 254 MB RAM. Upgrading allows the firmware to make use of the extra memory if available.

The `free -h` command will detail the RAM available to the main processor (the total RAM is split between the GPU and ARM cores) and will give the following output:

```
                 total     used     free    shared   buffers    cached
Mem:              183M     125M      58M        0B      9.1M       96M
-/+ buffers/cache:          19M     164M
Swap:              99M       0B      99M
```

You can then recheck the preceding output following a reboot to confirm if they have been updated (although they may have already been the latest).

How to do it...

Before running any upgrades or installing any packages, it is worth ensuring you have the latest list of packages in the repository. The `update` command gets the latest list of available software and versions:

```
sudo apt-get update
```

If you just want to obtain an upgrade of your current packages, `upgrade` will bring them all up to date:

```
sudo apt-get upgrade
```

To ensure that you are running the latest release of Raspbian, you can run `dist-upgrade` (be warned; this can take an hour or so, depending on the amount that needs to be upgraded). This will perform all the updates that `upgrade` will perform but will also remove redundant packages and clean up:

```
sudo apt-get dist-upgrade
```

Both methods will upgrade the software, including the firmware used at boot and startup (`bootcode.bin` and `start.elf`).

2

Starting with Python Strings, Files, and Menus

In this chapter, we will cover:

- ▸ Working with text and strings
- ▸ Using files and handling errors
- ▸ Creating a boot-up menu
- ▸ Creating a self-defining menu

Introduction

In this chapter, we shall jump into using Python to perform some basic encryption by scrambling letters. This will introduce some basic string manipulation, user input, progressing on to creating reusable modules, and finally graphical user interfaces.

To follow, we shall create some useful Python scripts that can be added to run as the Raspberry Pi boots or as an easy-to-run command that will provide quick shortcuts to common or frequently used commands. Taking this further, we shall make use of threading to run multiple tasks and introduce classes to define multiple objects.

Since it is traditional to start any programming exercise with a **Hello World** example, we shall kick off with that now.

Create the `hellopi.py` file using `nano` as follows:

```
nano -c hellopi.py
```

Within our `hellopi.py` file, add the following code:

```
#!/usr/bin/python
#hellopi.py
print ("Hello Raspberry Pi")
```

When done, save and exit (*Ctrl + X, Y,* and *Enter*). To run the file, use the following command:

python3 hellopi.py

Congratulations, you've created your first program!

You should have a similar result to that shown in the following screenshot:

The Hello Raspberry Pi output

Working with text and strings

A good starting point with Python is to get to grips with basic text handling and strings. A string is a block of characters stored together as a value. As you will see, they can be viewed as a simple list of characters.

We will create a script to obtain the user's input, use string manipulation to switch around the letters, and print out a coded version of the message. We then extend this example by demonstrating how encoded messages can be passed between parties without revealing the encoding methods, while also showing how we can reuse sections of code within other Python modules.

Getting ready

You can use most text editors to write Python code. They can be used directly on the Raspberry Pi or remotely through VNC or SSH.

The following are a few text editors that are available with the Raspberry Pi:

▸ **nano**: This text editor is available from the terminal and includes syntax highlighting and line numbers (with the `-c` option). Refer to the following screenshot:

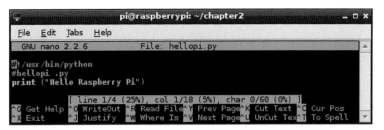

The nano command-line editor

▸ **IDLE3**: This Python editor includes the syntax highlighting feature, context help, and will run scripts directly from the editor (on pressing *F5*). This program requires X-Windows (the Debian desktop) or X11-forwarding to run remotely. We will be using Python 3 throughout this book, so ensure you run IDLE3 (rather than IDLE), which will use Python 3 to run the scripts. Refer to the following screenshot:

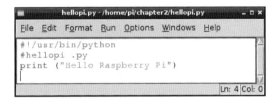

The IDLE3 Python editor

▸ **Geany**: This text editor provides an **IDE** (**Integrated Development Environment**) that supports a range of programming languages, syntax highlighting, autocompletion, and easy code navigation. This is a feature-rich editor but can be difficult to use for beginners and may sometimes be slow when running on the Raspberry Pi. Again, you will need to run this editor with the Debian desktop or X11-forwarding. Refer to the following screenshot:

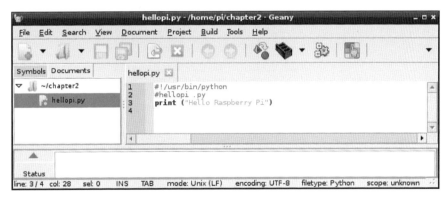

The Geany Integrated Development Environment

To install Geany, use the following command (then run Geany from the **Programming** menu item):

```
sudo apt-get install geany
```

To ensure Geany uses Python 3 when you click on the **Execute** button (to run your scripts), you will need to change the **Build** commands. Load `hellopi.py` and then click on the **Build** menu and select **Set Build Commands**. In the window that appears, which is shown in the following screenshot, change `python` to `python3` in the **Compile** and **Execute** sections. Python is always compiled automatically when it is run (producing the temporary `.pyc` files), so you should never need to use the **Compile** button, except maybe to check the syntax of the code.

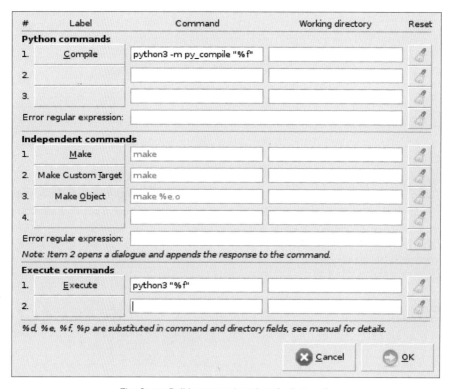

The Geany Build command settings for Python 3

If you have the `home` directory of the Raspberry Pi shared across the network (refer to the *Sharing the home folder of the Raspberry Pi with SMB* recipe in *Chapter 1, Getting Started with a Raspberry Pi Computer*), you can edit files on another computer. However, note that if you use Windows, you must use an editor that supports Linux line endings, such as Notepad++ (you should not use the standard Notepad program).

To create a space for your Python scripts, we will add a folder named `python_scripts` to your `home` directory with the following command:

```
mkdir ~/python_scripts
```

Now you can open this folder and list the files whenever you need to, using the following commands:

```
cd ~/python_scripts
ls
```

 You can use the *Tab* key to help complete commands in the terminal; for example, typing in `cd ~/pyt` and then pressing the *Tab* key will finish the command for you. If there are multiple options that start with `pyt`, pressing the *Tab* key again will list them.

To repeat or edit older commands, use the up and down arrow keys to switch between older and newer commands as required.

How to do it...

Create the `encryptdecrypt.py` script as follows:

```python
#!/usr/bin/python3
#encryptdecrypt.py

#Takes the input_text and encrypts it, returning the result
def encryptText(input_text,key):
  input_text=input_text.upper()
  result = ""
  for letter in input_text:
    #Ascii Uppercase 65-90  Lowercase 97-122 (Full range 32-126)
    ascii_value=ord(letter)
    #Exclude non-characters from encryption
    if (ord("A") > ascii_value) or (ascii_value > ord("Z")):
      result+=letter
    else:
      #Apply encryption key
      key_val = ascii_value+key
      #Ensure we just use A-Z regardless of key
      if not((ord("A")) < key_val < ord("Z")):
        key_val=ord("A")+(key_val-ord("A"))%(ord("Z")-ord("A")+1)
      #Add the encoded letter to the result string
      result+=str(chr(key_val))
```

```
      return result
#Test function
def main():
  print ("Please enter text to scramble:")
  #Get user input
  try:
    user_input = input()
    scrambled_result = encryptText(user_input,10)
    print ("Result: " + scrambled_result)
    print ("To un-scramble, press enter again")
    input()
    unscrambled_result = encryptText(scrambled_result,-10)
    print ("Result: " + unscrambled_result)
  except UnicodeDecodeError:
    print ("Sorry: Only ASCII Characters are supported")

main()
#End
```

> Within the *There's more...* section, we change `main()` to the following code:
> ```
> if __name__=="__main__":
>     main()
> ```
> If you skip the section, ensure you include this change in the
> `encryptdecrypt.py` file as we use it later.

How it works...

The preceding script implements a very basic method to scramble text using a simple form
of character substitution, called a **Caesar Cypher**. Dating back to the Romans, Julius Caesar
used the same method to send secret orders to his armies.

The file defines two functions, `encryptText()` and `main()`.

When the script is running, the `main()` function obtains the user's input by using the
`input()` command. The result is stored as a string in the `user_input` variable (the
command will wait until the user has pressed the *Enter* key before continuing) as follows:

```
user_input = input()
```

> The `input()` function will not handle non-ASCII characters, so we use
> `try...except` to handle this case, which will cause `UnicodeDecodeError`
> to be raised. For more information on using `try...except`, refer to the *Using
> files and handling errors* recipe.

We call the `encryptText()` function with two arguments, the text to be encrypted, and the key. After the text has been encrypted as follows, the result is printed:

```
scrambled_result = encryptText(user_input,10)
print ("Result: " + scrambled_result)
```

Finally, we use `input()` to wait for the user input again (in this case, a prompt to press *Enter*; any other input is ignored). Now, we unscramble the text by reversing the encryption, calling `encryptText()` again but with a negative version of the key, and displaying the result, which should be the original message.

The `encryptText()` function performs a simple form of encryption by taking the letters in the message and substituting each letter with another in the alphabet (determined by counting on from the number of letters specified by the encryption `key`). In this way, the letter A will become C when the encryption `key` is 2.

To simplify the process, the function converts all characters to uppercase. This allows us to use the ASCII character set to translate each character into numbers easily; the letter A is represented by 65 and Z by 90. This is achieved with `input_text=input_text.upper()` and then later by using `ord(letter)` to convert to an ASCII value, which gives us a number representation of the character. ASCII is a standard that maps the numbers 0 to 254 (an 8-bit value) and commonly used characters and symbols.

Next, we ensure we have an empty string in which we can build our result (`result = ""`) and we set our encryption `key` to our key value.

The variable `input_text` contains our string, which is stored as a list (this is similar to an array) of letters. We can access each item in the list using `input_text[0]` for the first item and so on; however, Python also allows us to loop through a list using `for...in`, accessing each item in turn.

The line `for the letter in input_text:` allows us to break up `input_text` by looping through it for each item inside (in this case, the letters in the string) and also setting the letter equal to that item. So if `input_text` equaled HELLO, it would run all the code that is indented below the command five times; each time, the variable letter would be set to H, E, L, L, and finally O. This allows us to read each letter separately, process it, and add the new encrypted letter to the result string.

The next part, `if (ord("A") > ascii_value) or (ascii_value > ord("Z")):`, checks to see if the letter we are looking at is not between A and Z, which means it is probably a number or punctuation mark. In that case, we shall exclude it from the encryption (we just add them to the result string unchanged).

If the letter is between A and Z, we can add the value of our encryption `key` to the value of our letter to obtain our new encoded letter. That is, for an encryption `key` of `10`, we end up with the following set of letters in the output:

```
Input Letter:   A B C D E F G H I J K L M N O P Q R S T U V W X Y Z

Output Letter:  K L M N O P Q R S T U V W X Y Z A B C D E F G H I J
```

Since we want the encrypted message to be easy to write out, we have limited the output to be between A and Z. So, if the letter starts as X, we want to it to wrap around and continue counting from A. We can achieve this by using the % (modulus) function, which gives us the remainder value if we divide a number by another. So, if X is `24` and we add `10`, we get `34`. The value of 34%26 (where 26 is the total number of letters) is 8. Counting on 8 from A, we reach H.

However, in ASCII, the letter A is the number `65`, so we remove this offset from `key_value` and then add it back on once we have the modulus value. The following code ensures that we limit the ASCII values to be between A and Z:

```
#Ensure we just use A-Z regardless of key
if (ord("A") > ascii_value) or (ascii_value > ord("Z")):
  key_value=ord("A") + (key_value-ord("A"))%26
```

This also works if the key is larger than `26` and if we are counting the opposite way too; for instance, if the encryption key was negative, and therefore the decryption key positive.

Finally, we can convert `key_value` back into a letter by using the `unichr()` function and adding it to the result string.

Of course, given very little time, such a simple encryption method could easily be broken. Remember that there are only 25 possible combinations to choose from before the result of the encryption is repeated (multiples of 26 will result in no encryption at all).

There's more...

You can try this simple experiment. Currently, with this basic form of encryption, you would supply the method and the key to anyone you wish to read your message. However, what happens if you want to send a secure transmission without sending the method and the key?

The answer is to send the same message back and forth three times as demonstrated in the following diagram:

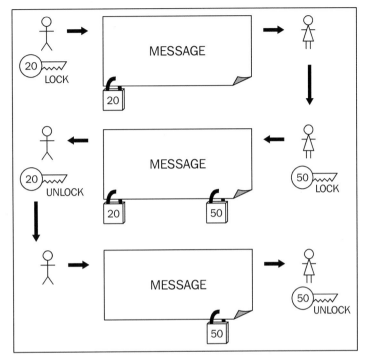

We do not need to exchange encryption keys with the other person

The first time, we encrypt it and send it over to the other party. They then encrypt it again with their own encryption and send it back. The message at this stage has two layers of encryption applied to it. We can now remove our encryption and return it. Finally, they receive the message with just their encryption, which they can remove and read the message.

Just remember that there are only 25 useful encryption combinations with the Caesar Cypher, so it is possible that they could decrypt the message by accident.

We can make use of our previous file as a module by using the import command as follows:

```
import encryptdecrypt as ENC
```

This will allow access to any functions inside the `encryptdecrypt` file using the `ENC` as reference. When such a file is imported, it will run any code that would normally be run; in this case, the `main()` function.

 To avoid this, we can change the call to `main()` only to occur when the file is run directly.

If the file is run directly, Python will set the global attribute __name__ to "__main__". By using the following code, we can reuse the functions in this Python script in other scripts without running any other code:

```
if __name__=="__main__":
    main()
```

Create the keypassing.py script using the following code file in the same directory as encryptdecrypt.py:

```
#!/usr/bin/python3
#keypassing.py
import encryptdecrypt as ENC

KEY1 = 20
KEY2 = 50


print ("Please enter text to scramble:")
#Get user input
user_input = input()
#Send message out
encodedKEY1 = ENC.encryptText(user_input,KEY1)
print ("USER1: Send message encrypted with KEY1 (KEY1): " +
    encodedKEY1)
#Receiver encrypts the message again
encodedKEY1KEY2 = ENC.encryptText(encodedKEY1,KEY2)
print ("USER2: Encrypt with KEY2 & returns it (KEY1+KEY2): " +
    encodedKEY1KEY2)
#Remove the original encoding
encodedKEY2 = ENC.encryptText(encodedKEY1KEY2,-KEY1)
print ("USER1: Removes KEY1 & returns with just KEY2 (KEY2): " +
    encodedKEY2)
#Receiver removes their encryption
message_result = ENC.encryptText(encodedKEY2,-KEY2)
print ("USER2: Removes KEY2 & Message received: " + message_result)
#End
```

On running the preceding script, we can see that the other person never needs to know the encryption key that we are using, and anyone who intercepts the message will not be able to see its contents. The script produces the following output:

```
Please enter text to scramble:
"A message to a friend."
USER1: Send message encrypted with KEY1 (KEY1): U GYMMUAY NI U ZLCYHX.
```

```
USER2: Encrypt with KEY2 & returns it (KEY1+KEY2): S EWKKSYW LG S XJAWFV.

USER1: Removes KEY1 & returns with just KEY2 (KEY2): Y KCQQYEC RM Y DPGCLB.

USER2: Removes KEY2 & Message received: A MESSAGE TO A FRIEND.
```

This method is known as the **three-pass protocol**, developed by Adi Shamir in 1980 (http://en.wikipedia.org/wiki/Three-pass_protocol). One particular disadvantage in this method is that it is possible for a third party to intercept the messages (the so-called man-in-the-middle attack) and characterize the encryption method by inserting known values and analyzing the responses.

Using files and handling errors

In addition to easy string handling, Python allows you to read, edit, and create files easily. So, by building upon the previous scripts, we can make use of our encryptText() function to encode whole files.

Since reading and writing to files can be quite dependent on factors that are outside of the direct control of the script, such as if the file we are trying to open exists or if the filesystem has space to store a new file, we will also take a look at how to handle exceptions and protect operations that may result in errors.

Getting ready

The following script will allow you to specify a file through the command line, which will be read and encoded to produce an output file. Create a small text file named infile.txt and save it so that we can test the script. It should include a short message like the following:

`This is a short message to test our file encryption program.`

How to do it...

Create the fileencrypt.py script using the following code:

```
#!/usr/bin/python3
#fileencrypt.py
import sys #Imported to obtain command line arguments
import encryptdecrypt as ENC

#Define expected inputs
ARG_INFILE=1
ARG_OUTFILE=2
ARG_KEY=3
```

```
ARG_LENGTH=4

def covertFile(infile,outfile,key):
    #Convert the key text to an integer
    try:
        enc_key=int(key)
    except ValueError:
        print ("Error: The key %s should be an integer value!"
            % (key))
    #Code put on to two lines
    else:
        try:
            #Open the files
            with open(infile) as f_in:
                infile_content=f_in.readlines()
        except IOError:
            print ("Unable to open %s" % (infile))
        try:
            with open(outfile,'w') as f_out:
                for line in infile_content:
                    out_line = ENC.encryptText(line,enc_key)
                    f_out.writelines(out_line)
        except IOError:
            print ("Unable to open %s" % (outfile))
        print ("Conversion complete: %s" % (outfile))
    finally:
        print ("Finish")

#Check the arguments
if len(sys.argv) == ARG_LENGTH:
    print ("Command: %s" %(sys.argv))
    covertFile(sys.argv[ARG_INFILE], sys.argv[ARG_OUTFILE],
            sys.argv[ARG_KEY])
else:
    print ("Usage: fileencrypt.py infile outfile key")
#End
```

To run the script, use the following command (here, `infile` can be any text file we want to encrypt, `outfile` is our encrypted version, and `key` is the key value we wish to use):

```
python3 fileencrypt.py infile outfile key
```

For example, to encrypt `infile.txt` and output it as `encrypted.txt` using `30` as the key, use the following command:

```
python3 fileencrypt.py infile.txt encrypted.txt 30
```

To view the result, use `less encrypted.txt`. Press *Q* to exit.

To decrypt `encrypted.txt` and output it as `decrypted.txt` using `-30` as the key, use the following command:

```
python3 fileencrypt.py encrypted.txt decrypted.txt -30
```

To view the result, use `less decrypted.txt`. Press *Q* to exit.

How it works...

The script requires us to use arguments that are provided on the command line. We will access them by importing the Python module called `sys`. Just like before, we also `import` our `encryptdecrypt` module using the import command. We use the `as` part to allow us to reference it using `ENC`.

Next, we set values to define what each command-line argument will represent. When you run it, you will see that `sys.argv[]` is a list of values shown in the following array:

```
['fileencrypt.py', 'infile.txt', 'encrypted.txt', '30']
```

So, the input file is at the index `1` in the list (indexing always starts at `0`), then the output file, and finally the key, with the total number of arguments being `ARG_LENGTH=4`.

Next, we define the `convertFile()` function, which we will call in a minute from the next block of code.

To avoid errors, we check if the length of the `sys.argv` value matches the expected number of arguments from the command line. This will ensure that the user has supplied us with enough and we don't try to reference items in the `sys.argv[]` list that don't exist. Otherwise, we return a short message explaining what we are expecting.

We now call the `convertFile()` function using the command-line values and making use of Python's built-in exception handling features to ensure errors are responded to accordingly.

The `try...except` code allows you to try running some code and to handle any exceptions (errors) within the program itself, rather than everything coming to a sudden stop.

The `try` code is accompanied by the following four optional sections:

> ▶ `except ValueError:` – When an error occurs, a specific type of exception can be specified and handled with the action depending on the error we wish to handle (that is, for `ValueError`, we could check if the value is a float value and convert it to an integer or prompt for a new one). Multiple exceptions can be caught using `except (ValueError, IOError)` as required.

- ▶ `except:` – This is a catch-all case where any other exceptions that we haven't handled can be dealt with. For situations where the code may be called from other places, we may also want to raise the exception again using the `raise` command so it can be dealt with by other parts of the program (for instance, as part of the GUI, we can warn the user that the input was not correct without needing to do so at this stage). Typically, you should either deal with a specific exception or ensure you raise it again so the particular error is visible on a failure; if not handled at all, Python will report it on the terminal along with the trace to the function where it occurred.

- ▶ `else:` – This section of code is always executed if the `try` code was successful; however, any errors in this code will not be handled by the `try...except` section it is part of.

- ▶ `finally:` – This code is always executed, regardless of whether an exception was raised or the `try` code ran without problems.

If you are familiar with other languages, you will find `try...except` similar to `try...catch`, and `raise` and `throw` as equivalents. Dealing with exceptions can be quite an art form; however, making your code able to handle problems gracefully and effectively is all part of good design. In many cases, catching the situations where things go wrong is just as important as performing the intended function successfully.

If there is no problem with converting the key argument into an integer, we continue to open the input file specified and read the contents into the `infile_content` list. This will contain the contents of the file split into separate lines as a list.

In this example, we use a slightly different method to display values within the `print` statement.

Consider the following code as an example:

```
print ("Error: The key %s should be an integer value!"
% (key))
```

This allows us to use the `%s` symbol to determine where the key value is printed and also to specify the format (`%s` is a string). For numerical values, such as floats and integers, we can use `%d` to display integers, `%f` for floats, or even `%.4f` to limit the value to four decimal places.

You may have noticed that we opened the file using the `with...as...:` section. This is a special way to open a file, which will ensure that it is closed once it has finished (even if there is an error). Refer to the following code:

```
try:
    #Open the files
    with open(infile) as f_in:
        infile_content=f_in.readlines()
except IOError:
    print ("Unable to open %s" % (infile))
```

This is equivalent to:

```
try:
  f_in = open(infile)
  try:
    infile_content=f_in.readlines()
    finally:
      f_in.close()
  except IOerror:
    print ("Unable to open %s" % (infile))
```

If there is an exception in opening the file (if it doesn't exist, for example, it will raise IOerror), we can flag to the user that there was a problem with the filename/path provided. We also use except: on its own to deal with any other problems we may have with the file, such as the encoding type or non-text based files.

Next, we open a file for our output using 'w' to open it as a writable file. If it doesn't exist, it will create a new file; otherwise, it will overwrite the file. We also have the option to append to the file instead, using 'a'. We step through each item in infile_content, converting each line by passing it through our ENC.encryptText() function and writing the line to the f_out file. Once again, when we finish the with...as...: section, the file is closed and the conversion is complete.

Creating a boot-up menu

We shall now apply the methods introduced in the previous scripts and reapply them to create a menu that we can customize to present a range of quick-to-run commands and programs.

How to do it...

Create the menu.py script using the following code:

```
#!/usr/bin/python3
#menu.py
from subprocess import call

filename="menu.ini"
DESC=0
KEY=1
CMD=2


print ("Start Menu:")
try:
```

```
    with open(filename) as f:
      menufile = f.readlines()
  except IOError:
    print ("Unable to open %s" % (filename))
  for item in menufile:
    line = item.split(',')
    print ("(%s):%s" % (line[KEY],line[DESC]))
  #Get user input
  running = True
  while(running):
    user_input = input()
    #Check input, and execute command
    for item in menufile:
      line = item.split(',')
      if (user_input == line[KEY]):
        print ("Command: " + line[CMD])
        #call the script
        #e.g. call(["ls", "-l"])
        commands = line[CMD].rstrip().split()
        print (commands)
        running = False
        #Only run command is one if available
        if len(commands):
            call(commands)
    if (running==True):
      print ("Key not in menu.")
  print ("All Done.")
  #End
```

Create a `menu.ini` file that will contain the following menu items and commands:

```
Start Desktop,d,startx

Show IP Address,i,hostname -I

Show CPU speed,s,cat /sys/devices/system/cpu/cpu0/cpufreq/scaling_cur_
freq

Show Core Temperature,t,sudo /opt/vc/bin/vcgencmd measure_temp

Exit,x,
```

You can add your own commands to the list, creating your own custom start-up menu.

How it works...

In order to execute other programs from within a Python script, we need to use the `call` command. This time, we only wish to use the `call` part of the `subprocess` module, so we can simply use `from subprocess import call`. This just imports the part we need.

We open the file and read all the lines into a list named `menufile`. We can then process each item (or line of the file) using `item.split(',')`, which will create a new list consisting of each section of the line divided by the `','` symbol as follows:

```
line = ['Start Desktop', 'd', 'startx\n']
```

As shown by the `print` statement, we can now access each section independently, so we can print the key we need to press for a specific command and the description of the command.

Once we have printed the entire menu of commands, we wait for the user's input. This is done inside a `while` loop; it will continue to run until we set the condition inside `running` to `False`. This means if an invalid key is pressed, we can enter another key until a command is selected or the exit item is used. We then check the `input` key to see if it matches the allocated key for the `menu` item as follows:

```
user_input == line[KEY]
```

If there is a match, we extract the command we wish to call. The `call` command requires a command and its arguments to also be a list, so we use `.split()` to break up the command part into a list (where each space in the command is a new item in the list). Also note that there is a `/n` at the end of the line; this is the end of the line character from the `menu.ini` file. We remove this first using `.rstrip()`, which removes any whitespace (spaces, tabs, or line endings) from the end of a string.

Once the command is formatted into a list of arguments, we set `running` to `False` (so the `while` loop will not enter another loop), execute our command, and finish the script. If the user selects `x`, there will be no `commands` set, allowing us to exit menu without calling anything. The script produces a small menu of options as follows:

```
Start Menu:
(d):Start Desktop
(i):Show IP Address
(s):Show CPU speed
(t):Show Core Temperature
(x):Exit
g
Key not in menu.
i
Command: hostname -I
['hostname', '-I']
All Done.
```

There's more...

To make the script run each time we start the Raspberry Pi, we can call it from
`.bash_profile`, which is a bash script that runs when the user's profile is loaded.

Create or edit the file as follows:

```
nano -c ~/.bash_profile
```

Add the following command:

```
python3 menu.py
```

When done, save and exit (*Ctrl + X, Y,* and *Enter*).

The next time you power up your Raspberry Pi, you will have a menu to run your favorite
commands from, without needing to remember them.

> You can also run Python scripts directly, without the `python3` command,
> making them executable, as follows:
>
> ```
> chmod +x menu.py
> ```
>
> Now type in `./menu.py` and the script will run using the program defined
> within the file by the first line, as follows:
>
> ```
> #!/usr/bin/python3
> ```

Creating a self-defining menu

While the previous menu is very useful for defining the most common commands and
functions we may use when running the Raspberry Pi, we will often change what we are doing
or develop scripts to automate complex tasks.

To avoid the need to continuously update and edit the `menu.ini` file, we can create a
menu that can list installed scripts and dynamically build a menu from it. Refer to the
following screenshot:

```
pi@raspberrypi: ~/chapter2                           _ □ x

File  Edit  Tabs  Help

pi@raspberrypi ~/chapter2 $ python3 menuadv.py
Start Menu:
1: encryptdecrypt.py
2: keypassing.py
3: hellopi.py
4: menu.py
5: fileencrypt.py
6: encryptdecrypt-1stpart.py
Enter script number to run: 1-6 (x to exit)
```

A menu of all the Python scripts in the current directory

How to do it...

Create the `menuadv.py` script using the following code:

```python
#!/usr/bin/python3
#menuadv.py
import os
from subprocess import call

SCRIPT_DIR="." #Use current directory
SCRIPT_NAME=os.path.basename(__file__)

print ("Start Menu:")
scripts=[]
item_num=1
for files in os.listdir(SCRIPT_DIR):
  if files.endswith(".py"):
    if files != SCRIPT_NAME:
      print ("%s:%s"%(item_num,files))
      scripts.append(files)
      item_num+=1
running = True
while (running):
  print ("Enter script number to run: 1-%d (x to exit)" %
    (len(scripts)))
  run_item = input()
  try:
    run_number = int(run_item)
    if len(scripts) >= run_number > 0:
      print ("Run script number:" + run_item)
      commands = ["python3",scripts[run_number-1]]
      print (commands)
      call(commands)
      running = False
  except ValueError:
    #Otherwise, ignore invalid input
    if run_item == "x":
      running = False
      print ("Exit")
#End
```

How it works...

This script allows us to take a different approach. Rather than predefining a list of commands or applications, we can simply keep a folder of useful scripts and scan it to create a list to pick from. In this case, the menu will list just Python scripts and call them without any command-line options.

To be able to access the list of files in a directory, we can use the `os` module's `os.listdir()` function. This function allows us to specify a directory and it will return a list of the files and directories within it.

Using `SCRIPT_DIR="."` will allow us to search the current directory (the one the script is being run from). We can specify an absolute path (that is, `"//home/pi/python_scripts"`), a relative path (that is, `"./python_scripts_subdirectory"`), or navigate from the current directory to others in the structure (that is, `"../more_scripts"`, where the `..` symbol would move up a level from the current directory and then into the `more_scripts` directory if it existed).

If the directory does not exist, an exception (`OSError`) will be raised. Since this menu is intended to simply run and display the list, we are better off letting the exception cause an error and stop the script. This will encourage the user to fix the directory rather than try to handle the error (perhaps by prompting for another path each time). It will also be easier for the user to locate and correct the path when the script isn't running.

We also get the name of the script using `os.path.basename(__file__)`; this allows us to later exclude the `menuadv.py` script from the list options.

We create an empty list named `scripts` and ensure that we initialize `item_num` to 1. Now, we call `os.listdir(SCRIPT_DIR)` directly within a `for...in` loop so we can process each directory or filename returned by it. Next, we can check the end of each item using the `endswith()` function (another useful string function), which allows us to look for a specific ending to the string (in this case, the ending for Python scripts). At this point, we can also exclude the `menuadv.py` script from the list, if found.

We print the name of the script along with `index_num` and add it to the script list, finally incrementing `index_num` so it is correct for the next item.

We now prompt the user to enter the relevant script number (between 1 and the total number of scripts) and wait for the user input from `input()`. The script will check for a valid input. If it is a number, it will stay in the `try` section, and we can then check if the number is in the correct range (one of the listed script numbers). If correct, the script is called using `['python3', 'scriptname.py']` and the `call()` function, as before. If the input is not a number (for example, `"x"`), it will raise the `ValueError` exception. Within the `ValueError` exception, we can check if `"x"` was pressed and exit the `while` loop by setting `running` to `False` (otherwise, the loop will reprint the prompt and wait for new input).

The script is now complete.

You can adjust the preceding script to support other types of scripts, if required. Simply add other file extensions, such as `".sh"`, to the scripts `list` and `call` using `"sh"` or `"bash"` instead of `"python3"`.

There's more...

We can extend this example further by placing all our useful scripts in a single place and adding the `menu` script to the path.

Alternative script locations

While not entirely necessary (by default, the script will look in the current directory), it will be useful to create a suitable location to keep your scripts that you would like to use with the menu. This can be a location within your `home` folder (~ is short for the `home` folder path, which is `/home/pi` by default). An example is shown in the following command line:

```
mkdir ~/menupy
cd ~/menupy
```

To copy files, you can use `cp sourcefile targetfile`. If you use the `-r` option, it will also create the directory if it doesn't exist. To move or rename the files, use `mv sourcefile targetfile`. To delete the files, use `rm targetfile`. You must use the `-r` option to delete a directory.

Just ensure that if the script is not within the same location, the path is updated for `SCRIPT_DIR` to refer to the required location.

Adding scripts to PATH

As before, we could add this script to a start-up file, such as `.bash_profile`, and have the menu appear when the user logs in to the Raspberry Pi. Alternatively, we can place such scripts into a folder such as `~/bin`, which we can add to the global value call PATH. The PATH settings are a list of directories that scripts and programs will check when trying to locate a file that isn't in the current directory (typically, installed programs and software, but also common configuration files and scripts).

This will allow us to run the script regardless of what directory we are currently in.

We can see the current PATH settings using the following command:

```
echo $PATH
/usr/local/sbin:/usr/local/bin:/usr/sbin:/usr/bin:/sbin:/bin:/usr/local/
games:/usr/games
```

We can temporarily add to this until the next boot with the following command:

```
PATH=$PATH:~/bin
```

Or we can add this to `.bash_profile` to set it every time for the current user as follows:

```
PATH=$PATH:$HOME/bin
export PATH
```

The next time we reboot, the PATH settings will be (for a user with the name `pi`) as follows:

```
/usr/local/sbin:/usr/local/bin:/usr/sbin:/usr/bin:/sbin:/bin:/usr/local/
games:/usr/games:/home/pi/bin
```

 When items are automatically located through PATH, it can be difficult to find a specific version of a file or program. To overcome this, use `whereis` before the filename/command, and it will list all the locations in which it can be found.

Finally, if you do move the script to the `bin` directory, ensure that you update the path in `os.listdir("//home/pi/bin")` to locate and list the scripts you wish to display in the menu.

3
Using Python for Automation and Productivity

In this chapter, we will cover:

- ▶ Using Tkinter to create graphical user interfaces
- ▶ Creating a graphical application Start menu
- ▶ Displaying photo information in an application
- ▶ Organizing your photos automatically

Introduction

Until now, we have focused purely on command-line applications; however, there is much more to the Raspberry Pi than just the command line. By using **graphical user interfaces (GUIs)**, it is often easier to obtain input from a user and provide feedback in a more natural way. After all, we continuously process multiple inputs and outputs all the time, so why limit ourselves to the procedural format of the command line when we don't have to.

Fortunately, Python can support this. Much like other programming languages, such as Visual Basic and C/C++/C#, this can be achieved using prebuilt objects that provide standard controls. We will use a module called **Tkinter** that provides a good range of controls (also referred to as **widgets**) and tools for creating graphical applications.

First, we will take our previous example, the encryptdecrypt.py module discussed in the *How to do it...* section in the *Working with text and strings* recipe in *Chapter 2, Starting with Python Strings, Files, and Menus*, and demonstrate how useful modules can be written and reused in a variety of ways. This is a test of good coding practice. We should aim to write code that can be tested thoroughly and then reused in many places.

Next, we will extend our previous examples by creating a small graphical Start menu application to run our favorite applications from.

Then, we will explore using **classes** within our applications to display and then to organize photos.

Using Tkinter to create graphical user interfaces

We will create a small GUI to allow the user to enter information, and the program can then be used to encrypt and decrypt it.

Getting ready

You will need to ensure that you have completed the instructions in the *There's more...* section of the *Working with text and strings* recipe in *Chapter 2, Starting with Python Strings, Files, and Menus*, where we created the reusable module encryptdecrypt.py. You must ensure that this file is placed in the same directory as the following script.

Since we are using Tkinter (one of many available add-ons of Python), we need to ensure that it is installed. It should be installed by default on the standard Raspbian image. We can confirm it is installed by importing it from the Python prompt, as follows:

```
python3
>>> import tkinter
```

If it is not installed, an ImportError exception will be raised, in which case you can install it using the following command (use *Ctrl + Z* to exit the Python prompt):

```
sudo apt-get install python3-tk
```

If the module did load, you can use the following command to read more about the module (use *Q* to quit when you are done reading):

```
>>>help(tkinter)
```

You can also get information about all the classes, functions, and methods within the module from the following command:

```
>>>help(tkinter.Button)
```

The following dir command will list any valid commands or variables that are in scope of the module:

```
>>>dir(tkinter.Button)
```

You will see that our own modules will have the information about the functions marked by triple quotes; this will show up if we use the help command.

The command line will not be able to display the graphical displays created in this chapter, so you will have to start the Raspberry Pi desktop (using the command `startx`), or if you are using it remotely, ensure you have **X11 Forwarding** enabled and an X server running (see *Chapter 1, Getting Started with a Raspberry Pi Computer*).

How to do it...

To create a GUI, create the following `tkencryptdecrypt.py` script:

```python
#!/usr/bin/python3
#tkencryptdecrypt.py
import encryptdecrypt as ENC
import tkinter as TK

def encryptButton():
    encryptvalue.set(ENC.encryptText(encryptvalue.get(),
                                     keyvalue.get()))


def decryptButton():
    encryptvalue.set(ENC.encryptText(encryptvalue.get(),
                                     -keyvalue.get()))
#Define Tkinter application
root=TK.Tk()
root.title("Encrypt/Decrypt GUI")
#Set control & test value
encryptvalue = TK.StringVar()
encryptvalue.set("My Message")
keyvalue = TK.IntVar()
keyvalue.set(20)
prompt="Enter message to encrypt:"
key="Key:"

label1=TK.Label(root,text=prompt,width=len(prompt),bg='green')
textEnter=TK.Entry(root,textvariable=encryptvalue,
                   width=len(prompt))
encryptButton=TK.Button(root,text="Encrypt",command=encryptButton)
decryptButton=TK.Button(root,text="Decrypt",command=decryptButton)
label2=TK.Label(root,text=key,width=len(key))
keyEnter=TK.Entry(root,textvariable=keyvalue,width=8)
#Set layout
label1.grid(row=0,columnspan=2,sticky=TK.E+TK.W)
textEnter.grid(row=1,columnspan=2,sticky=TK.E+TK.W)
encryptButton.grid(row=2,column=0,sticky=TK.E)
```

```
decryptButton.grid(row=2,column=1,sticky=TK.W)
label2.grid(row=3,column=0,sticky=TK.E)
keyEnter.grid(row=3,column=1,sticky=TK.W)

TK.mainloop()
#End
```

How it works...

We start by importing two modules; the first is our own `encryptdecrypt` module and the second is the `tkinter` module. To make it easier to see which items have come from where, we use ENC/TK. If you want to avoid the extra reference, you can use `from <module_name> import *` to refer to the module items directly.

The functions `encryptButton()` and `decryptButton()` will be called when we click on the **Encrypt** and **Decrypt** buttons; they are explained in the following sections.

The main Tkinter window is created using the `Tk()` command, which returns the main window where all the widgets/controls can be placed.

We will define six controls as follows:

- ▸ `Label`: This displays the prompt **Enter message to encrypt:**
- ▸ `Entry`: This provides a textbox to receive the user's message to be encrypted
- ▸ `Button`: This is an **Encrypt** button to trigger the message to be encrypted
- ▸ `Button`: This is a **Decrypt** button to reverse the encryption
- ▸ `Label`: This displays the **Key:** field to prompt the user for an encryption key value
- ▸ `Entry`: This provides a second textbox to receive values for the encryption keys

These controls will produce a GUI similar to the one shown in the following screenshot:

The graphical user interface to encrypt/decrypt messages

Let's take a look at the first `label1` definition:

```
label1=TK.Label(root,text=prompt,width=len(prompt),bg='green')
```

All controls must be linked to the application window; hence, we have to specify our Tkinter window `root`. The text used for the label is set by `text`; in this case, we have set it to a string named `prompt`, which has been defined previously with the text we require. We also set the `width` to match the number of characters of the message (while not essential, it provides a neater result if we add more text to our labels later), and finally, we set the background color using `bg='green'`.

Next, we define the text `Entry` box for our message:

```
textEnter=TK.Entry(root,textvariable=encryptvalue,
                   width=len(prompt))
```

We will define `textvariable`—a useful way to link a variable to the contents of the box—which is a special string variable. We could access the `text` directly using `textEnter.get()`, but we shall use a `Tkinter StringVar()` object instead to access it indirectly. If required, this will allow us to separate the data we are processing from the code that handles the GUI layout. The `enycrptvalue` variable automatically updates the `Entry` widget it is linked to whenever the `.set()` command is used (and the `.get()` command obtains the latest value from the `Entry` widget).

Next, we have our two `Button` widgets, **Encrypt** and **Decrypt**, as follows:

```
encryptButton=TK.Button(root,text="Encrypt",command=encryptButton)
decryptButton=TK.Button(root,text="Decrypt",command=decryptButton)
```

In this case, we can set a function to be called when the `Button` widget is clicked by setting the `command` attribute. We can define the two functions that will be called when each button is clicked. In the following code snippet, we have the `encryptButton()` function, which will set the `encryptvalue` StringVar that controls the contents of the first `Entry` box. This string is set to the result we get by calling `ENC.encryptText()` with the message we want to encrypt (the current value of `encryptvalue`) and the `keyvalue` variable. The `decrypt()` function is exactly the same, except we make the `keyvalue` variable negative to decrypt the message:

```
def encryptButton():
    encryptvalue.set(ENC.encryptText(encryptvalue.get(),
                                     keyvalue.get()))
```

We then set the final Label and `Entry` widgets in a similar way. Note that `textvariable` can also be an integer (numerical value) if required, but there is no built-in check to ensure that only numbers can be entered. You will get a `ValueError` exception when the `.get()` command is used.

After we have defined all the widgets to be used in the Tkinter window, we have to set the layout. There are three ways to define the layout in Tkinter: place, pack, and grid.

The place layout allows us to specify the positions and sizes using exact pixel positions. The pack layout places the items in the window in the order that they have been added in. The grid layout allows us to place the items in a specific layout. It is recommended that you avoid the place layout wherever possible since any small change to one item can have a knock-on effect on the positions and sizes of all the other items; the other layouts account for this by determining their positions relative to the other items in the window.

We will place the items as laid out in the following screenshot:

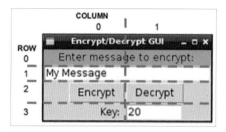

Grid layout for the Encrypt/Decrypt GUI

The positions of first two items in the GUI are set using the following code:

```
label1.grid(row=0,columnspan=2,sticky= TK.E+TK.W)
textEnter.grid(row=1,columnspan=2,sticky= TK.E+TK.W)
```

We can specify that the first `Label` and `Entry` box will span both columns (`columnspan=2`), and we can set the sticky values to ensure they span right to the edges. This is achieved by setting both the `TK.E` for the east and `TK.W` for the west sides. We'd use `TK.N` for the north and `TK.S` for the south sides if we needed to do the same vertically. If the `column` value is not specified, the grid function defaults to `column=0`. The other items are similarly defined.

The last step is to call `TK.mainloop()`, which allows Tkinter to run; this allows the buttons to be monitored for clicks and Tkinter to call the functions linked to them.

Creating a graphical application Start menu

The example in this recipe shows how we can define our own variations of the Tkinter objects to generate custom controls and dynamically construct a menu with them. We will also take a quick look at using threads, to allow other tasks to continue to function while a particular task is being executed.

Getting ready

To view the GUI display, you will need a monitor displaying the Raspberry Pi desktop or need to be connected to another computer running the X server.

How to do it...

To create a graphical Start menu application, create the following `graphicmenu.py` script:

```python
#!/usr/bin/python3
# graphicmenu.py
import tkinter as tk
from subprocess import call
import threading

#Define applications ["Display name","command"]
leafpad = ["Leafpad","leafpad"]
scratch = ["Scratch","scratch"]
pistore = ["Pi Store","pistore"]
app_list = [leafpad,scratch,pistore]
APP_NAME = 0
APP_CMD  = 1

class runApplictionThread(threading.Thread):
    def __init__(self,app_cmd):
        threading.Thread.__init__(self)
        self.cmd = app_cmd
    def run(self):
        #Run the command, if valid
        try:
            call(self.cmd)
        except:
            print ("Unable to run: %s" % self.cmd)

class appButtons:
    def __init__(self,gui,app_index):
        #Add the buttons to window
        btn = tk.Button(gui, text=app_list[app_index][APP_NAME],
                    width=30, command=self.startApp)
        btn.pack()
        self.app_cmd=app_list[app_index][APP_CMD]
    def startApp(self):
        print ("APP_CMD: %s" % self.app_cmd)
        runApplictionThread(self.app_cmd).start()
```

```
root = tk.Tk()
root.title("App Menu")
prompt = '        Select an application        '
label1 = tk.Label(root, text=prompt, width=len(prompt), bg='green')
label1.pack()
#Create menu buttons from app_list
for index, app in enumerate(app_list):
    appButtons(root,index)
#Run the tk window
root.mainloop()
#End
```

The previous code produces the following application:

The App Menu GUI

How it works...

We create the Tkinter window as we did before; however, instead of defining all the items separately, we create a special class for the application buttons.

The **class** we create acts as a blueprint or specification of what we want the appButtons items to include. Each item will consist of a string value for app_cmd, a function called startApp(), and an __init__() function. The __init__() function is a special function (called a **constructor**) that is called when we create an appButtons item; it will allow us to create any setup that is required.

In this case, the __init__() function allows us to create a new Tkinter button with the text to be set to an item in app_list and the command to be called in the startApp() function when the button is clicked. The keyword self is used so that the command called will be the one that is part of the item; this means that each button will call a locally defined function that has access to the local data of the item.

We set the value of `self.app_cmd` to the command from `app_list` and make it ready for use by the `startApp()` function. We now create the `startApp()` function. If we run the application command here directly, the Tkinter window will freeze until the application we have opened is closed again. To avoid this, we can use the Python **Threading** module, which allows us to perform multiple actions at the same time.

The `runApplicationThread()` class is created using the `threading.Thread` class as a template—this inherits all the features of the `threading.Thread` class into a new class. Just like our previous class, we provide an `__init__()` function for this as well. We first call the `__init__()` function of the inherited class to ensure it is set up correctly, and then we store the `app_cmd` value in `self.cmd`. After the `runApplicationThread()` function has been created and initialized, the `start()` function is called. This function is part of `threading.Thread`, which our class can use. When the `start()` function is called, it will create a separate application thread (that is, simulate running two things at the same time), allowing Tkinter to continue monitoring button clicks while executing the `run()` function within the class.

Therefore, we can place the code in the `run()` function to run the required application (using `call(self.cmd)`).

There's more...

One aspect that makes Python particularly powerful is that it supports the programming techniques used in **Object Orientated Design** (**OOD**). This is commonly used by modern programming languages to help translate the tasks we want our program to perform into meaningful constructs and structures in code. The principle of OOD lies in the fact that we think of most problems consisting of several objects (a GUI window, a button, and so on) that interact with each other to produce a desired result.

In the previous section, we found that we can use classes to create standardized objects that can be reused multiple times. We created an `appButton` class, which generated an object with all the features of the class, including its own personal version of `app_cmd` which will be used by the function `startApp()`. Another object of the `appButton` type will have its own unrelated [app_CMD] data that its `startApp()` function will use.

You can see that classes are useful to keep together a collection of related variables and functions in a single object, and the class will hold its own data in one place. Having multiple objects of the same type (class), each with their own functions, and data inside them results in better program structure. The traditional approach would be to keep all the information in one place and send each item back and forth for various functions to process; however, this may become cumbersome in large systems.

The following diagram shows the organization of related functions and data:

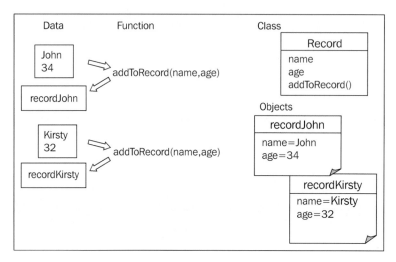

Related functions and data can be organized into classes and objects

So far, we have used Python modules to separate parts of our programs into different files; this allows us to conceptually separate different parts of the program (an interface, encoder/decoder, or library of classes, such as Tkinter). Modules can provide code to control a particular bit of hardware, define an interface for the Internet, or provide a library of common functionality; however, its most important function is to control the interface (the collection of functions, variables, and classes that are available when the item is imported). A well-implemented module should have a clear interface that is centered around how it is used rather than how it is implemented. This allows you to create multiple modules that can be swapped and changed easily since they share the same interface. In our previous example, imagine how easy it would be to change the `encryptdecrypt` module for another one just by supporting `encryptText(input_text,key)`. Complex functionality can be split into smaller, manageable blocks that can be reused in multiple applications.

Python makes use of classes and modules all the time. Each time you import a library, such as `sys` or Tkinter, or convert a value using `value.str()` and iterate through a list using `for...in`, you can use them without worrying about the details. You don't have to use classes or modules in every bit of code you write, but they are useful tools to keep in your programmer's toolbox for times when they fit what you are doing.

We will understand how classes and modules allow us to produce well-structured code that is easier to test and maintain by using them in the examples of this book.

Displaying photo information in an application

In this example, we shall create a utility class for handling photos that can be used by other applications (as a module) to access Photo metadata and display preview images easily.

Getting ready

The following script makes use of **Python Image Library** (**PIL**); a compatible version for Python 3 is **Pillow**.

Pillow has not been included in the Raspbian repository (used by `apt-get`); therefore, we will need to install Pillow using a **Python Package Manager** called **PIP**.

To install packages for Python 3, we will use the Python 3 version of PIP (this requires 50 MB of available space).

The following commands can be used to install PIP:

```
sudo apt-get update
sudo apt-get install python3-pip
```

Before you use PIP, ensure that you have installed `libjpeg-dev` to allow Pillow to handle JPEG files. You can do this using the following command:

```
sudo apt-get install libjpeg-dev
```

Now you can install Pillow using the following PIP command:

```
sudo pip-3.2 install pillow
```

PIP also makes it easy to uninstall packages using `uninstall`.

Finally, you can confirm that it has installed successfully by running `python3`:

```
>>>import PIL
>>>help(PIL)
```

You should not get any errors and see lots of information about PIL and its uses:

```
>>PIL.PILLOW_VERSION
```

You should see `2.1.0` (or similar).

PIP can also be used with Python 2 by installing pip-2.x using the following command:

`sudo apt-get install python-pip`

Any packages installed using `sudo pip install` will be installed just for Python 2.

How to do it...

To display photo information in an application, create the following `photohandler.py` script:

```python
##!/usr/bin/python3
#photohandler.py
from PIL import Image
from PIL import ExifTags
import datetime
import os

#set module values
previewsize=240,240
defaultimagepreview="./preview.ppm"
filedate_to_use="Exif DateTime"
#Define expected inputs
ARG_IMAGEFILE=1
ARG_LENGTH=2

class Photo:
    def __init__(self,filename):
        """Class constructor"""
        self.filename=filename
        self.filevalid=False
        self.exifvalid=False
        img=self.initImage()
        if self.filevalid==True:
            self.initExif(img)
            self.initDates()

    def initImage(self):
        """opens the image and confirms if valid, returns Image"""
        try:
            img=Image.open(self.filename)
            self.filevalid=True
```

```python
    except IOError:
        print ("Target image not found/valid %s" %
                (self.filename))
        img=None
        self.filevalid=False
    return img

def initExif(self,image):
    """gets any Exif data from the photo"""
    try:
        self.exif_info={
            ExifTags.TAGS[x]:y
            for x,y in image._getexif().items()
            if x in ExifTags.TAGS
        }
        self.exifvalid=True
    except AttributeError:
        print ("Image has no Exif Tags")
        self.exifvalid=False


def initDates(self):
    """determines the date the photo was taken"""
    #Gather all the times available into YYYY-MM-DD format
    self.filedates={}
    if self.exifvalid:
        #Get the date info from Exif info
        exif_ids=["DateTime","DateTimeOriginal",
                "DateTimeDigitized"]
        for id in exif_ids:
            dateraw=self.exif_info[id]
            self.filedates["Exif "+id]=
                            dateraw[:10].replace(":","-")
    modtimeraw = os.path.getmtime(self.filename)
    self.filedates["File ModTime"]="%s" %
        datetime.datetime.fromtimestamp(modtimeraw).date()
    createtimeraw = os.path.getctime(self.filename)
    self.filedates["File CreateTime"]="%s" %
        datetime.datetime.fromtimestamp(createtimeraw).date()

def getDate(self):
    """returns the date the image was taken"""
    try:
```

```
            date = self.filedates[filedate_to_use]
        except KeyError:
            print ("Exif Date not found")
            date = self.filedates["File ModTime"]
        return date

    def previewPhoto(self):
        """creates a thumbnail image suitable for tk to display"""
        imageview=self.initImage()
        imageview=imageview.convert('RGB')
        imageview.thumbnail(previewsize,Image.ANTIALIAS)
        imageview.save(defaultimagepreview,format='ppm')
        return defaultimagepreview
```

The previous code defines our `Photo` class; it is of no use to us until we run it in the *There's more...* section and in the next example.

How it works...

We define a general class called `Photo`; it contains details about itself and provides functions to access **Exchangeable Image File Format** (**EXIF**) information and generate a preview image.

In the `__init__()` function, we set values for our class variables and call `self.initImage()`, which will open the image using the `Image()` function from the PIL. We then call `self.initExif()` and `self.initDates()` and set a flag to indicate whether the file was valid or not. If not valid, the `Image()` function would raise an `IOError` exception.

The `initExif()` function uses PIL to read the EXIF data from the `img` object as shown in the following code snippet:

```
self.exif_info={
                ExifTags.TAGS[id]:y
                for id,y in image._getexif().items()
                if id in ExifTags.TAGS
                }
```

The previous code is a series of compound statements that result in `self.exif_info` being populated with a dictionary of tag names and their related values.

`ExifTag.TAGS` is a dictionary that contains a list of possible tag names linked with their IDs as shown in the following code snippet:

```
ExifTag.TAGS={
4096: 'RelatedImageFileFormat',
513: 'JpegIFOffset',
```

```
514: 'JpegIFByteCount',
40963: 'ExifImageHeight',
…etc…}
```

The image._getexif() function returns a dictionary that contains all the values set by the camera of the image, each linked to their relevant IDs, as shown in the following code snippet:

```
Image._getexif()={
256: 3264,
257: 2448,
37378: (281, 100),
36867: '2013:02:04 09:12:16',
…etc…}
```

The for loop will go through each item in the image's EXIF value dictionary and check for its occurrence in the ExifTags.TAGS dictionary; the result will get stored in self.exif_info. The code for the same is shown as follows:

```
self.exif_info={
'YResolution': (72, 1),
 'ResolutionUnit': 2,
 'ExposureMode': 0,
'Flash': 24,
…etc…}
```

Again, if there are no exceptions, we set a flag to indicate that the EXIF data is valid, or if there is no EXIF data, we raise an AttributeError exception.

The initDates() function allows us to gather all the possible file dates and dates from the EXIF data so that we can select one of them as the date we wish to use for the file. For example, it allows us to rename all the images to a filename in the standard date format. We create a dictionary self.filedates that we populate with three dates extracted from the EXIF information. We then add the filesystem dates (created and modified) just in case no EXIF data is available. The os module allows us to use os.path.getctime() and os.path.getmtime() to obtain an epoch value of the file creation—it can also be the date and time when the file was moved—and file modification—when it was last written to (for example, it often refers to the date when the picture was taken). The epoch value is the number of seconds since January 1, 1970, but we can use datetime.datetime.fromtimestamp() to convert it into years, months, days, hours, and seconds. Adding date() simply limits it to years, months, and days.

Now if the `Photo` class was to be used by another module, and we wished to know the date of the image that was taken, we could look at the `self.dates` dictionary and pick out a suitable date. However, this would require the programmer to know how the `self.dates` values are arranged, and if we later changed how they are stored, it would break their program. For this reason, it is recommended that we access data in a class through access functions so the implementation is independent of the interfaces (this process is known as **encapsulation**). We provide a function that returns a date when called; the programmer does not need to know that it could be one of the five available dates or even that they are stored as epoch values. Using a function, we can ensure that the interface will remain the same no matter how the data is stored or collected.

Finally, the last function we want the `Photo` class to provide is `previewPhoto()`. This function provides a method to generate a small thumbnail image and save it as a **Portable Pixmap Format** (**PPM**) file. As we will discover in a moment, Tkinter allows us to place images on its `Canvas` widget, but unfortunately, it does not support JPGs (and only supports GIF or PPM) directly. Therefore, we simply save a small copy of the image we want to display in the PPM format—with the added caveat that the image pallet must be converted to RGB too—and then get Tkinter to load it onto the `Canvas` when required.

To summarize, the `Photo` class we have created is as follows:

Operations	Description
`__init__(self,filename)`	This is the object initialization function
`initImage(self)`	This returns `img`, a PIL-type image object
`initExif(self,image)`	This extracts all the EXIF information, if any is present
`initDates(self)`	This creates a dictionary of all the dates available from the file and photo information
`getDate(self)`	This returns a string of the date when the photo was taken/created
`previewPhoto(self)`	This returns a string of the filename of the previewed thumbnail

The properties and their respective descriptions are as follows:

Properties	Description
`self.filename`	The filename of the photo
`self.filevalid`	This is set to `True` if the file is opened successfully
`self.exifvalid`	This is set to `True` if the Photo contains EXIF information
`self.exif_info`	This contains the EXIF information from the photo
`self.filedates`	This contains a dictionary of the available dates from the file and photo information

To test the new class, we will create some test code to confirm that everything is working as we expect; see the following section.

There's more...

We previously created the class `Photo`. Now we can add some test code to our module to ensure that it functions as we expect. We can use the `__name__ ="__main__"` attribute as before to detect whether the module has been run directly or not.

We can add the succeeding section of code at the end of the `photohandler.py` script to produce the following test application which looks as follows:

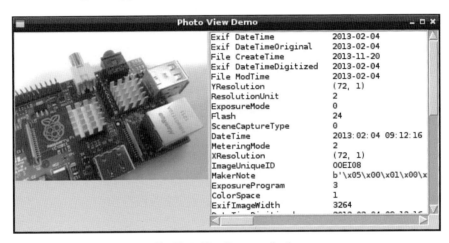

The Photo View Demo application

Add the following code at the end of `photohandler.py`:

```
#Module test code
def dispPreview(aPhoto):
    """Create a test GUI"""
    import tkinter as TK

    #Define the app window
    app = TK.Tk()
    app.title("Photo View Demo")

    #Define TK objects
    # create an empty canvas object the same size as the image
    canvas = TK.Canvas(app, width=previewsize[0],
                    height=previewsize[1])
    canvas.grid(row=0,rowspan=2)
    # Add list box to display the photo data
```

```python
    #(including xyscroll bars)
    photoInfo=TK.Variable()
    lbPhotoInfo=TK.Listbox(app,listvariable=photoInfo,
                           height=18,width=45,
                           font=("monospace",10))
    yscroll=TK.Scrollbar(command=lbPhotoInfo.yview,
                         orient=TK.VERTICAL)
    xscroll=TK.Scrollbar(command=lbPhotoInfo.xview,
                         orient=TK.HORIZONTAL)
    lbPhotoInfo.configure(xscrollcommand=xscroll.set,
                          yscrollcommand=yscroll.set)
    lbPhotoInfo.grid(row=0,column=1,sticky=TK.N+TK.S)
    yscroll.grid(row=0,column=2,sticky=TK.N+TK.S)
    xscroll.grid(row=1,column=1,sticky=TK.N+TK.E+TK.W)

    # Generate the preview image
    preview_filename = aPhoto.previewPhoto()
    photoImg = TK.PhotoImage(file=preview_filename)
    # anchor image to NW corner
    canvas.create_image(0,0, anchor=TK.NW, image=photoImg)

    # Populate infoList with dates and exif data
    infoList=[]
    for key,value in aPhoto.filedates.items():
        infoList.append(key.ljust(25) + value)
    if aPhoto.exifvalid:
        for key,value in aPhoto.exif_info.items():
            infoList.append(key.ljust(25) + str(value))
    # Set listvariable with the infoList
    photoInfo.set(tuple(infoList))

    app.mainloop()

def main():
    """"called only when run directly, allowing module testing"""
    import sys
    #Check the arguments
    if len(sys.argv) == ARG_LENGTH:
        print ("Command: %s" % (sys.argv))
        #Create an instance of the Photo class
        viewPhoto = Photo(sys.argv[ARG_IMAGEFILE])
        #Test the module by running a GUI
        if viewPhoto.filevalid==True:
            dispPreview(viewPhoto)
```

```
        else:
            print ("Usage: photohandler.py imagefile")

    if __name__=='__main__':
      main()
    #End
```

The previous test code will run the `main()` function, which takes the filename of a photo to use and create a new `Photo` object called `viewPhoto`. If `viewPhoto` is opened successfully, we will call `dispPreview()` to display the image and its details.

The `dispPreview()` function creates four Tkinter widgets to be displayed: a `Canvas` to load the thumbnail image, a `Listbox` widget to display the photo information, and two scroll bars to control the `Listbox`. First, we create a `Canvas` widget the size of the thumbnail image (`previewsize`).

Next, we create `photoInfo`, which will be our `listvariable` parameter linked to the `Listbox` widget. Since Tkinter doesn't provide a `ListVar()` function to create a suitable item, we use the generic type `TK.Variable()` and then ensure we convert it to a tuple type before setting the value. The `Listbox` widget gets added; we need to make sure that the `listvariable` parameter is set to `photoInfo` and also set the font to `monospace`. This will allow us to line up our data values using spaces, as `monospace` is a fixed width font, so each character takes up the same width as any other.

We define the two scroll bars, linking them to the `Listbox` widget, by setting the `Scrollbar` command parameters for vertical and horizontal scroll bars to `lbPhotoInfo.yview` and `lbPhotoInfo.xview`. Then, we adjust the parameters of the `Listbox` using the following command:

```
lbPhotoInfo.configure(xscrollcommand=xscroll.set,
                            yscrollcommand=yscroll.set)
```

The `configure` command allows us to add or change the widget's parameters after it has been created, in this case linking the two scroll bars so the `Listbox` widget can also control them if the user scrolls within the list.

As before, we make use of the grid layout to ensure that the `Listbox` widget has the two scroll bars placed correctly next to it and the `Canvas` widget is to the left of the `Listbox` widget.

We now use the `Photo` object to create the `preview.ppm` thumbnail file (using the `aPhoto.previewPhoto()` function) and create a `TK.PhotoImage` object that can then be added to the `Canvas` widget with the following command:

```
canvas.create_image(0,0, anchor=TK.NW, image=photoImg)
```

Finally, we use the date information that the `Photo` class gathers and the EXIF information (ensuring it is valid first) to populate the `Listbox` widget. We do this by converting each item into a list of strings that are spaced out using `.ljust(25)`—it adds a left justification to the name and pads it out to make the string 25 characters wide. Once we have the list, we convert it to a tuple type and set the `listvariable(photoInfo)` parameter.

As always, we call `app.mainloop()` to start the monitoring for events to respond to.

Organizing your photos automatically

Now that we have a class that allows us to gather information about photos, we can apply this information to perform useful tasks. In this case, we will use the file information to automatically organize a folder full of photos into a subset of folders based on the dates the photos were taken on. The following screenshot shows the output of the script:

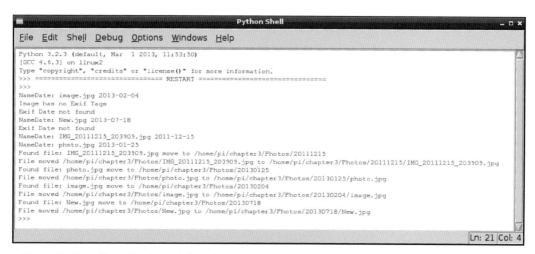

The application will use the photo's information to sort pictures into folders by the date on which they were taken

Getting ready

You will need a selection of photos placed in a folder on the Raspberry Pi. Alternatively, you can insert a USB memory stick or card reader with photos on it—they will be located under `/mnt/`. However, please make sure you test the scripts with a copy of your photos first, just in case there are any problems.

How to do it...

Create the following script in `filehandler.py` to automatically organize your photos:

```python
#!/usr/bin/python3
#filehandler.py
import os
import shutil
import photohandler as PH
from operator import itemgetter

FOLDERSONLY=True
DEBUG=True
defaultpath=""
NAME=0
DATE=1

class FileList:
  def __init__(self,folder):
    """Class constructor"""
    self.folder=folder
    self.listFileDates()

  def getPhotoNamedates(self):
    """returns the list of filenames and dates"""
    return self.photo_namedates

  def listFileDates(self):
    """Generate list of filenames and dates"""
    self.photo_namedates = list()
    if os.path.isdir(self.folder):
      for filename in os.listdir(self.folder):
        if filename.lower().endswith(".jpg"):
          aPhoto = PH.Photo(os.path.join(self.folder,filename))
          if aPhoto.filevalid:
            if (DEBUG):print("NameDate: %s %s"%
                             (filename,aPhoto.getDate()))
            self.photo_namedates.append((filename,
                                        aPhoto.getDate()))
            self.photo_namedates = sorted(self.photo_namedates,
                              key=lambda date: date[DATE])
```

```python
    def genFolders(self):
        """function to generate folders"""
        for i,namedate in enumerate(self.getPhotoNamedates()):
            #Remove the - from the date format
            new_folder=namedate[DATE].replace("-","")
            newpath = os.path.join(self.folder,new_folder)
            #If path does not exist create folder
            if not os.path.exists(newpath):
                if (DEBUG):print ("New Path: %s" % newpath)
                os.makedirs(newpath)
            if (DEBUG):print ("Found file: %s move to %s" %
                              (namedate[NAME],newpath))
            src_file = os.path.join(self.folder,namedate[NAME])
            dst_file = os.path.join(newpath,namedate[NAME])
            try:
                if (DEBUG):print ("File moved %s to %s" %
                                  (src_file, dst_file))
                if (FOLDERSONLY==False):shutil.move(src_file, dst_file)
            except IOError:
                print ("Skipped: File not found")


def main():
    """called only when run directly, allowing module testing"""
    import tkinter as TK
    from tkinter import filedialog
    app = TK.Tk()
    app.withdraw()
    dirname = TK.filedialog.askdirectory(parent=app,
        initialdir=defaultpath,
        title='Select your pictures folder')
    if dirname != "":
        ourFileList=FileList(dirname)
        ourFileList.genFolders()


if __name__=="__main__":
    main()
#End
```

How it works...

We shall make a class called `FileList`; it will make use of the `Photo` class to manage the photos within a specific folder. There are two main steps for this: we first need to find all the images within the folder, and then generate a list containing both the filename and the photo date. We will use this information to generate new subfolders and move the photos into these folders.

When we create the `FileList` object, we will create the list using `listFileDates()`. We will then confirm that the folder provided is valid and use `os.listdir` to obtain the full list of files within the directory. We will check that each file is a `.jpg` file and obtain each photo's date (using the function defined in the `Photo` class). Next, we will add the filename and date as a tuple to the `self.photo_namedates` list.

Finally, we will use the built-in `sorted` function to place all the files in order of their date. While we don't need to do this here, this function would make it easier to remove duplicate dates if we were to use this module elsewhere.

The `sorted` function requires the list to be sorted, and in this case, we want to sort it by the `date` values.

`sorted(self.photo_namedates,key=lambda date: date[DATE])`

We will substitute `date[DATE]` with `lambda date:` as the value to sort by.

Once the `FileList` object has been initialized, we can use it by calling `genFolders()`. First, we convert the date text into a suitable format for our folders (YYYYMMDD), allowing our folders to be easily sorted in order of their date. Next, it will create the folders within the current directory if they don't already exist. Finally, it will move each of the files into the required subfolder.

We end up with our `FileList` class that is ready to be tested:

Operations	Description
`__init__(self,folder)`	This is the object initialization function
`getPhotoNamedates(self)`	This returns a list of the filenames of the dates of the photos
`listFileDates(self)`	This creates a list of the filenames and dates of the photos in the folder
`genFolders(self)`	This creates new folders based on a photo's date and moves the files into them

The properties are mentioned as follows:

Properties	Description
`self.folder`	The folder we are working with
`self.photo_namedates`	This contains a list of the filenames and dates

Tkinter filediaglog.askdirectory() is used to select the photo directory

To test this, we use the Tkinter `filedialog.askdirectory()` widget to allow us to select a target directory of pictures. We use `app.withdrawn()` to hide the main Tkinter window since it isn't required this time. We just need to create a new `FileList` object and then call `genFolders()` to move all our photos to new locations!

> Two additional flags have been defined in this script that provide an extra control for testing. DEBUG allows us to enable or disable extra debugging messages by setting them to either `True` or `False`. Apart from this, FOLDERSONLY when set to `True` only generates the folders and doesn't move the files (this is helpful for testing whether the new subfolders are correct).

Once you have run the script, you can check if all the folders have been created correctly. Finally, change FOLDERSONLY to `True`, and your program will automatically move and organize your photos according to their dates the next time. It is recommended that you only run this on a copy of your photos, just in case you get an error.

4

Creating Games and Graphics

In this chapter, we will cover:

- ▸ Using IDLE3 to debug your programs
- ▸ Drawing lines using a mouse on a Tkinter Canvas
- ▸ Creating a bat and ball game
- ▸ Creating an overhead scrolling game

Introduction

Games are often a great way to explore and extend your programming skills as they present an inherent motivating force to modify and improve your creation, add new features, and create new challenges. They are also great for sharing your ideas with others, even if they aren't interested in programming.

This chapter focuses on using the Tkinter Canvas widget to create and display objects on screen for the user to interact with. Using these techniques, a wide variety of games and applications can be created that are limited only by your own creativity.

We also take a quick look at using the debugger built into IDLE, a valuable tool to test and develop your programs without the need to write extensive test code.

The first example demonstrates how we can monitor and make use of the mouse to create objects and draw directly on the `Canvas` widget. Next, we create a bat and ball game, which shows how the positions of objects can be controlled and how interactions between them can be detected and responded to. Finally, we take things a little further and use Tkinter to place our own graphics onto the `Canvas` widget to create an overhead view treasure hunt game.

Using IDLE3 to debug your programs

A key aspect of programming is being able to test and debug your code, and a useful tool to achieve this is a debugger. The IDLE editor (make sure you use IDLE3 to support the Python3 code we use in this book) includes a basic debugger. It allows you to step through your code, observe the values of local and global variables, and set breakpoints.

How to do it...

To enable the debugger, start IDLE3 and select **Debugger** from the **Debug** menu; it will open up the following window (if you are currently running some code, you will need to stop it first):

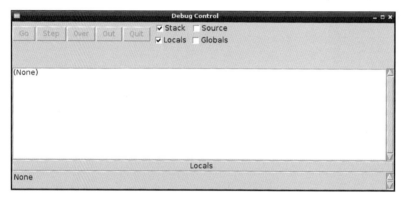

The IDLE3 debugger window

Open up the code you want to test (via **File | Open...**) and try running it (*F5*). You will find that the code will not start since the debugger has automatically stopped at the first line The following screenshot shows the debugger has stopped on the first line of code in filehandler.py which is line 4:import os, shutil.

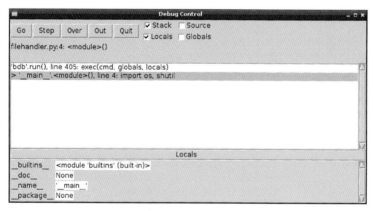

The IDLE3 debugger at the start of the code

How it works...

The control buttons shown in the following screenshot allow you to run and/or jump through the code.

Debugger controls

The functions of the control buttons are as follows:

- **Go**: This button will execute the code as normal.
- **Step**: This button will execute the line of code one step at a time and then stop again. If a function is called, it will enter that function and allow you to step through that too.
- **Over**: This button is like the `Step` command, but if there is a function call, it will execute the whole function and stop at the following line.
- **Out**: This button will keep executing the code until it has completed the function it is currently in, allowing you to continue until you come out of the function.
- **Quit**: This button ends the program immediately.

In addition to the previously mentioned controls, you can **Set Breakpoint** and **Clear Breakpoint** directly within the code. A breakpoint is a marker that you can insert in the code (by right-clicking on the editor window), which the debugger will always break on (stop at) when it is reached.

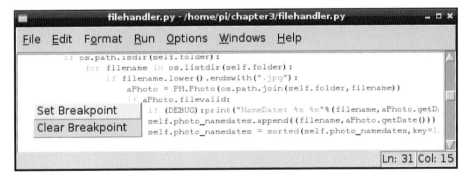

Set and clear breakpoints directly in your code

The checkboxes (on the right-hand side of the control buttons) allow you to choose what information to display when you step through the code or when the debugger stops somewhere due to a breakpoint. **Stack** is shown in the main window, which is similar to what you would see if the program hit an unhandled exception. The **Stack** option shows all the function calls made to get to the current position in the code, right up to the line it has stopped at. The **Source** option highlights the line of code currently being executed and, in some cases, the code inside the imported modules too (if they are noncompiled libraries).

You can also select whether to display **Locals** and/or **Globals**. By default, the **Source** and **Globals** options are usually disabled as they can make the process quite slow if there is a lot of data to display.

Python uses the concept of Local and Global variables to define the scope (where and when the variables are valid). Global variables are defined at the top level of the file and are visible from any point in the code after it has been defined. However, in order to alter its value from anywhere other than the top level, Python requires you to use the global keyword first. Without the global keyword, you will create a local copy with the same name (the value of which will be lost when you exit the function). Local variables are defined when you create a variable within a function; once outside of the function, the variable is destroyed and is not visible anymore.

Below **Stack** data are the **Locals**, in this case aPhoto, filename, and self. Then (if enabled), we have all the global values that are currently valid providing useful details about the status of the program (DATE = 1, DEBUG = True, FOLDERSONLY = True, and so on).

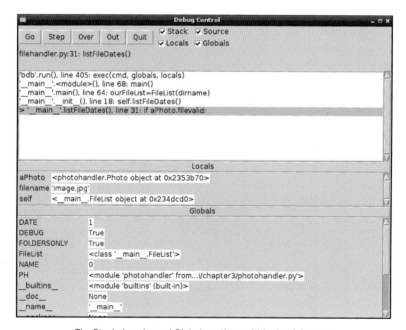

The Stack, Locals, and Globals options within the debugger

The debugger isn't particularly advanced as it does not allow you to expand complex objects such as the `photohandler.Photo` object to see what data it contains. However, if required, you can adjust your code and assign the data you want to observe to some temporary variables during testing.

It is worth learning how to use the debugger as it is a much easier way to track down particular problems and check whether or not things are functioning as you expect them to.

Drawing lines using a mouse on Tkinter Canvas

The Tkinter Canvas widget provides an area to create and draw objects on. The following script demonstrates how to use `mouse` events to interact with Tkinter. By detecting the mouse clicks, we can use Tkinter to draw a line that follows the movement of the mouse.

A simple drawing application using Tkinter

Getting ready

As before, we need to have Tkinter installed and either the Raspbian desktop running (`startx` from the command line) or an SSH session with X11 Forwarding and an X server running (see *Chapter 1, Getting Started with a Raspberry Pi Computer*). We will also need a mouse connected.

How to do it...

Create the following script, `painting.py`:

```
#!/usr/bin/python3
#painting.py
import tkinter as TK
```

```
#Set defaults
btn1pressed = False
newline = True

def main():
  root = TK.Tk()
  the_canvas = TK.Canvas(root)
  the_canvas.pack()
  the_canvas.bind("<Motion>", mousemove)
  the_canvas.bind("<ButtonPress-1>", mouse1press)
  the_canvas.bind("<ButtonRelease-1>", mouse1release)
  root.mainloop()

def mouse1press(event):
  global btn1pressed
  btn1pressed = True

def mouse1release(event):
  global btn1pressed, newline
  btn1pressed = False
  newline = True

def mousemove(event):
  if btn1pressed == True:
    global xorig, yorig, newline
    if newline == False:
      event.widget.create_line(xorig,yorig,event.x,event.y,
                                         smooth=TK.TRUE)

    newline = False
    xorig = event.x
    yorig = event.y

if __name__ == "__main__":
  main()
#End
```

How it works...

The Python code creates a Tkinter window that contains a Canvas object called
the_canvas. We use the bind function here, which will bind a specific event that occurs
on this widget (the_canvas) to a specific action or key press. In this case, we bind the
<Motion> function of the mouse plus the click and release of the first mouse button
(<ButtonPress-1> and <ButtonRelease-1>). Each of these events are then used
to call the mouse1press(), mouse1release() and mousemove() functions.

The logic here is as follows. We track the status of the mouse button using the `mouse1press()` and `mouse1release()` functions and within the `mousemove()` function. We then check the status of the button.

If the mouse has been clicked, the function `mousemove()` will check to see whether we are drawing a new line (we set new coordinates for this) or continuing an old one (we draw a line from the previous coordinates to the coordinates of the current event that has triggered `mousemove()`). We just need to ensure that we reset to the `newline` command whenever the mouse button is released to reset the start position of the line.

Creating a bat and ball game

A classic bat and ball game can be created using the drawing tools of canvas and by detecting the collisions of the objects. The user will be able to control the green paddle using the left and right cursor keys to aim the ball at the bricks and hit them until they have all been destroyed.

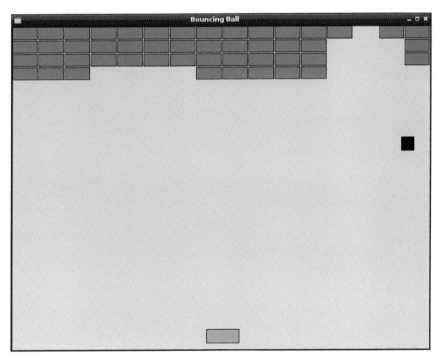

Control the bat to aim the ball at the bricks

Getting ready

This example requires a screen and keyboard attached to the Raspberry Pi or X11 Forwarding and X server.

How to do it...

Create the following script, `bouncingball.py`:

```python
#!/usr/bin/python3
# bouncingball.py
import tkinter as TK
import time

VERT,HOREZ=0,1
xTOP,yTOP = 0,1
xBTM,yBTM = 2,3
MAX_WIDTH,MAX_HEIGHT = 640,480
xSTART,ySTART = 100,200
BALL_SIZE=20
RUNNING=True

def close():
  global RUNNING
  RUNNING=False
  root.destroy()

def move_right(event):
  if canv.coords(paddle)[xBTM]<(MAX_WIDTH-7):
    canv.move(paddle, 7, 0)

def move_left(event):
  if canv.coords(paddle)[xTOP]>7:
    canv.move(paddle, -7, 0)

def determineDir(ball,obj):
  global delta_x,delta_y
  if (ball[xTOP] == obj[xBTM]) or (ball[xBTM] == obj[xTOP]):
    delta_x = -delta_x
  elif (ball[yTOP] == obj[yBTM]) or (ball[yBTM] == obj[yTOP]):
    delta_y = -delta_y

root = TK.Tk()
```

```
root.title("Bouncing Ball")
root.geometry('%sx%s+%s+%s' %(MAX_WIDTH, MAX_HEIGHT, 100, 100))
root.bind('<Right>', move_right)
root.bind('<Left>', move_left)
root.protocol('WM_DELETE_WINDOW', close)

canv = TK.Canvas(root, highlightthickness=0)
canv.pack(fill='both', expand=True)

top = canv.create_line(0, 0, MAX_WIDTH, 0, fill='blue',
                       tags=('top'))
left = canv.create_line(0, 0, 0, MAX_HEIGHT, fill='blue',
                        tags=('left'))
right = canv.create_line(MAX_WIDTH, 0, MAX_WIDTH, MAX_HEIGHT,
                      fill='blue', tags=('right'))
bottom = canv.create_line(0, MAX_HEIGHT, MAX_WIDTH, MAX_HEIGHT,
                      fill='blue', tags=('bottom'))

ball = canv.create_rectangle(0, 0, BALL_SIZE, BALL_SIZE,
                      outline='black', fill='black', tags=('ball'))
paddle = canv.create_rectangle(100, MAX_HEIGHT - 30, 150, 470,
                      outline='black', fill='green', tags=('rect'))

brick=list()
for i in range(0,16):
  for row in range(0,4):
    brick.append(canv.create_rectangle(i*40, row*20,
                ((i+1)*40)-2, ((row+1)*20)-2,
                outline='black', fill='red',
                tags=('rect')))

delta_x = delta_y = 1
xold,yold = xSTART,ySTART
canv.move(ball, xold, yold)

while RUNNING:
  objects = canv.find_overlapping(canv.coords(ball)[0],
                                  canv.coords(ball)[1],
                                  canv.coords(ball)[2],
                                  canv.coords(ball)[3])

  #Only change the direction once (so will bounce off 1st
  # block even if 2 are hit)
  dir_changed=False
```

```
for obj in objects:
  if (obj != ball):
    if dir_changed==False:
      determineDir(canv.coords(ball),canv.coords(obj))
      dir_changed=True
    if (obj >= brick[0]) and (obj <= brick[len(brick)-1]):
      canv.delete(obj)
    if (obj == bottom):
      text = canv.create_text(300,100,text="YOU HAVE MISSED!")
      canv.coords(ball, (xSTART,ySTART,
                         xSTART+BALL_SIZE,ySTART+BALL_SIZE))
      delta_x = delta_y = 1
      canv.update()
      time.sleep(3)
      canv.delete(text)
  new_x, new_y = delta_x, delta_y
  canv.move(ball, new_x, new_y)

  canv.update()
  time.sleep(0.005)
#End
```

How it works...

We create a Tkinter application that is 640 x 480 pixels and bind the `<Right>` and `<Left>` cursor keys to the `move_right()` and `move_left()` functions. We use `root.protocol('WM_DELETE_WINDOW', close)` to detect when the window is closed so that we can cleanly exit the program (via `close()`, which sets `RUNNING` to `False`).

We then add a `Canvas` widget to the application that will hold all our objects. We create the following objects: `top`, `left`, `right`, and `bottom`. These make up our bounding sides for our game area. The canvas coordinates are `0,0` in the top-left corner and `640,480` in the bottom-right corner, so the start and end coordinates can be determined for each side (using `canv.create_line(xStart, yStart, xEnd, yEnd)`).

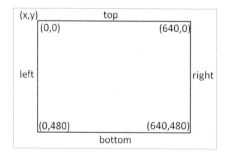

The coordinates of the Canvas widget

You can also add multiple `tags` to the objects; `tags` are often useful for defining specific actions or behaviors of objects. For instance, they allow for different types of events to occur when specific objects or bricks are hit. We see more uses of `tags` in the next example.

Next, we define the ball and paddle objects, which are added using `canv.create_rectangle()`. This requires two sets of coordinates that define the opposite corners of the objects (in this case, the top-left and bottom-right corners).

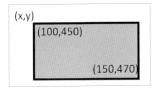

Finally, we can create the bricks!

We want our bricks to be 40 x 20 pixels wide so we can fit 16 bricks across our game area of 640 pixels (in four rows). We can create a list of brick objects with their positions defined automatically as shown in the following code:

```
brick=list()
for i in range(0,16):
    for row in range(0,4):
        brick.append(canv.create_rectangle(i*40, row*20,
            ((i+1)*40)-2, ((row+1)*20)-2, outline='black',
                fill='red', tags=('rect')))
```

A brick-like effect is provided by making the bricks slightly smaller (`-2`) to create a small gap.

Four rows of 16 bricks are generated at the top of Canvas

We now set the default settings before starting the main control loop. The movement of the ball will be governed by `delta_x` and `delta_y`, which are added or subtracted to the ball's previous position in each cycle.

Next, we set the starting position of the ball and use the `canv.move()` function to move the ball by that amount. The `move()` function will add `100` to the x and y coordinates of the ball object, which was originally created at position `0,0`.

Now that everything is set up, the main loop can run; this will check that the ball has not hit anything (using the `canv.find_overlapping()` function), make any adjustments to the `delta_x` or `delta_y` values, and then apply them to move the ball to the next location.

The sign of `delta_x` and `delta_y` determines the direction of the ball. Positive values will make the ball travel diagonally downwards and towards the right. While `-delta_x` will make it travel towards the left, either downwards or upwards depending on whether `delta_y` is positive or negative.

After the ball has been moved, we use `canv.update()` to redraw any changes made to the display, and `time.sleep()` allows a small delay before checking and moving the ball again.

Object collisions are detected using the `canv.find_overlapping()` function. This returns a list of canvas objects that are found to be overlapping the bounds of a rectangle defined by the supplied coordinates. For example, in the case of the square ball, are any of the co-ordinates of the canvas objects within the rectangle?

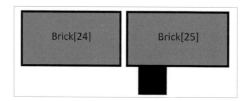

If the ball is found to be overlapping another object, such as the walls, the paddle, or one or more of the bricks, we need to determine which direction the ball should next travel in. Since we are using the coordinates of the ball as the area within which to check, they will always be listed so that we ignore them when we check the list of objects.

We use the `dir_changed` flag to ensure that if we hit two bricks at the same time, we do not change direction twice before we move the ball. Otherwise, this would cause the ball to continue moving in the same direction even though it has collided with the bricks.

So if the ball is overlapping something else, we can call `determineDir()` with the coordinates of the ball and the object to work out what the new direction should be.

When the ball collides with something, we want the ball to bounce off it; fortunately, this is easy to simulate as we just need to change the sign of either `delta_x` or `delta_y` depending on whether we have hit something on the sides or the top/bottom. If the ball hits the bottom of another object, it means we were travelling upwards and should now travel downwards. However, we will continue to travel in the same direction on the x axis (be it left or right or just up) as it can be seen from the following code:

```
if (ball[xTOP] == obj[xBTM]) or (ball[xBTM] == obj[xTOP]):
        delta_x = -delta_x
```

The `determineDir()` function looks at the coordinates of the ball and the object and looks for a match between either the left and right x coordinates or the top and bottom y coordinates. This is enough to say whether the collision is on the sides or top/bottom, and we can set the `delta_x` or `delta_y` signs accordingly as it can be seen from the following code:

```
if (obj >= brick[0]) and (obj <= brick[-1]):
            canv.delete(obj)
```

Next, we can determine if we have hit a brick by checking whether the overlapping object ID is between the first and last ID bricks. If it was a brick, we can remove it using `canv.delete()`.

 Python allows the index values to wrap around rather than access the invalid memory, so an index value of `-1` will provide us with the last item in the list.

We also check to see whether the object being overlapped is on the bottom line (in which case, the player has missed the ball with the paddle), so a short message is displayed briefly. We reset the position of the `ball` and `delta_x`/`delta_y` values. The `canv.update()` function ensures that the display is refreshed with the message before it is deleted (3 seconds later).

Finally, the ball is moved by the `delta_x`/`delta_y` distance and the display is updated. A small delay is added here to reduce the rate of updates and the CPU time used. Otherwise, you will find that your Raspberry Pi will become unresponsive if it is spending 100 percent of its effort in running the program.

When the user presses the cursor keys, the `move_right()` and `move_left()` functions are called. They check the position of the paddle object, and if the objects are not at the edge, they will move the paddle accordingly. If the ball hits the paddle, the collision detection will ensure that the ball bounces off just like one of the bricks.

You can extend this game further by adding a score for each block destroyed, allow the player a finite number of lives which are lost when they miss the ball and even write some code to read in new brick layouts.

Creating an overhead scrolling game

By using objects and images in our programs, we can create many types of 2D graphical games.

In this recipe, we will create a treasure hunt game where the player is trying to find buried treasure (by pressing *Enter* to dig for it). Each time the treasure has not been found, the player is given a clue to how far away the treasure is; they can then use the cursor keys to move around and search until they find it.

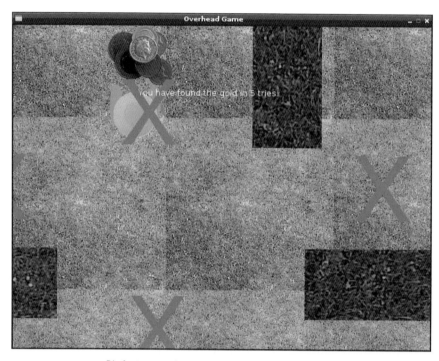

Dig for treasure in your own overhead scrolling game!

Although this is a basic concept for a game, it could easily be extended to include multiple layouts, traps, and enemies to avoid, perhaps even additional tools or puzzles to solve. With a few adjustments to the graphics, the character could be exploring a dungeon or spaceship or hopping through the clouds collecting rainbows!

Getting ready

The following example uses a number of images; these are available as part of the book's resources. You will need to place the nine images in the same directory as the Python script.

The required image files can be seen in the code bundle of this chapter.

How to do it...

Create the following script, `scroller.py`:

1. Begin by importing the required libraries and parameters:

```python
#!/usr/bin/python3
# scroller.py
import tkinter as TK
import time
import math
from random import randint

STEP=7
xVAL,yVAL=0,1
MAX_WIDTH,MAX_HEIGHT=640,480
SPACE_WIDTH=MAX_WIDTH*2
SPACE_HEIGHT=MAX_HEIGHT*2
LEFT,UP,RIGHT,DOWN=0,1,2,3
SPACE_LIMITS=[0,0,SPACE_WIDTH-MAX_WIDTH,
              SPACE_HEIGHT-MAX_HEIGHT]
DIS_LIMITS=[STEP,STEP,MAX_WIDTH-STEP,MAX_HEIGHT-STEP]
BGN_IMG="bg.gif"
PLAYER_IMG=["playerL.gif","playerU.gif",
            "playerR.gif","playerD.gif"]
WALL_IMG=["wallH.gif","wallV.gif"]
GOLD_IMG="gold.gif"
MARK_IMG="mark.gif"
newGame=False
checks=list()
```

2. Provide functions to handle the movement of the player:

```python
def move_right(event):
  movePlayer(RIGHT,STEP)
def move_left(event):
  movePlayer(LEFT,-STEP)
def move_up(event):
  movePlayer(UP,-STEP)
def move_down(event):
  movePlayer(DOWN,STEP)

def foundWall(facing,move):
  hitWall=False
  olCoords=[canv.coords(player)[xVAL],
            canv.coords(player)[yVAL],
```

```
                    canv.coords(player)[xVAL]+PLAYER_SIZE[xVAL],
                    canv.coords(player)[yVAL]+PLAYER_SIZE[yVAL]]
      olCoords[facing]+=move
      objects = canv.find_overlapping(olCoords[0],olCoords[1],
                                      olCoords[2],olCoords[3])
      for obj in objects:
        objTags = canv.gettags(obj)
        for tag in objTags:
          if tag == "wall":
            hitWall=True
      return hitWall


  def moveBackgnd(movement):
    global bg_offset
    bg_offset[xVAL]+=movement[xVAL]
    bg_offset[yVAL]+=movement[yVAL]
    for obj in canv.find_withtag("bg"):
      canv.move(obj, -movement[xVAL], -movement[yVAL])


  def makeMove(facing,move):
    if facing == RIGHT or facing == LEFT:
      movement=[move,0]  #RIGHT/LEFT
      bgOffset=bg_offset[xVAL]
      playerPos=canv.coords(player)[xVAL]
    else:
      movement=[0,move]  #UP/DOWN
      bgOffset=bg_offset[yVAL]
      playerPos=canv.coords(player)[yVAL]
    #Check Bottom/Right Corner
    if facing == RIGHT or facing == DOWN:
      if (playerPos+PLAYER_SIZE[xVAL]) < DIS_LIMITS[facing]:
        canv.move(player, movement[xVAL], movement[yVAL])
      elif bgOffset < SPACE_LIMITS[facing]:
        moveBackgnd(movement)
    else:    #Check Top/Left Corner
      if (playerPos) > DIS_LIMITS[facing]:
        canv.move(player, movement[xVAL], movement[yVAL])
      elif bgOffset > SPACE_LIMITS[facing]:
        moveBackgnd(movement)


  def movePlayer(facing,move):
    hitWall=foundWall(facing,move)
    if hitWall==False:
      makeMove(facing,move)
    canv.itemconfig(player,image=playImg[facing])
```

3. Add functions to check how far the player is from the hidden gold:

```python
def check(event):
  global checks,newGame,text
  if newGame:
    for chk in checks:
      canv.delete(chk)
    del checks[:]
    canv.delete(gold,text)
    newGame=False
    hideGold()
  else:
    checks.append(
            canv.create_image(canv.coords(player)[xVAL],
                              canv.coords(player)[yVAL],
                              anchor=TK.NW, image=checkImg,
                              tags=('check','bg')))
    distance=measureTo(checks[-1],gold)
    if(distance<=0):
      canv.itemconfig(gold,state='normal')
      canv.itemconfig(check,state='hidden')
      text = canv.create_text(300,100,fill="white",
                      text=("You have found the gold in"+
                            " %d tries!"%len(checks)))
      newGame=True
    else:
      text = canv.create_text(300,100,fill="white",
                  text=("You are %d steps away!"%distance))
    canv.update()
    time.sleep(1)
    canv.delete(text)

def measureTo(objectA,objectB):
  deltaX=canv.coords(objectA)[xVAL]-\
                    canv.coords(objectB)[xVAL]
  deltaY=canv.coords(objectA)[yVAL]-\
                    canv.coords(objectB)[yVAL]
  w_sq=abs(deltaX)**2
  h_sq=abs(deltaY)**2
  hypot=math.sqrt(w_sq+h_sq)
  return round((hypot/5)-20,-1)
```

4. Add functions to help find a location to hide the gold in:

```python
def hideGold():
  global gold
  goldPos=findLocationForGold()
  gold=canv.create_image(goldPos[xVAL], goldPos[yVAL],
                         anchor=TK.NW, image=goldImg,
                         tags=('gold','bg'), state='hidden')

def findLocationForGold():
  placeGold=False
  while(placeGold==False):
    goldPos=[randint(0-bg_offset[xVAL],
          SPACE_WIDTH-GOLD_SIZE[xVAL]-bg_offset[xVAL]),
          randint(0-bg_offset[yVAL],
          SPACE_HEIGHT-GOLD_SIZE[yVAL]-bg_offset[yVAL])]
    objects = canv.find_overlapping(goldPos[xVAL],
                         goldPos[yVAL],
                         goldPos[xVAL]+GOLD_SIZE[xVAL],
                         goldPos[yVAL]+GOLD_SIZE[yVAL])
    findNewPlace=False
    for obj in objects:
      objTags = canv.gettags(obj)
      for tag in objTags:
        if (tag == "wall") or (tag == "player"):
          findNewPlace=True
    if findNewPlace == False:
      placeGold=True
  return goldPos
```

5. Create the Tkinter application window and bind the keyboard events:

```python
root = TK.Tk()
root.title("Overhead Game")
root.geometry('%sx%s+%s+%s' %(MAX_WIDTH,
                              MAX_HEIGHT,
                              100, 100))
root.resizable(width=TK.FALSE, height=TK.FALSE)
root.bind('<Right>', move_right)
root.bind('<Left>', move_left)
root.bind('<Up>', move_up)
root.bind('<Down>', move_down)
root.bind('<Return>', check)

canv = TK.Canvas(root, highlightthickness=0)
canv.place(x=0,y=0,width=SPACE_WIDTH,height=SPACE_HEIGHT)
```

6. Initialize all the game objects (the background tiles, the player, the walls, and the gold):

```
#Create background tiles
bgnImg = TK.PhotoImage(file=BGN_IMG)
BGN_SIZE = bgnImg.width(),bgnImg.height()
background=list()
COLS=int(SPACE_WIDTH/BGN_SIZE[xVAL])+1
ROWS=int(SPACE_HEIGHT/BGN_SIZE[yVAL])+1
for col in range(0,COLS):
  for row in range(0,ROWS):
    background.append(canv.create_image(col*BGN_SIZE[xVAL],
                     row*BGN_SIZE[yVAL], anchor=TK.NW,
                     image=bgnImg, tags=('background','bg')))
bg_offset=[0,0]

#Create player
playImg=list()
for img in PLAYER_IMG:
  playImg.append(TK.PhotoImage(file=img))
#Assume images are all same size/shape
PLAYER_SIZE=playImg[RIGHT].width(),playImg[RIGHT].height()
player = canv.create_image(100,100, anchor=TK.NW,
                           image=playImg[RIGHT], tags=('player'))

#Create walls
wallImg=[TK.PhotoImage(file=WALL_IMG[0]),
         TK.PhotoImage(file=WALL_IMG[1])]
WALL_SIZE=[wallImg[0].width(),wallImg[0].height()]
wallPosH=[(0,WALL_SIZE[xVAL]*1.5),
          (WALL_SIZE[xVAL],WALL_SIZE[xVAL]*1.5),
          (SPACE_WIDTH-WALL_SIZE[xVAL],WALL_SIZE[xVAL]*1.5),
          (WALL_SIZE[xVAL],SPACE_HEIGHT-WALL_SIZE[yVAL])]
wallPosV=[(WALL_SIZE[xVAL],0),(WALL_SIZE[xVAL]*3,0)]
wallPos=[wallPosH,wallPosV]
wall=list()
for i,img in enumerate(WALL_IMG):
  for item in wallPos[i]:
    wall.append(canv.create_image(item[xVAL],item[yVAL],
             anchor=TK.NW, image=wallImg[i], tags=('wall','bg')))

#Place gold
goldImg = TK.PhotoImage(file=GOLD_IMG)
GOLD_SIZE=[goldImg.width(),goldImg.height()]
hideGold()
#Check mark
checkImg = TK.PhotoImage(file=MARK_IMG)
```

7. Finally, start the `mainloop()` command to allow Tkinter to monitor for events:

```
#Wait for actions from user
root.mainloop()
#End
```

How it works...

As before, we create a new Tkinter application that contains a `Canvas` widget that we can add all the objects of the game. We ensure that we bind the right, left, up, down and *Enter* keys, which will be our controls in the game.

First, we place our background image (`bg.gif`) onto the canvas widget. We calculate the number of images we can fit along the length and width to tile the whole canvas space and locate them using suitable coordinates.

Next, we create the player image (by creating `playImg`, a list of Tkinter image objects for each direction the player can turn in) and place it on the canvas.

We now create the walls, the positions of which are defined by the `wallPosH` and `wallPosV` lists. These could be defined using the exact coordinates, perhaps even read from a file to provide an easy method to load different layouts for levels if required. By iterating through the lists, the horizontal and vertical wall images are put in position on the canvas.

To complete the layout, we just need to hide the gold somewhere. Using the `hideGold()` function, we randomly determine a suitable place to locate the gold. Within `findLocationForGold()`, we use `randint(0,value)` to create a pseudo-random number (it is not totally random but good enough for this use) between 0 and `value`. In our case, the value we want is between 0 and the edge of our canvas space minus the size of the gold image and any `bg_offset` that has been applied to the canvas. This ensures it is not beyond the edge of the screen. We then check the potential location using the `find_overlapping()` function to see whether any objects with `wall` or `player` tags are in the way. If so, we pick a new location. Otherwise, we place the gold on the canvas but with the `state="hidden"` value, which will hide it from view.

We then create `checkImg` (a Tkinter image) and use it while checking for gold to mark the area we have checked. Finally, we just wait for the user to press one of the keys.

The character will move around the screen whenever one of the cursor keys is pressed. The player's movement is determined by the `movePlayer()` function; it will first check whether the player is trying to move into a wall, then determine (within the `makeMove()` function) if the player is at the edge of the display or canvas space.

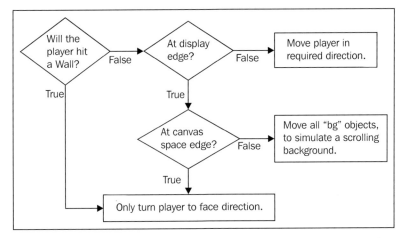

Every time a cursor key is pressed, we use the logic shown in the diagram to determine what to do

The `foundWall()` function works out whether the player will hit a wall by checking for any objects with `"wall"` tags within the area being covered by the player image, plus a little extra for the area that the player will be moving to next. The following diagram shows how the `olCoords` coordinates are determined:

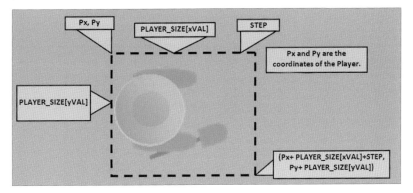

The coordinates to check for objects that overlap (olCoords) are calculated

The `makeMove()` function checks if the player will be moving to the edge of the display (as defined by `DIS_LIMITS`) and whether they are at the edge of the canvas space (as defined by `SPACE_LIMITS`). Within the display, the player can be moved in the direction of the cursor, or all the objects tagged with `"bg"` within the canvas space are moved in the opposite direction, simulating scrolling behind the player. This is done by the `moveBackground()` function.

When the player presses *Enter*, we'll want to check for gold in the current location. Using the `measureTo()` function, the position of the player and the gold are compared (the distance between the x and y coordinates of each is calculated).

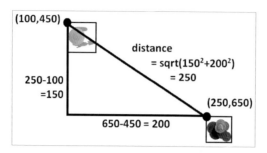

The result is scaled to provide a rough indication of how far away the player is from the gold. If the distance is greater than zero, we display how far away the player is from the gold and leave a cross to show where we have checked. If the player has found the gold, we display a message saying so and set `newGame` to `True`. The next time the player presses *Enter*, the places marked with a cross are removed and the gold is relocated to somewhere new.

With the gold hidden again, the player is ready to start again!

5
Creating 3D Graphics

In this chapter, we will cover:

- ▶ Starting with 3D coordinates and vertices
- ▶ Creating and importing 3D models
- ▶ Creating a 3D world to roam in
- ▶ Building 3D maps and mazes

Introduction

The chip at the heart of the Raspberry Pi (a Broadcom BCM2835 processor) was originally designed to be a **Graphical Processing Unit** (**GPU**) for mobile and embedded applications. The ARM core that drives most of the Raspberry Pi's functionality was added because some extra space was available on the chip; this enabled this powerful GPU to be used as a **System-On-Chip** (**SoC**) solution.

As you can imagine, if the ARM core (**ARM1176JZF-S**, which is the **ARMv6** architecture) consists of only a small part of the chip on the Raspberry Pi, you would be right in thinking that the GPU must perform rather well. The **VideoCore IV GPU** consists of 48 purpose-built processors, with some providing support for 1080p high-definition encoding and decoding of video while others supporting **OpenGL ES 2.0** that provide fast calculations for 3D graphics. It has been said that its graphics processing power is equivalent to that of an Apple iPhone 4s and also the original Microsoft Xbox. This is even more apparent if you run **Quake 3** or **OpenArena** on the Raspberry Pi (go to `http://www.raspberrypi.org/archives/3131` for details).

In this chapter, I hope to show you that while you can achieve a lot by performing operations using the ARM side of the Raspberry Pi, if you venture into the side where the GPU is hidden, you may see that there is even more to this little computer than first appears.

The Pi3D library created by the Pi3D team (Patrick Gaunt, Tom Swirly, Tim Skillman, and others) provides a way to put the GPU to work by creating 3D graphics.

The Pi3D wiki and documentation pages can be found at the following link:

```
http://pi3d.github.io/html/index.html
```

The support/development group can be found at the following link:

```
https://groups.google.com/forum/#!forum/pi3d
```

The library contains many features, so it will not be possible to cover everything that is available in the following examples. It is recommended that you also take some time to try out the demos. You can have a look through some of the Python modules, which make up the library itself (described in the documentation or the code on GitHub), to discover more options for the creation and handling of the 3D graphics. It is hoped that this chapter will introduce you to enough concepts to illustrate some of the raw potential available to you.

Starting with 3D coordinates and vertices

The world around us is three dimensional; so in order to simulate parts of the world, we can create a 3D representation and display it on our 2D screen.

The Raspberry Pi enables us to simulate a 3D space, place 3D objects within it, and observe them from a selected viewpoint. We will use the GPU to produce a representation of the 3D view as a 2D image to display it on the screen.

The following example will show how we can use **Pi3D** (an OpenGL ES library for the Raspberry Pi) to place a single 3D object and display it within the 3D space. We will then allow the mouse to rotate the view around the object.

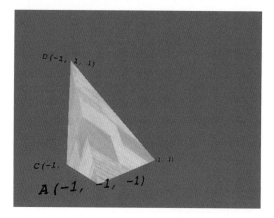

Getting ready

The Raspberry Pi must be directly connected to a display, either via the HDMI or an analog video output. The 3D graphics rendered by the GPU will be only displayed on a local display, even if you are connecting to the Raspberry Pi remotely over a network. You will also need to use a locally connected keyboard/mouse for control.

The first time we use Pi3D, we will need to download and install it with the following steps:

1. The Pi3D library uses Pillow, a version of the Python Imaging Library that is compatible with Python 3 to import graphics used in models (such as textures and backgrounds).

   The installation of Pillow has been covered in the *Getting ready* section of *Chapter 3, Using Python for Automation and Productivity*.

   The commands to do the installation are shown in the following code (if you've installed them before, it will skip them and continue):

   ```
   sudo apt-get update
   sudo apt-get install python3-pip
   sudo apt-get install libjpeg-dev
   sudo pip-3.2 install pillow
   ```

2. We can now use PIP to install Pi3D using the following command:

   ```
   sudo pip-3.2 install pi3d
   ```

   The Pi3D team is continuously developing and improving the library; if you are experiencing problems, it may mean that a new release is not compatible with the previous ones.

   You can also check in the *Appendix, Hardware and Software List*, to confirm which version of Pi3D you have and, if required, install the same version listed. Alternatively, contact the Pi3D team on the Google group; they will be happy to help!

3. Obtain Pi3D demos from the GitHub site as shown in the following command lines. You will need around 90 MB of free space to download and extract the files:

   ```
   cd ~
   wget https://github.com/pi3d/pi3d_demos/archive/master.zip
   unzip master.zip
   rm master.zip
   ```

You will find that the demos have been unpacked to `pi3d_demos-master`. By default, the demos are expected to be located at `home/pi/pi3d`; therefore, we will rename this directory to `pi3d` as shown in the following command:

```
mv pi3d_demos-master pi3d
```

4. Finally, check the Raspberry Pi memory split.

Run **raspi-config** (`sudo raspi-config`) and ensure that your memory split is set to 128. (You should only need to do this if you have changed it in the past, as 128 MB is the default.) This ensures that you have plenty of RAM allocated for the GPU, so it will be able to handle lots of 3D objects if required.

5. Test if everything is working properly.

You should now be able to run any of the scripts in the `pi3d_demos-master` directory. See the Pi3D wiki pages for details of how they function (`http://pi3d.github.io/html/ReadMe.html`).

To get the best performance, it is recommended that the scripts are run from the command prompt (without loading the desktop).

Many of the demos require mouse and keyboard control; these scripts will require `sudo` privileges to access the input devices. Therefore, the scripts should be run using `sudo` as follows:

```
sudo python3 pi3d/Shapes.py
```

Although it would be perfectly reasonable to use the methods from *Chapter 4, Creating Games and Graphics*, for mouse and keyboard input using **Tkinter**, many of the demos in the Pi3D library use **InputEvent** objects to provide additional support for joysticks and gamepads. As noted within the examples, `inputs` may detect multiple input devices, so you may need to adjust the device number to select the correct device using get_mouse_movement(1) or perhaps get_mouse_movement(2).

6. Configure the setup for your own scripts.

Since we will use some of the textures and models from the demos, it is recommended that you create your scripts within the `pi3d` directory. If you have a username different from the default Pi account, you will need to adjust `/pi3d/demo.py`.

Replace the `pi` part with your own username as follows:

```
nano ~/pi3d/demo.py
import sys
sys.path.append('/home/pi/pi3d')
```

If you want to relocate your files somewhere else, ensure that you add a copy of `demo.py` in the folder with the correct path to any resource files you require.

How to do it...

Create the following `3dObject.py` script:

```python
#!/usr/bin/python3
""" Create a 3D space with a Tetrahedron inside and rotate the
    view around using the mouse.
"""
from math import sin, cos, radians
import demo
import pi3d

DISPLAY = pi3d.Display.create(x=50, y=50)
#capture mouse and key presses
inputs=pi3d.InputEvents()

def main():
  CAMERA = pi3d.Camera.instance()
  tex = pi3d.Texture("textures/stripwood.jpg")
  flatsh = pi3d.Shader("uv_flat")

  #Define the coordinates for our shape (x,y,z)
  A=(-1.0,-1.0,-1.0)
  B=(1.0,-1.0,1.0)
  C=(-1.0,-1.0,1.0)
  D=(-1.0,1.0,1.0)
  ids=["A","B","C","D"]
  coords=[A,B,C,D]
  myTetra = pi3d.Tetrahedron(x=0.0, y=0.0, z=0.0,
                             corners=(A,B,C,D))
  myTetra.set_draw_details(flatsh,[tex])
  # Load ttf font and set the font to black
  arialFont = pi3d.Font("fonts/FreeMonoBoldOblique.ttf",
                   "#000000")
  mystring=[]
  #Create string objects to show the coordinates
  for i,pos in enumerate(coords):
    mystring.append(pi3d.String(font=arialFont,
                          string=ids[i]+str(pos),
                          x=pos[0], y=pos[1],z=pos[2]))
    mystring.append(pi3d.String(font=arialFont,
```

```
                              string=ids[i]+str(pos),
                              x=pos[0], y=pos[1],z=pos[2], ry=180))
      for string in mystring:
        string.set_shader(flatsh)

      camRad = 4.0 # radius of camera position
      rot = 0.0 # rotation of camera
      tilt = 0.0 # tilt of camera

      # main display loop
      while DISPLAY.loop_running() and not \
                                inputs.key_state("KEY_ESC"):
        inputs.do_input_events()
        #Note:Some mouse devices will be located on
        #get_mouse_movement(1) or (2) etc.
        mx,my,mv,mh,md=inputs.get_mouse_movement()

        rot -= (mx)*0.2
        tilt -= (my)*0.2
        CAMERA.reset()
        CAMERA.rotate(-tilt, rot, 0)
        CAMERA.position((camRad * sin(radians(rot)) *
                        cos(radians(tilt)),
                        camRad * sin(radians(tilt)),
                        -camRad * cos(radians(rot)) *
                        cos(radians(tilt))))
        #Draw the Tetrahedron
        myTetra.draw()
        for string in mystring:
          string.draw()

try:
  main()
finally:
  inputs.release()
  DISPLAY.destroy()
  print("Closed Everything. END")
#End
```

To run the script, use `sudo python3 3dObject.py`.

How it works...

We import the math modules (for angle calculations—used to control the view based on mouse movements). We also import the demo, which just provides the path to the **shaders** and **textures** in this example.

We start by defining some key elements that will be used by Pi3D to generate and display our object. The space in which we shall place our object is the `pi3d.Display` object; this defines the size of the space and initializes the screen to generate and display OpenGL ES graphics.

Next, we define a `pi3d.Camera` object, which will allow us to define how we view the object within our space. To render our object, we define a texture to be applied to the surface and a shader that will apply the texture to the object. The shader is used to apply all the effects and lighting to the object, and it is coded to use the GPU's OpenGL ES core instead of the ARM processor.

We define the `inputs` object using `pi3d.InputEvents()` so that we can respond to the keyboard and mouse input. The main loop, when running, will check if the *Esc* key is pressed and then close everything down (including calling `DISPLAY.destroy()` to release the screen). We use the `try: finally:` method to ensure that the display is closed correctly even if there is an exception within `main()`.

The mouse movement is collected in the main display loop using `inputs.get_mouse_movement()`, which returns the x and y movement (along with wheel movements and so on). The x and y movement is used to rotate around the object.

The mouse movements determine the position and angle of the camera. Any adjustment to the forward/backward position of the mouse is used to move it over or under the object and change the angle of the camera (using `tilt`) so it remains pointing at the object. Similarly, any sideways movement will move the camera around the object using the `CAMERA.reset()` function. This ensures that the display updates the camera view with the new position, `CAMERA.rotate()`, to change the angle and uses `CAMERA.position()` to move the camera to a position around the object, with the `camRad` units away from its center.

We will draw a three-dimensional object called a **tetrahedron**, a shape made up of four triangles to form a pyramid with a triangular base. The four corners of the shape (three around the base and one at the top) will be defined by the three-dimensional coordinates A, B, C, and D as shown in the following figure:

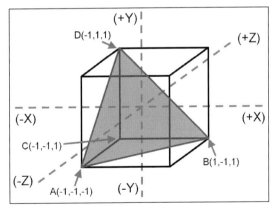

The tetrahedron placed within the X, Y, and Z axes

The pi3d.Tetrahedron object is defined by specifying coordinates to position it in the space and then specify the corners that will be joined to form four triangles that make up the shape.

Using set_draw_details(flatsh, [tex]), we apply the shader(s) we wish to use and the texture(s) for the object. In our example, we are just using a single texture, but some shaders can use several textures for complex effects.

To help highlight where the coordinates are, we will add some pi3d.String objects (by setting the string text to specify the ID and coordinates next to them and placing it at the required location). We will create two string objects for each location, one facing forward and another facing backwards (ry=180 rotates the object by 180 degrees on the y axis). The pi3d.String objects are single sided, so if we only had one side facing forward, it wouldn't be visible from behind when the view was rotated and would just disappear (plus the text would be backwards anyway). Again, we use the flatsh shader to render it using the set_shader() string object.

All that is left to do now is to draw our tetrahedron and the string objects while checking for any keyboard events. Each time the while loop completes, DISPLAY.loop_running() is called, which will update the display with any adjustments to the camera as required.

There's more...

In addition to introducing how to draw a basic object within the 3D space, the preceding example makes use of the following four key elements used in 3D graphics programming.

Camera

The camera represents our view in the 3D space; one way to explore and see more of the space is by moving the camera. The Camera class is defined as follows:

```
pi3d.Camera.Camera(at=(0, 0, 0), eye=(0, 0, -0.1),
                   lens=None, is_3d=True, scale=1.0)
```

The camera is defined by providing two locations, one to look at (usually the object we wish to see—defined by at) and another to look from (the object's position—defined by eye). Other features of the camera, such as its field of view (lens) and so on, can be adjusted or used with the default settings.

 If we didn't define a camera in our display, a default one will be created that points at the origin (the center of the display, that is, 0,0,0) positioned slightly in front of it (0,0,-0.1).

See the Pi3D documentation regarding the camera module for more details.

Shaders

Shaders are very useful as they allow a lot of the complex work required to apply textures and lighting to an object by offloading the task to the more powerful GPU in the Raspberry Pi. The Shader class is defined as follows:

```
class pi3d.Shader.Shader(shfile=None, vshader_source=None,
                                      fshader_source=None)
```

This allows you to specify a shader file (`shfile`) and specific vertex and fragment shaders (if required) within the file.

There are several shaders included in the Pi3D library, some of which allow multiple textures to be used for reflections, close-up details, and transparency effects. The implementation of the shader will determine how the lights and textures are applied to the object (and in some cases, such as `uv_flat`, the shader will ignore any lighting effects).

The shader files are listed in the `pi3d\shaders` directory. Try experimenting with different shaders such as `mat_reflect`, which will ignore the textures/fonts but still apply the lighting effects; or `uv_toon`, which will apply a cartoon effect to the texture.

Each shader consists of two files; the `vs` (vertex shader) and `fs` (fragment shader), written in C-like code. They work together to apply the effects to the object as desired. The vertex shader is responsible for mapping the 3D location of the vertices to the 2D display. The fragment shader (or sometimes called the pixel shader) is responsible for applying lighting and texture effects to the pixels themselves. The construction and operation of these shaders are well beyond the scope of this chapter, but there are several example shaders that you can compare, change, and experiment with within the `pi3d\shaders` directory.

Lights

Lighting is very important in a 3D world; it could range from simple general lighting (as used in our example) to multiple lights angled from different directions providing different strengths and colors. How lights interact with objects and the effects they produce will be determined by the textures and shaders used to render them.

Lights are defined by their direction, their color and brightness, and also by an ambient light to define the background (non-directional) light. The Light class is defined as follows:

```
class pi3d.Light.Light(lightpos=(10, -10, 20),
                       lightcol=(1.0, 1.0, 1.0),
                       lightamb=(0.1, 0.1, 0.2))
```

By default, the display will define a light that has the following properties:

- ► `lightpos=(10, -10, 20)`: This is a light that shines from the front of the space (near the top-left side) down towards the back of the space (towards the right).
- ► `lightcol=(1.0, 1.0, 1.0)`: This is a bright, white, directional light (the direction is defined in the preceding dimension, and it is the color defined by the RGB values `1.0, 1.0, 1.0`).
- ► `lightamb=(0.1, 0.1, 0.2)`: This is overall a dull, slightly bluish light.

Textures

Textures are able to add realism to an object by allowing fine detail to be applied to the object's surface; this could be an image of bricks for a wall or a person's face to be displayed on the character. When a texture is used by the shader, it can often be scaled and reflection can be added to it; some shaders even allow you to apply surface detail.

We can apply multiple textures to an object to combine them and produce different effects; it will be up to the shader to determine how they are applied.

Creating and importing 3D models

Creating complex shapes directly from code can often be cumbersome and time consuming. Fortunately, it is possible to import prebuilt models into your 3D space.

It is even possible to use graphical 3D modeling programs to generate models and then export them as a suitable format for you to use. This example produces a Newell Pi Teapot in the Raspberry Pi theme as shown in the following screenshot:

Newell Raspberry Pi teapot

Getting ready

We shall use 3D models of a teapot (both `teapot.obj` and `teapot.mdl`) located in `pi3d\models`.

> Modeling a teapot is the traditional 3D equivalent of displaying *Hello World*. Computer graphics researcher Martin Newell first created the Newell Teapot in 1975 as a basic test model for his work. The Newell Teapot soon became the standard model to quickly check if a 3D rendering system is working correctly (it even appeared in Toy Story and a 3D episode of The Simpsons).

Other models are available in the `pi3d\models` directory (`monkey.obj/mdl` that has been used later on is available in the book resource files).

How to do it...

Create and run the following `3dModel.py` script:

```python
#!/usr/bin/python3
""" Wavefront obj model loading. Material properties set in
    mtl file.
"""
import demo
import pi3d
from math import sin, cos, radians

# set up display and initialize pi3d
DISPLAY = pi3d.Display.create()
# Fetch key presses
inputs=pi3d.InputEvents()

def main():
  #Model textures and shaders
  shader = pi3d.Shader("uv_reflect")
  bumptex = pi3d.Texture("textures/floor_nm.jpg")
  shinetex = pi3d.Texture("textures/stars.jpg")
  # load model
  mymodel = pi3d.Model(file_string='models/teapot.obj', z=10)
  mymodel.set_shader(shader)
  mymodel.set_normal_shine(bumptex, 4.0, shinetex, 0.5)
```

```
    #Create environment box
    flatsh = pi3d.Shader("uv_flat")
    ectex=pi3d.loadECfiles("textures/ecubes","sbox")
    myecube = pi3d.EnvironmentCube(size=900.0, maptype="FACES",
                                   name="cube")
    myecube.set_draw_details(flatsh, ectex)

    CAMERA = pi3d.Camera.instance()
    rot = 0.0 # rotation of camera
    tilt = 0.0 # tilt of camera

    while DISPLAY.loop_running() and not \
                                inputs.key_state("KEY_ESC"):
      #Rotate camera
      inputs.do_input_events()
      # camera steered by mouse
      #Note:Some mice devices will be located on
      #get_mouse_movement(1) or (2) etc.
      mx,my,mv,mh,md=inputs.get_mouse_movement()

      rot -= (mx)*0.2
      tilt -= (my)*0.2
      CAMERA.reset()
      CAMERA.rotate(tilt, rot, 0)
      #Rotate object
      mymodel.rotateIncY(2.0)
      mymodel.rotateIncZ(0.1)
      mymodel.rotateIncX(0.3)
      #Draw objects
      mymodel.draw()
      myecube.draw()

try:
  main()
finally:
  inputs.release()
  DISPLAY.destroy()
  print("Closed Everything. END")
#End
```

How it works...

Like the `3dObject.py` example, we define the DISPLAY shader (this time using `uv_reflect`) and some additional textures—`bumptex` (`floor_nm.jpg`) and `shinetex` (`stars.jpg`)—to use later. We define a model that we want to import, placing it at `z=10` (if no coordinates are given, it will be placed at `(0,0,0)`. Since we do not specify a camera position, the default will place it within the view (see the section regarding the camera for more details).

We apply the shader using the `set_shader()` function. Next, we add some textures and effects using `bumptex` as a surface texture (scaled by 4). We apply an extra shiny effect using `shinetex` and apply a reflection strength of 0.5 (the strength ranges from weakest 0.0 to 1.0 strongest) using the `set_normal_shine()` function. If you look closely at the surface of the model, the `bumptex` texture provides additional surface detail and the `shinetex` texture can be seen as the reflection on the surface.

To display our model within something more interesting than a default blue space, we create an `EnvironmentCube` object. This defines a large space that has a special texture applied to the inside space (in this instance, it will load the `sbox_front/back/bottom/left` and `sbox_right` images from the `textures\ecubes` directory), so it effectively encloses the objects within. The result is that you get a pleasant backdrop for your object.

Again, we define a default `CAMERA` object with `rot` and `tilt` variables to control the view. Within the `DISPLAY.loop_running()` section, we can control the view of the `CAMERA` object using the mouse and rotate the model on its axis at different rates to let it spin and show all its sides (using the `RotateIncX/Y/Z()` function to specify the rate of rotation). Finally, we ensure that the DISPLAY is updated by drawing the model and the environment cube.

There's more...

We can create a wide range of objects to place within our simulated environment. Pi3D provides methods to import our own models and apply multiple textures to them.

Creating or loading your own objects

If you wish to use your own models in this example, you shall need to create one in the correct format; Pi3D supports **obj** (wavefront object files) and **egg** (Panda3D).

An excellent, free, 3D modeling program is called **Blender** (available at `http://www.blender.org`). There are lots of examples and tutorials on their website to get you started with basic modeling (`http://www.blender.org/education-help/tutorials`).

The Pi3D model support is limited and will not support all the features that Blender can embed in an exported model, for example, deformable meshes. Therefore, only basic multipart models are supported. There are a few steps required to simplify the model so it can be loaded by Pi3D.

To create a suitable `.obj` model to use with Pi3D, proceed with the following steps:

1. Create or load a model in Blender—try starting with a simple object before attempting more complex models.

2. Select each **Object** and switch to the **Edit** mode (press *Tab*).

3. Select all vertices (press *A*) and uv-map them (press *U* and then select **Unwrap**).

4. Return to the **Object** mode (press *Tab*).

5. Export it as **obj (wavefront object file)**—from the **File** menu at the top, select **Export** and then **Wavefront (.obj)**. Ensure that **Include Normals** is also checked in the list of options in the bottom-left list.

6. Click on **Save** and place the `.obj` and `.mtl` files in the `pi3d\models` directory, and ensure that you update the script with the model's filename as follows:

```
mymodel = pi3d.Model(file_string='models/monkey.obj',
   name='monkey', z=4)
```

When you run your updated script, you will see your model displayed in the 3D space. For example the, `monkey.obj` model is shown in the following screenshot:

A monkey head model created in Blender and displayed by Pi3D

Changing the object's textures and .mtl files

The texture that is applied to the surface of the model is contained within the `.mtl` file of the model. This file defines the textures and how they are applied as set by the modeling software. Complex models may contain multiple textures for various parts of the object.

If no material is defined, the first texture in the shader is used (in our example, this is the `bumptex` texture). To add a new texture to the object, add (or edit) the following line in the `.mtl` file (that is, to use `water.jpg`):

```
map_Kd ../textures/water.jpg
```

More information about `.mtl` files and `.obj` files can be found on the following Wikipedia link:

```
https://en.wikipedia.org/wiki/Wavefront_.obj_file
```

Taking screenshots

The Pi3D library includes a useful screenshot function to capture the screen in a `.jpg` or `.png` file. We can add a new key event to trigger it and call `pi3d.screenshot("filename.jpg")` to save an image (or use a counter to take multiple screenshots) as shown in the following code:

```
shotnum = 0 #Set counter to 0
while DISPLAY.loop_running()
...
  if inputs.key_state("KEY_P"):
    while inputs.key_state("KEY_P"):
      inputs.do_input_events()                # wait for key to go up
      pi3d.screenshot("screenshot%04d.jpg"%( shotnum))
      shotnum += 1
...
```

Creating a 3D world to roam in

Now that we are able to create models and objects within our 3D space, as well as generate backgrounds, we may want to create a more interesting environment within which to place them.

3D terrain maps provide an elegant way to define very complex landscapes. The terrain is defined using a grayscale image to set the elevation of the land. The following example shows how we can define our own landscape and simulate flying over it, or even walk on its surface:

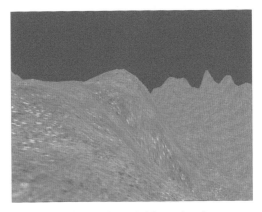

A 3D landscape generated from a terrain map

Getting ready

You will need to place the `Map.png` file in the `pi3d/textures` directory of the Pi3D library. Alternatively, you can use one of the elevation maps already present—replace the reference to `Map.png` for another one of the elevation maps, such as `testislands.jpg`.

How to do it...

Create the following `3dWorld.py` script:

```python
#!/usr/bin/python3
from __future__ import absolute_import, division
from __future__ import print_function, unicode_literals
""" An example of generating a 3D environment using a elevation map
"""
from math import sin, cos, radians
import demo
import pi3d

DISPLAY = pi3d.Display.create(x=50, y=50)
#capture mouse and key presses
inputs=pi3d.InputEvents()

def limit(value,min,max):
  if (value < min):
    value = min
  elif (value > max):
    value = max
  return value

def main():
  CAMERA = pi3d.Camera.instance()
  tex = pi3d.Texture("textures/grass.jpg")
  flatsh = pi3d.Shader("uv_flat")
  # Create elevation map
  mapwidth,mapdepth,mapheight=200.0,200.0,50.0
  mymap = pi3d.ElevationMap("textures/Map.png",
            width=mapwidth, depth=mapdepth, height=mapheight,
            divx=128, divy=128, ntiles=20)
  mymap.set_draw_details(flatsh, [tex], 1.0, 1.0)

  rot = 0.0 # rotation of camera
  tilt = 0.0 # tilt of camera
  height = 20
  viewhight = 4
  sky = 200
```

```
    xm,ym,zm = 0.0,height,0.0
    onGround = False
    # main display loop
    while DISPLAY.loop_running() and not \
                            inputs.key_state("KEY_ESC"):
      inputs.do_input_events()
      #Note:Some mice devices will be located on
      #get_mouse_movement(1) or (2) etc.
      mx,my,mv,mh,md=inputs.get_mouse_movement()

      rot -= (mx)*0.2
      tilt -= (my)*0.2
      CAMERA.reset()
      CAMERA.rotate(-tilt, rot, 0)
      CAMERA.position((xm,ym,zm))
      mymap.draw()
      if inputs.key_state("KEY_W"):
        xm -= sin(radians(rot))
        zm += cos(radians(rot))
      elif inputs.key_state("KEY_S"):
        xm += sin(radians(rot))
        zm -= cos(radians(rot))
      elif inputs.key_state("KEY_R"):
        ym += 2
        onGround = False
      elif inputs.key_state("KEY_T"):
        ym -= 2
      ym-=0.1 #Float down!
      #Limit the movement
      xm=limit(xm,-(mapwidth/2),mapwidth/2)
      zm=limit(zm,-(mapdepth/2),mapdepth/2)
      if ym >= sky:
        ym = sky
      #Check onGround
      ground = mymap.calcHeight(xm, zm) + viewhight
      if (onGround == True) or (ym <= ground):
        ym = mymap.calcHeight(xm, zm) + viewhight
        onGround = True

try:
  main()
finally:
  inputs.release()
  DISPLAY.destroy()
  print("Closed Everything. END")
#End
```

How it works...

Once we have defined the display, camera, textures, and shaders that we are going to use, we can define the `ElevationMap` object.

It works by assigning a height to the terrain image based on the pixel value of selected points of the image. For example, a single line of an image will provide a slice of the `ElevationMap` object and a row of elevation points on the 3D surface.

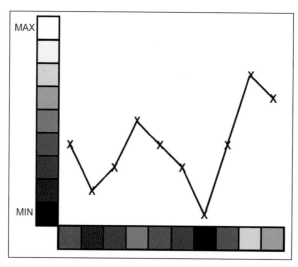

Mapping the map.png pixel shade to the terrain height

We create an `ElevationMap` object by providing the filename of the image we will use for the gradient information (`textures/Map.png`), and we also create the dimensions of the map (`width`, `depth`, and `height`—which is how high the white spaces will be compared to the black spaces).

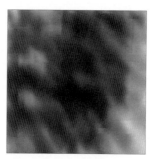

The light parts of the map will create high points and the dark ones will create low points.

The `Map.png` texture provides an example terrain map, which is converted into a three-dimensional surface.

We also specify `divx` and `divy`, which determines how much detail of the terrain map is used (how many points from the terrain map are used to create the elevation surface). Finally, `ntiles` specifies that the texture used will be scaled to fit `20 times` across the surface.

Within the main `DISPLAY.loop_running()` section, we will control the camera, draw `ElevationMap`, respond to inputs, and limit movements in our space.

As before, we use an `InputEvents` object to capture mouse movements and translate them to control the camera. We will also use `inputs.key_state()` to determine if *W*, *S*, *R*, and *T* have been pressed, which allow us to move forward, backwards, as well as rise up and down.

To ensure that we do not fall through the `ElevationMap` object when we move over it, we can use `mymap.calcHeight()` to provide us with the height of the terrain at a specific location (`x,y,z`). We can either follow the ground by ensuring the camera is set to equal this, or fly through the air by just ensuring that we never go below it. When we detect that we are on the ground, we ensure that we remain on the ground until we press *R* to rise again.

Building 3D maps and mazes

We've seen that the Pi3D library can be used to create lots of interesting objects and environments. Using some of the more complex classes (or by constructing our own), whole custom spaces can be designed for the user to explore.

In the following example, we use a special module called **Building**, which has been designed to allow you to construct a building using a single image file to provide the layout.

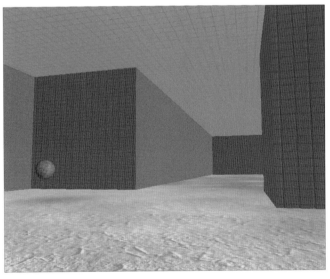

Explore the maze and find the sphere that marks the exit

Getting ready

You will need to ensure that you have the following files in the pi3d/textures directory:

▶ squareblocksred.png

▶ floor.png

▶ inside_map0.png, inside_map1.png, inside_map2.png

These files are available as part of the book resources placed at Chapter05\resource\ source_files\textures.

How to do it...

Let's run the following 3dMaze.py script by performing the following steps:

1. First, we set up the display and settings for the model using the following code:

```
#!/usr/bin/python3
"""Small maze game, try to find the exit
"""
from math import sin, cos, radians
import demo
import pi3d
from pi3d.shape.Building import Building, SolidObject
from pi3d.shape.Building import Size, Position

# Set up display and initialize pi3d
DISPLAY = pi3d.Display.create()
#Load shader
shader = pi3d.Shader("uv_reflect")
flatsh = pi3d.Shader("uv_flat")
# Load textures
ceilingimg = pi3d.Texture("textures/squareblocks4.png")
wallimg = pi3d.Texture("textures/squareblocksred.png")
floorimg = pi3d.Texture("textures/dunes3_512.jpg")
bumpimg = pi3d.Texture("textures/mudnormal.jpg")
startimg = pi3d.Texture("textures/rock1.jpg")
endimg = pi3d.Texture("textures/water.jpg")
# Create elevation map
mapwidth=1000.0
mapdepth=1000.0
#We shall assume we are using a flat floor in this example
mapheight=0.0
```

```
mymap = pi3d.ElevationMap(mapfile="textures/floor.png",
            width=mapwidth, depth=mapdepth, height=mapheight,
            divx=64, divy=64)
mymap.set_draw_details(shader, [floorimg, bumpimg],128.0, 0.0)
levelList=["textures/inside_map0.png","textures/inside_map1.png",
            "textures/inside_map2.png"]
avhgt = 5.0
aveyelevel = 4.0
MAP_BLOCK = 15.0
aveyeleveladjust = aveyelevel - avhgt/2
PLAYERHEIGHT=(mymap.calcHeight(5, 5) + avhgt/2)
#Start the player in the top-left corner
startpos=[(8*MAP_BLOCK),PLAYERHEIGHT,(8*MAP_BLOCK)]
endpos=[0,PLAYERHEIGHT,0] #Set the end pos in the centre
person = SolidObject("person", Size(1, avhgt, 1),
            Position(startpos[0],startpos[1],startpos[2]), 1)
#Add spheres for start and end; the end must also have a solid
#object so we can detect when we hit it
startobject=pi3d.Sphere(name="start",x=startpos[0],
            y=startpos[1]+avhgt,z=startpos[2])
startobject.set_draw_details(shader, [startimg, bumpimg],
            32.0, 0.3)
endobject=pi3d.Sphere(name="end",x=endpos[0],
            y=endpos[1],z=endpos[2])
endobject.set_draw_details(shader, [endimg, bumpimg], 32.0, 0.3)
endSolid = SolidObject("end", Size(1, avhgt, 1),
            Position(endpos[0],endpos[1],endpos[2]), 1)
mazeScheme = {"#models": 3,
        (1,None): [["C",2]],        #white cell : Ceiling
        (0,1,"edge"): [["W",1]],    #white cell on edge next
                                    #   black cell : Wall
        (1,0,"edge"): [["W",1]],    #black cell on edge next
                                    #   to white cell : Wall
        (0,1):[["W",0]]}            #white cell next
                                    #   to black cell : Wall


details = [[shader, [wallimg], 1.0, 0.0, 4.0, 16.0],
            [shader, [wallimg], 1.0, 0.0, 4.0, 8.0],
            [shader, [ceilingimg], 1.0, 0.0, 4.0, 4.0]]


arialFont = pi3d.Font("fonts/FreeMonoBoldOblique.ttf",
            "#ffffff", font_size=10)
inputs = pi3d.InputEvents()
```

2. We then create functions to allow us to reload the levels and display messages to the player using the following code:

```
def loadLevel(next_level):
  print(">>> Please wait while maze is constructed...")
  next_level=next_level%len(levelList)
  building = pi3d.Building(levelList[next_level], 0, 0, mymap,
      width=MAP_BLOCK, depth=MAP_BLOCK, height=30.0,
      name="", draw_details=details, yoff=-15, scheme=mazeScheme)
  return building


def showMessage(text,rot=0):
  message = pi3d.String(font=arialFont, string=text,
                        x=endpos[0],y=endpos[1]+(avhgt/4),
                        z=endpos[2], sx=0.05, sy=0.05,ry=-rot)
  message.set_shader(flatsh)
  message.draw()
```

3. Within the main function, we set up the 3D environment and draw all the objects using the following code:

```
def main():
  #Load a level
  level=0
  building = loadLevel(level)
  lights = pi3d.Light(lightpos=(10, -10, 20),
                      lightcol =(0.7, 0.7, 0.7),
                      lightamb=(0.7, 0.7, 0.7))
  rot=0.0
  tilt=0.0
  CAMERA = pi3d.Camera.instance()
  while DISPLAY.loop_running() and not \
                            inputs.key_state("KEY_ESC"):
    CAMERA.reset()
    CAMERA.rotate(tilt, rot, 0)
    CAMERA.position((person.x(), person.y(),
                    person.z() - aveyeleveladjust))
    #draw objects
    person.drawall()
    building.drawAll()
    mymap.draw()
    startobject.draw()
    endobject.draw()
    #Apply the light to all the objects in the building
    for b in building.model:
```

```
      b.set_light(lights, 0)
  mymap.set_light(lights, 0)

  inputs.do_input_events()
  #Note:Some mouse devices will be located on
  #get_mouse_movement(1) or (2) etc.
  mx,my,mv,mh,md=inputs.get_mouse_movement()

  rot -= (mx)*0.2
  tilt -= (my)*0.2
  xm = person.x()
  ym = person.y()
  zm = person.z()
```

4. Finally, we monitor for key presses, handle any collisions with objects, and move within the maze as follows:

```
  if inputs.key_state("KEY_APOSTROPHE"):  #key '
    tilt -= 2.0
  if inputs.key_state("KEY_SLASH"):  #key /
    tilt += 2.0
  if inputs.key_state("KEY_A"):
    rot += 2
  if inputs.key_state("KEY_D"):
    rot -= 2
  if inputs.key_state("KEY_H"):
    #Use point_at as help - will turn the player to face
    #  the direction of the end point
    tilt, rot = CAMERA.point_at([endobject.x(), endobject.y(),
                                endobject.z()])
  if inputs.key_state("KEY_W"):
    xm -= sin(radians(rot))
    zm += cos(radians(rot))
  if inputs.key_state("KEY_S"):
    xm += sin(radians(rot))
    zm -= cos(radians(rot))

  NewPos = Position(xm, ym, zm)
  collisions = person.CollisionList(NewPos)
  if collisions:
    #If we reach the end, reset to start position!
    for obj in collisions:
      if obj.name == "end":
        inputs.do_input_events() #clear any pending inputs
```

```
            #Required to remove the building walls from the
            #  solidobject list
            building.remove_walls()
            showMessage("Loading Level",rot)
            DISPLAY.loop_running()
            level+=1
            building = loadLevel(level)
            showMessage("")
            person.move(Position(startpos[0],startpos[1],
                                 startpos[2]))
        else:
          person.move(NewPos)

try:
  main()
finally:
  inputs.release()
  DISPLAY.destroy()
  print("Closed Everything. END")
#End
```

How it works...

We define many of the elements we used in the preceding examples, such as the display, textures, shaders, font, and lighting. We also define the objects, such as the building itself, the `ElevationMap` object, as well as the start and end points of the maze. We also use **SolidObjects** to help detect movement within the space. See the *Using SolidObjects to detect collisions* subsection in the *There's more...* section of this recipe for more information.

Finally, we create the actual `Building` object based on the selected map image (using the `loadLevel()` function) and locate the camera (which represents our first-person viewpoint) at the start. See the *The Building module* subsection in the *There's more...* section of this recipe for more information.

Within the main loop, we draw all the objects in our space and apply the lighting effects. We will also monitor the inputs events for movement in the mouse (to control the tilt and rotation of the camera) or the keyboard to move the player (or exit/provide help).

The controls are as follows:

- ▸ **Mouse movement**: This changes the camera tilt and rotation.
- ▸ **' or / key**: This changes the camera to tilt either downwards or upwards.
- ▸ **A or D**: This changes the camera to rotate from left to right or vice versa.

- ▶ **W or S**: This moves the player forwards or backwards.
- ▶ **H**: This helps the player by rotating them to face the end of the maze. The useful `CAMERA.point_at()` function is used to quickly rotate and tilt the camera's viewpoint towards the provided coordinates (the end position).

Whenever the player moves, we check if the new position (`NewPos`) collides with another `SolidObject` using `CollisionList(NewPos)`. The function will return a list of any other SolidObjects that overlap the coordinates provided.

If there are no SolidObjects in the way, we make the player move; otherwise, we check to see if one of the SolidObject's names is the `end` object, in which case we have reached the end of the maze.

When the player reaches the end, we clear the inputs, remove the walls from the old `Building` object, and display a loading message. If we forget to remove the walls, all the SolidObjects belonging to the previous `Building` will still remain, creating invisible obstacles in the next level.

We use the `showMessage()` function to inform the user that the next level will be loaded soon (since it can take a while for the building object to be constructed). We need to ensure that we call `DISPLAY.loop_running()` after we draw the message so that it is displayed on screen before we start loading the level (at which point the person will be unable to move and so on). We need to ensure that the message is always facing the player regardless of the side they collide with the `end` object, by using the camera rotation (`rot`) for its angle.

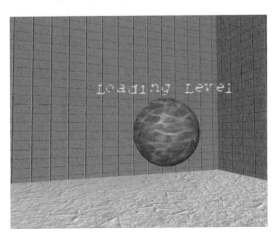

When the exit ball is found, the next level is loaded

When the next level in the list has been loaded (or the first level has been loaded again when all the levels have been completed), we replace the message with a blank one to remove it and reset the person's position back to the start.

You can design and add your own levels by creating additional map files (20 x 20 PNG files with walls marked out with black pixels and walkways in white) and listing them in `levelList`. The player will start at the top-left corner of the map, and the exit is placed at the center.

You will notice that loading the levels can take quite a long time; this is the relatively slow ARM processor in the Raspberry Pi performing all the calculations required to construct the maze and locate all the components. As soon as the maze has been built, the more powerful GPU takes over, which results in fast and smooth graphics as the player explores the space.

There's more...

The preceding example creates a building for the player to explore and interact with. In order to achieve this, we use the Building module of Pi3D to create a building and use SolidObject to detect collisions.

The Building module

The `pi3d.Building` module allows you to define a whole level or floor of a building using map files. Like the terrain maps used in the preceding example, the color of the pixels will be converted into different parts of the level. In our case, black is for the walls and white is for the passages and halls, complete with ceilings.

The building layout is defined by the pixels in the image

The sections built by the `Building` object are defined by the **Scheme** used. The Scheme is defined by two sections, by the number of models, and then by the definitions for various aspects of the model, as seen in the following code:

```
mazeScheme = {"#models": 3,
    (1,None): [["C",2]],      #white cell : Ceiling
    (0,1,"edge"): [["W",1]], #white cell on edge by black cell : Wall
    (1,0,"edge"): [["W",1]], #black cell on edge by white cell : Wall
    (0,1):[["W",0]]}          #white cell next to black cell : Wall
```

The first **tuple** defines the type of cell/square that the selected model should be applied to. Since there are two pixel colors in the map, the squares will either be black (0) or white (1). By determining the position and type of a particular cell/square, we can define which models (wall, ceiling, or roof) we want to apply.

We define three main types of cell/square locations:

- A whole square (1, None): This is a white cell representing open space in the building.
- One cell bordering another, on the edge (0, 1, "edge"): This is a black cell next to a white one on the map edge. This also includes (1, 0, "edge"). This will represent the outer wall of the building.
- Any black cell that is next to a white cell (0, 1): This will represent all the internal walls of the building.

Next, we allocate a type of object(s) to be applied for that type (W or C):

- **Wall** (W): This is a vertical wall that is placed between the specified cells (such as between black and white cells).
- **Ceiling** (C): This is a horizontal section of the ceiling to cover the current cell.
- **Roof** (R): This is an additional horizontal section that is placed slightly above the ceiling to provide a roofing effect. It is typically used for buildings that may need to be viewed from the outside (this is not used in our example).
- **Ceiling Edge** (CE): This is used to join the ceiling sections to the roof around the edges of the building (it is not used in our example since ours is an indoor model).

Finally, we specify the model that will be used for each object. We are using three models in this example (normal walls, walls on an edge, and the ceiling), so we can define the model used by specifying 0, 1, or 2.

Each of the models are defined in the `details` array, which allows us to set the required textures and shaders for each one (this contains the same information that would normally be set by the `.set_draw_details()` function), as shown in the following code:

```
details = [[shader, [wallimg], 1.0, 0.0, 4.0, 16.0],
           [shader, [wallimg], 1.0, 0.0, 4.0, 8.0],
           [shader, [ceilingimg], 1.0, 0.0, 4.0, 4.0]]
```

In our example, the inside walls are allocated to the `wallimg` texture (`textures/squareblocksred.png`) and the ceilings are allocated to the `ceilingimg` texture (`textures/squareblocks4.png`). You may be able to note from the following screenshot that we can apply different texture models (in our case, just of a slightly different scaling) for different types of blocks. The walls that border the outside of the maze (with the edge identifier—which is the wall on the left-hand side of the image) will use the second model texture rather than the first (like the other walls that are in the middle and on the right-hand side of the image).

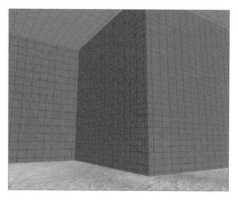

The outward facing wall on the left has a different scaling applied compared to the other walls

Both `scheme` and `draw_details` are set when the `pi3d.Building` object is created as shown in the following code:

```
building = pi3d.Building(levelList[next_level], 0, 0, mymap,
    width=MAP_BLOCK, depth=MAP_BLOCK, height=30.0, name="",
        draw_details=details, yoff=-15, scheme=mazeScheme)
```

Using the map file (`levelList[next_level]`), the scheme (`mazeScheme`), and draw details (`details`), the entire building is created within the environment.

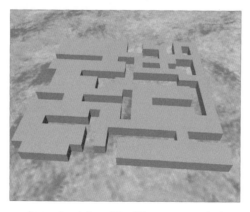

An overhead view of the 3D maze we created

Although we use just black and white in this example, other colored pixels can also be used to define additional block types (and therefore different textures, if required). If another color (such as gray) is added, the indexing of the color mapping is shifted so that black blocks are referenced as 0, the new colored blocks as 1, and the white blocks as 2. See the **Silo** example in the Pi3D demos for details.

We also need to define an `ElevationMap` object—mymap. The `pi3d.Building` module makes use of the `ElevationMap` object's `calcHeight()` function to correctly place the walls on top of the `ElevationMap` object's surface. In this example, we will apply a basic `ElevationMap` object using `textures/floor.png`, which will generate a flat surface that the `Building` object will be placed on.

Using SolidObjects to detect collisions

In addition to the `Building` object, we will define an object for the player and also define two objects to mark the start and end points of the maze. Although the player's view is the first-person viewpoint (that is, we don't actually see them since the view is effectively through their eyes), we need to define a **SolidObject** to represent them.

A SolidObject is a special type of invisible object that can be checked to determine if the space that would be occupied by one SolidObject has overlapped another. This will allow us to use `person.CollisionList(NewPos)` to get a list of any other SolidObjects that the `person` object will be in contact with at the `NewPos` position. Since the `Building` class defines SolidObjects for all the parts of the `Building` object, we will be able to detect when the player tries to move through a wall (or for some reason the roof/ceiling) and stop them from moving through it.

We also use SolidObjects for the starting and end locations in the maze. The place where the player starts is set as the top-left corner of the map (the white-space pixel from the top left of the map) and is marked by the `startpos` object (a small `pi3d.Sphere` with the `rock1.jpg` texture) placed above the person's head. The end of the maze is marked with another `pi3d.Sphere` object (with the `water.jpg` texture) located at the center of the map. We also define another SolidObject at the end so that we can detect when the player reaches it and collides with it (and load the next level!).

6
Using Python to Drive Hardware

In this chapter, we will cover:

- ▶ Controlling an LED
- ▶ Responding to a button
- ▶ A controlled shutdown button
- ▶ The GPIO keypad input
- ▶ Multiplexed color LEDs

Introduction

One of the key features of a Raspberry Pi computer that sets it apart from most other home/office computers is that it has the ability to directly interface with other hardware. The hardware **General Purpose Input/Output** (**GPIO**) pins on the Raspberry Pi can control a wide range of low-level electronics, from **Light Emitting Diodes** (**LEDs**) to switches, sensors, motors, servos, and even extra displays.

This chapter will focus on connecting the Raspberry Pi with some simple circuits and getting to grips with using Python to control and respond to the connected components.

The Raspberry Pi hardware interface consists of 26 pins (**P1**) located to the side of the analog video connector.

The **Model B Rev 2** version of the board (and **Model A**) also includes a secondary set of eight holes (**P5**) located next to **P1**. If an additional connector is soldered in place, it will be able to provide four additional GPIO pins (see *Relocating to the P5 header* in the *A controlled shutdown button* recipe for details).

P1			
GPIO.BOARD			
3V3	1	2	5V
SDA0/1	3	4	5V
SCL0/1	5	6	GND
	7	8	TX
GND	9	10	RX
	11	12	PWM0
	13	14	GND
	15	16	
3v3	17	18	
SPI MOSI	19	20	GND
SPI MISO	21	22	
SPI SCLK	23	24	SPI CE0
GND	25	26	SPI CE1

Raspberry Pi P1 GPIO header pins (pin functions)

The layout of the P1 connector is shown in the previous diagram; the pin numbers are shown as seen from the top of the Raspberry Pi. **Pin 1** is at the end that is nearest to the SD card as shown in the following image:

The Raspberry Pi P1 GPIO header location

Care should be taken when using the P1 header, since it also includes power pins (3V3 and 5V) as well as ground pins (GND). Several of the GPIO pins can be used as standard GPIO, but they also have special functions; these are labeled and highlighted with different colors.

 It is common for engineers to use a 3V3 notation to specify values in schematics to avoid using decimal places that could easily be missed (using 33 volts rather than 3.3 volts would cause severe damage). The same can applied to other values such as resistors, so for example, 1.2k ohms can be written as 1k2 ohms.

There are **TX** and **RX** pins that are used for serial RS232 communications, and with the aid of a voltage level convertor, information can be transferred via a serial cable to another computer or device.

We have **SDA** and **SCL** that are able to support a two-wire bus communication protocol called **I²C** (which is I²C **Bus 0** on Model B Rev1 boards and **Bus 1** on Model A and Model B Rev 2 boards). There are also the **SPI MOSI**, **SPI MISO**, **SPI SCLK**, **SPI CE0**, and **SPI CE1** pins that support another type of bus protocol called **SPI** for high-speed data. Finally, we have **PWM0** that allows a **pulse width modulation** signal to be generated, which is useful for servos and generating analog signals.

However, we will focus on using just the standard GPIO functions in this chapter. The GPIO pin layout is shown in the following diagram:

GPIO.BCM (Rev1/2)		GPIO.BOARD			GPIO.BCM
		P1			
<50mA	3V3	1	2	5V	
BCM GPIO00/02	SDA0/1	3	4	5V	
BCM GPIO01/03	SCL0/1	5	6	GND	
BCM GPIO04		7	8	TX	BCM GPIO14
	GND	9	10	RX	BCM GPIO15
BCM GPIO17		11	12	PWM0	BCM GPIO18
BCM GPIO21/27		13	14	GND	
BCM GPIO22		15	16		BCM GPIO23
<50mA	3v3	17	18		BCM GPIO24
BCM GPIO10	SPIMOSI	19	20	GND	
BCM GPIO9	SPIMISO	21	22		BCM GPIO25
BCM GPIO11	SPI SCLK	23	24	SPI CE0 N	BCM GPIO08
	GND	25	26	SPI CE1 N	BCM GPIO07
GPIO.BCM		**P5**			**GPIO.BCM**
<50mA	3V3	2	1	5V	
BCM GPIO29	SCL0	4	3	SDA0	BCM GPIO28
BCM GPIO31		6	5		BCM GPIO30
	GND	8	7	GND	

Raspberry Pi P1 GPIO header pins (GPIO.BOARD and GPIO.BCM)

The **RPi.GPIO** library can reference the pins on the Raspberry Pi using one of two systems. The numbers shown in the center are the physical position of the pins and are also the numbers referenced by RPi.GPIO when in the **GPIO.BOARD** mode. Although there are BOARD numbers for P1, there aren't any for P5 yet. The numbers on the outside (**BCM GPIO**) are the actual references for the physical ports of the processor to which the pins are wired (which is why they are not in any specific order). They are used when the mode is set to **GPIO.BCM** and allow control of the P1 pins as well as the pins on P5, and also any peripherals connected to other GPIO lines . This includes the LED on the add-on camera on BCM GPIO 4, the status LED on the board, and also the GPIO lines used for reading/writing to the SD card, which would cause serious errors if interfered with.

Pins 3, 5, and 13 on the Model B Revision 1 boards are wired to different parts of the processor, so the GPIO.BCM references are different (as indicated by the Rev 1/2 numbers). When using GPIO.BOARD references, the software will adjust automatically, so the same pin number can be used for both. This is the preferred choice (where possible).

If you use other programming languages to access the GPIO pins, the numbering may be different, so it will be helpful if you are aware of the BCM GPIO references, which refer to the physical GPIO port of the processor.

Be sure to check out the *Appendix, Hardware and Software List*, which lists all the items used in this chapter and the places you can obtain them from.

Controlling an LED

The hardware equivalent of `hello world` is an LED flash, which is a great test to ensure that everything is working and that you have wired it correctly. To make it a little more interesting, I've suggested using an RGB LED (it has red, green, and blue LEDs combined into a single unit), but feel free to use separate LEDs if that is all you have available.

Getting ready

You will need the following equipment:

- 4x DuPont female to male patch wires
- Mini breadboard (170 tie points) or a larger one
- RGB LED (common cathode) / 3 standard LEDs (ideally red/green/blue)
- Breadboarding wire (solid core)
- 3x 470 ohm resistors

Each of the previous components should only cost a few dollars and can be reused for other projects afterwards. The breadboard is a particularly useful item that allows you to try out your own circuits without needing to solder them.

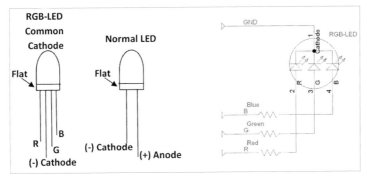

The diagrams of an RGB LED, standard LED, and RGB circuit

The following diagram shows the breadboard circuitry:

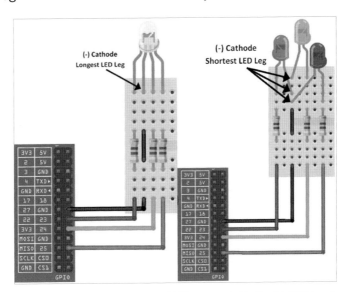

The wiring of an RGB LED / standard LEDs connected to the P1 GPIO header

There are several variations of RGB LEDs available, so check the datasheet of your component to confirm the pin order and type you have. Some are Red, Blue, and Green (RBG), so ensure that you wire accordingly or adjust the RGB_ pin settings in the code. You can also get common anode variants, which will require the anode to be connected to 3V3 (P1-Pin1) for it to light up (and require RGB_ENABLE and RGB_DISABLE to be set as 0 and 1).

The breadboard and component diagrams of this book have been created using a free tool called **Fritzing** (www.fritzing.org); it is great for planning your own Raspberry Pi projects.

How to do it...

Create the ledtest.py script as follows:

```python
#!/usr/bin/python3
#ledtest.py
import time
import RPi.GPIO as GPIO
# RGB LED module
#HARDWARE SETUP
# P1
# 2[======XRG=B==]26
# 1[============]25
# X=GND R=Red G=Green B=Blue

#Setup Active States
#Common Cathode RGB-LED (Cathode=Active Low)
RGB_ENABLE = 1; RGB_DISABLE = 0

#LED CONFIG - Set GPIO Ports
RGB_RED = 16; RGB_GREEN = 18; RGB_BLUE = 22
RGB = [RGB_RED,RGB_GREEN,RGB_BLUE]

def led_setup():
  #Setup the wiring
  GPIO.setmode(GPIO.BOARD)
  #Setup Ports
  for val in RGB:
    GPIO.setup(val,GPIO.OUT)

def main():
  led_setup()
  for val in RGB:
    GPIO.output(val,RGB_ENABLE)
    print("LED ON")
    time.sleep(5)
    GPIO.output(val,RGB_DISABLE)
    print("LED OFF")

try:
  main()
finally:
  GPIO.cleanup()
  print("Closed Everything. END")
#End
```

The `RPi.GPIO` library will require `sudo` permissions to access the GPIO pin hardware, so you will need to run the script using the following command:

```
sudo python3 ledtest.py
```

When you run the script, you should see the red, green, and blue parts of the LED (or each LED, if using separate ones) light up in turn. If not, double-check your wiring or confirm if the LED is working by temporarily connecting the red, green, or blue wire to the 3V3 pin (Pin 1 of the P1 header).

The `sudo` command is required for most hardware-related scripts because it isn't normal for users to directly control hardware at such a low level. For example, setting or clearing a control pin that is part of the SD card controller could corrupt data being written to it. Therefore, for security purposes, super user permissions are required to stop programs from using hardware by accident (or with malicious intent).

How it works...

To access the GPIO pins using Python, we import `RPi.GPIO`, which allows direct control of the pins through the module functions. We also require the `time` module to pause the program for a set number of seconds.

We define values for the LED wiring and active states (see *Controlling the GPIO current* in the *There's more...* section of this recipe).

Before the GPIO pins are used by the program, we need to set them up by specifying the numbering method (`GPIO.BOARD`) and the direction—`GPIO.OUT` or `GPIO.IN` (in this case, we set all the RGB pins to outputs). If a pin is configured as an output, we will be able to set the pin state; similarly, if it is configured as an input, we will be able to read the pin state.

Next, we control the pins using `GPIO.ouput()` by stating the number of the GPIO pin and the state we want it to be in (1 = high/on and 0 = low/off). We switch each LED on, wait 5 seconds, and then switch it back off.

Finally, we use `GPIO.cleanup()` to return the GPIO pins back to their original default state and release control of the pins for use by other programs.

There's more...

Using the GPIO pins on the Raspberry Pi must be done with care since these pins are directly connected to the main processor of the Raspberry Pi without any additional protection. Caution must be used, as any incorrect wiring will likely damage the Raspberry Pi processor and cause it to stop functioning altogether.

Alternatively, you could use one of the many modules available that plug directly onto the GPIO header pins (reducing the chance of wiring mistakes). See the *Appendix, Hardware and Software List*, for a list of Raspberry Pi hardware retailers.

Controlling the GPIO current

Each GPIO pin is only able to handle a certain level of current before it will burn out (not greater than 16 mA from a single pin or 30 mA in total), and similarly, the RGB LED should be limited to no more than 100 mA. By adding a resistor before or after an LED, we will be able to limit the amount of current that will be passed through it and also control how bright it is (more current will equal a brighter LED).

Since we may wish to drive more than one LED at a time, we typically aim to set the current as low as we can get away with while still providing enough power to light up the LED.

We can use Ohm's law to tell us how much resistance to use to provide a particular current. The law is as shown in the following diagram:

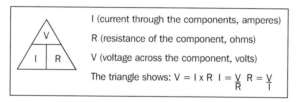

I (current through the components, amperes)

R (resistance of the component, ohms)

V (voltage across the component, volts)

The triangle shows: $V = I \times R$ $I = \dfrac{V}{R}$ $R = \dfrac{V}{I}$

Ohm's law describes the relationship between the current, resistance, and voltage in electrical circuits

We will aim for a minimum current (3mA) and maximum current (16mA) while still producing a reasonably bright light from each of the LEDs. To get a balanced output for the RGB LEDs, I tested different resistors until they provided a near white light (when viewed through a card). A 470 ohm resistor was selected for each one (your LEDs may differ slightly).

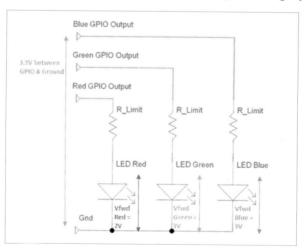

Resistors are needed to limit the current that passes through the LEDs

The voltage across the resistor is equal to the GPIO voltage (Vgpio = 3.3V) minus the voltage drop on the particular LED (Vfwd); we can then use this resistance to calculate the current used by each of the LEDs as shown in the following diagram:

$$V_{R\_Limit} = (Vgpio\text{-}Vfwd)$$

$$I = \frac{V_{R\_Limit}}{R} = \frac{(3.3\text{-}2)}{470} = \frac{1.3}{470} = 2.8mA \text{ for the Red LED}$$

$$I = \frac{V_{R\_Limit}}{R} = \frac{(3.3\text{-}3)}{470} = \frac{0.3}{470} = 0.64mA \text{ each for the Green and Blue LEDs}$$

We can calculate the current drawn by each of the LEDs

Responding to a button

Many applications using the Raspberry Pi require that actions be activated without a keyboard and screen attached to it. The GPIO pins provide an excellent way for the Raspberry Pi to be controlled by your own buttons and switches without the need for a mouse/keyboard and screen.

Getting ready

You will need the following equipment:

▸ 2x DuPont female to male patch wires

▸ Mini breadboard (170 tie points) or a larger one

▸ Push button to make a switch and momentary switch (or a wire connection to make/break the circuit)

▸ Breadboarding wire (solid core)

▸ 1k ohm resistor

The switches are as seen in the following diagram:

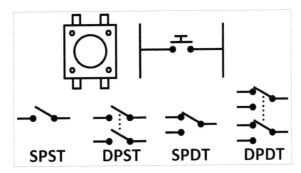

The push button switch and other types of switches

The switches used in the following examples are **single pole single throw** (**SPST**) momentary close push button switches. **Single pole** (**SP**) means that there is one set of contacts that makes a connection. In the case of the push switch used here, the legs on each side are connected together with a single pole switch in the middle. A **double pole** (**DP**) switch acts just like a single pole switch, except that the two sides are separated electrically, allowing you to switch two separate components on/off at the same time.

Single throw (**ST**) means the switch will make a connection with just one position; the other side will be left open. **Double throw** (**DT**) means both positions of the switch will connect to different parts.

A momentary close means that the button will close the switch when pressed and automatically open it when released. A latched push button switch will remain closed until it is pressed again.

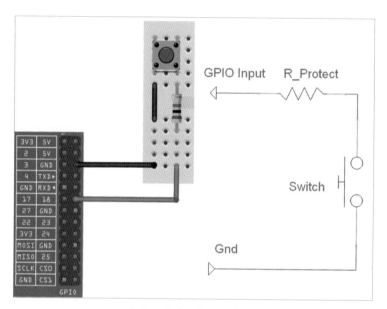

The layout of the button circuit

We will use sound in this example, so you will also need speakers or headphones attached.

You will need to install a program called `flite` using the following command, which will let us make the Raspberry Pi "talk":

```
sudo apt-get install flite
```

After it has been installed, you can test it with the following command:

```
sudo flite -t "hello I can talk"
```

If it is a little too quiet (or too loud), you can adjust the volume (0-100 percent) using the following command:

```
amixer set PCM 100%
```

How to do it...

Create the `btntest.py` script as follows:

```
#!/usr/bin/python3
#btntest.py
import time
import os
import RPi.GPIO as GPIO
#HARDWARE SETUP
# P1
# 2[==X==1=======]26
# 1[=============]25
#Button Config
BTN = 12

def gpio_setup():
  #Setup the wiring
  GPIO.setmode(GPIO.BOARD)
  #Setup Ports
  GPIO.setup(BTN,GPIO.IN,pull_up_down=GPIO.PUD_UP)


def main():
  gpio_setup()
  count=0
  btn_closed = True
  while True:
    btn_val = GPIO.input(BTN)
    if btn_val and btn_closed:
      print("OPEN")
      btn_closed=False
    elif btn_val==False and btn_closed==False:
      count+=1
      print("CLOSE %s" % count)
      os.system("flite -t '%s'" % count)
      btn_closed=True
    time.sleep(0.1)
```

```
try:
  main()
finally:
  GPIO.cleanup()
  print("Closed Everything. END")
#End
```

How it works...

As in the previous recipe, we set up the GPIO pin as required, but this time as an input, and we also enable the internal pull-up resistor (see *Pull-up and pull-down resistor circuits* in the *There's more...* section of this recipe for more information) using the following code:

```
GPIO.setup(BTN,GPIO.IN,pull_up_down=GPIO.PUD_UP)
```

After the GPIO pin is set up, we create a loop that will continuously check the state of `BTN` using `GPIO.input()`. If the value returned is `false`, the pin has been connected to 0V (ground) through the switch, and we will use `flite` to count out loud for us each time the button is pressed.

Since we have called the main function from within a `try/finally` condition, it will still call `GPIO.cleanup()` even if we close the program using *Ctrl + Z*.

 We use a short delay in the loop; this ensures that any noise from the contacts on the switch is ignored. When we press the button, there isn't always perfect contact as we press or release it, and it may produce several triggers if we check it fast enough. This is known as **software debouncing**; we ignore the "bounce" in the signal here.

There's more...

The Raspberry Pi GPIO pins must be used with care; voltages used for inputs should be within specific ranges, and any current drawn from them should be minimized using protective resistors.

Safe voltages

We must ensure that we only connect inputs that are between 0 (Ground) and 3.3 volts. Some processors use voltages between 0 and 5 volts, so extra components are required to interface safely with them. Never connect an input or component that uses 5V unless you are certain it is safe, or you will damage the GPIO ports of the Raspberry Pi.

Pull-up and pull-down resistor circuits

The previous code sets the GPIO pins to use an internal pull-up resistor. Without a pull-up resistor (or pull-down resistor) on the GPIO pin, the voltage is free to float somewhere between 3.3 V and 0 V, and the actual logical state remains undetermined (sometimes 1 and sometimes 0).

Raspberry Pi's internal pull-up resistors are 50k ohm - 65k ohm and the pull-down resistors are 50k ohm - 65k ohm. External pull-up/pull-down resistors are often used in GPIO circuits (as shown in the following diagram), typically using 10k ohm or larger for similar reasons (giving a very small current draw when not active).

A pull-up resistor allows a small amount of current to flow through the GPIO pin and provide a high voltage when the switch isn't pressed. When the switch is pressed, the small current is replaced by the larger one flowing to 0 V, so we get a low voltage on the GPIO pin instead (the switch is active low and logic 0 when pressed). It works as shown in the following diagram:

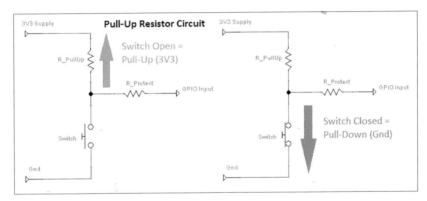

A pull-up resistor circuit

Pull-down resistors work in the same way, except the switch is active high (the GPIO pin is logic 1 when pressed). It works as shown in the following diagram:

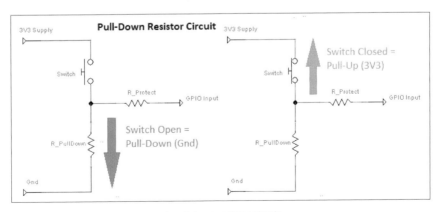

A pull-down resistor circuit

Protection resistors

In addition to the switch, the circuit includes a resistor in series with the switch to protect the GPIO pin as shown in the following diagram:

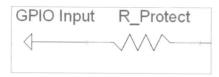

A GPIO protective current-limiting resistor

The purpose of the protection resistor is to protect the GPIO pin if it is accidentally set as an output rather than an input. Imagine, for instance, that we have our switch connected between the GPIO and ground. Now the GPIO pin is set as an output and switched on (driving it to 3.3 V) as soon as we press the switch; without a resistor present, the GPIO pin will directly be connected to 0 V. The GPIO will still try to drive it to 3.3 V; this would cause the GPIO pin to burn out (since it would use too much current to drive the pin to high state). If we use a 1k ohm resistor here, the pin is able to be driven high using an acceptable amount of current ($I = V/R = 3.3/1k = 3.3mA$).

A controlled shutdown button

The Raspberry Pi should always be shut down correctly to avoid the SD card being corrupted (by losing power when writing to the card). This can pose a problem if you don't have a keyboard or screen connected (if you are running an automated program or controlling it remotely over a network and forget to turn it off) as you can't type the command or see what you are doing. By adding our own buttons and LED indicator, we can easily command a shutdown, reset, and start up again to indicate when the system is active.

Getting ready

You will need the following equipment:

- 3x Dupont female to male patch wires
- Mini breadboard (170 tie points) or a larger one
- Push button
- Standard LED (for example, a red one)
- 2x 470 ohm resistors
- Breadboarding wire (solid core)

The entire layout of the shutdown circuit will look as shown in the following figure:

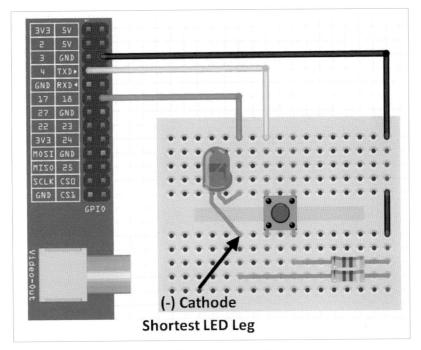

(-) Cathode
Shortest LED Leg

The controlled shutdown circuit layout

How to do it...

Create the shtdwn.py script as follows:

```
#!/usr/bin/python3
#shtdown.py
import time
import RPi.GPIO as GPIO
import os

# Shutdown Script
DEBUG=True #Simulate Only
SNDON=True
#HARDWARE SETUP
# P1
# 2[==X==L=======]26
# 1[===1=========]25
#BTN CONFIG - Set GPIO Ports
GPIO_MODE=GPIO.BOARD
```

```
SHTDWN_BTN = 7   #1
LED = 12         #L

def gpio_setup():
  #Setup the wiring
  GPIO.setmode(GPIO_MODE)
  #Setup Ports
  GPIO.setup(SHTDWN_BTN,GPIO.IN,pull_up_down=GPIO.PUD_UP)
  GPIO.setup(LED,GPIO.OUT)

def doShutdown():
  if(DEBUG):print("Press detected")
  time.sleep(3)
  if GPIO.input(SHTDWN_BTN):
    if(DEBUG):print("Ignore the shutdown (<3sec)")
  else:
    if(DEBUG):print ("Would shutdown the RPi Now")
    GPIO.output(LED,0)
    time.sleep(0.5)
    GPIO.output(LED,1)
    if(SNDON):os.system("flite -t 'Warning commencing power down'")
    if(DEBUG==False):os.system("sudo shutdown -h now")
    if(DEBUG):GPIO.cleanup()
    if(DEBUG):exit()

def main():
  gpio_setup()
  GPIO.output(LED,1)
  while True:
    if(DEBUG):print("Waiting for >3sec button press")
    if GPIO.input(SHTDWN_BTN)==False:
        doShutdown()
    time.sleep(1)

try:
  main()
finally:
  GPIO.cleanup()
  print("Closed Everything. END")
#End
```

To get this script to run automatically (once we have tested it), we can place the script in `~/bin` (we can use `cp` instead of `mv` if we just want to copy it) and add it to `crontab` with the following code:

```
mkdir ~/bin
mv shtdwn.py ~/bin/shtdwn.py
crontab -e
```

At the end of the file, we add the following code:

```
@reboot sudo python3 ~/bin/shtdwn.py
```

How it works...

This time when we set up the GPIO pin, we define the pin connected to the shutdown button as an input and the pin connected to the LED as an output. We turn the LED on to indicate that the system is running.

By setting the DEBUG flag to True, we can test the functionality of our script without causing an actual shutdown (by reading the terminal messages); we just need to ensure to set DEBUG to False when using the script for real.

We enter a `while` loop and check every second to see if the GPIO pin is set to LOW (the switch has been pressed); if so, we enter the `doShutdown()` function.

The program will wait for 3 seconds and then test again to see if the button is still being pressed. If the button is no longer being pressed, we return to the previous `while` loop. However, if it is still being pressed after 3 seconds, the program will flash the LED and trigger the shutdown (also providing an audio warning using `flite`).

When we are happy with how the script is operating, we can disable the DEBUG flag (by setting it to False) and add the script to `crontab`. Crontab is a special program that runs in the background that allows us to schedule (at specific times, dates, or periodically) programs and actions when the system is started (@reboot). This allows the script to be started automatically every time the Raspberry Pi is powered up. When we press and hold the shutdown button for more than 3 seconds, it safely shuts down the system and enters a low power state (the LED switches off just before this, indicating it is safe to remove the power shortly after). To restart the Raspberry Pi, we briefly remove the power; this will restart the system, and the LED will light up when the Raspberry Pi has loaded.

There's more...

We can extend this example further using the reset header by adding extra functionality and making use of additional GPIO connections (if available).

Resetting and rebooting Raspberry Pi

The Model B Rev 2 Raspberry Pi (and all of Model A) has holes for mounting a reset header (marked **P6** on the unit), which allow the device to be reset using a switch rather than by removing the micro USB connector each time to cycle the power.

To make use of it, you will need to solder a wire or pin header to the Raspberry Pi and connect a switch/button to it (or briefly touch a wire between the two holes of P6 each time). Alternatively, we can extend our previous circuit as shown in the following diagram:

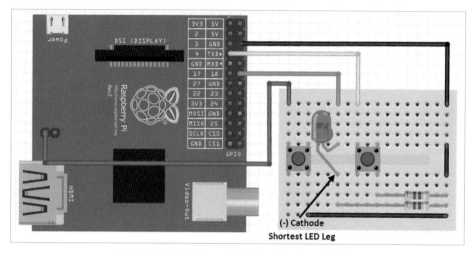

The controlled shutdown circuit layout and reset button

We can add this extra button to our circuit, which can be connected to connection 1 of the P6 reset header (the hole closest to the edge). This pin, when pulled low by connecting to ground (such as the hole next to it or another ground point such as Pin 6 of the P1 header), will reset the Raspberry Pi and allow it to boot up again following a shutdown.

Adding extra functions

Since we now have the script monitoring the shutdown button all the time, we can add extra buttons/switches/jumpers to be monitored at the same time. This will allow us to trigger specific programs or set up particular states just by changing the inputs. The following example allows us to easily switch between automatic DHCP networking (the default networking setup) and using a direct IP address, as used in the *Networking directly to a laptop or computer* recipe of *Chapter 1, Getting Started with a Raspberry Pi Computer*, for direct LAN connections.

Add the following components to the previous circuit:

- A 470 ohm resistor
- Two pin headers with a jumper connector (or optionally a switch)
- A breadboarding wire (solid core)

After adding the previous components, our controlled shutdown circuit now looks as follows:

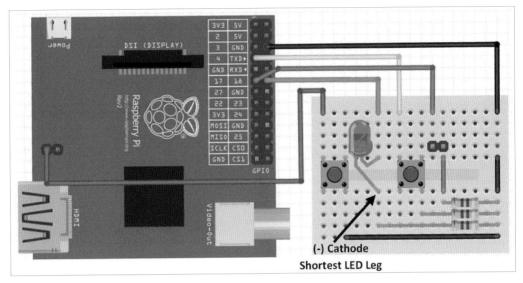

(-) Cathode
Shortest LED Leg

The controlled shutdown circuit layout, reset button, and jumper pins

In the previous script, we add an additional input to detect the status of the LAN_SWA pin (the jumper pins we added to the circuit) using the following code:

```
LAN_SWA = 11      #2
```

Ensure that it is set up as an input (with a pull-up resistor) in the gpio_setup() function using the following code:

```
GPIO.setup(LAN_SWA,GPIO.IN,pull_up_down=GPIO.PUD_UP)
```

Add a new function to switch between the LAN modes, and read out the new IP address. The doChangeLAN() function checks if the status of the LAN_SWA pin has changed since the last call, and if so, it sets the network adaptor to DHCP or sets the direct LAN settings accordingly (and uses flite to speak the new IP setting if available). Finally, the LAN being set for direct connection causes the LED to flash slowly while that mode is active. Use the following code to do so:

```
def doChangeLAN(direct):
  if(DEBUG):print("Direct LAN: %s" % direct)
  if GPIO.input(LAN_SWA) and direct==True:
    if(DEBUG):print("LAN Switch OFF")
    cmd="sudo dhclient eth0"
    direct=False
    GPIO.output(LED,1)
  elif GPIO.input(LAN_SWA)==False and direct==False:
    if(DEBUG):print("LAN Switch ON")
```

```
      cmd="sudo ifconfig eth0 169.254.69.69"
      direct=True
    else:
      return direct
    if(DEBUG==False):os.system(cmd)
    if(SNDON):os.system("hostname -I | flite")
    return direct
```

Add another function, `flashled()`, which will just toggle the state of the LED each time it is called. The code for this function is as follows:

```
def flashled(ledon):
  if ledon:
    ledon=False
  else:
    ledon=True
  GPIO.output(LED,ledon)
  return ledon
```

Finally, we adjust the main loop to also call `doChangeLAN()` and use the result, to decide if we call `flashled()` using `ledon` to keep track of the LED's previous state each time. The `main()` function should now be updated as follows:

```
def main():
  gpio_setup()
  GPIO.output(LED,1)
  directlan=False
  ledon=True
  while True:
    if(DEBUG):print("Waiting for >3sec button press")
    if GPIO.input(SHTDWN_BTN)==False:
      doShutdown()
    directlan= doChangeLAN(directlan)
    if directlan:
      flashled(ledon)
    time.sleep(1)
```

Relocating to the P5 header

The previous circuit can be very useful if permanently fitted to the Raspberry Pi, but it would get in the way if you intend to connect other components to the main GPIO header (P1). Fortunately, you can use the GPIO pins available on the P5 connections of the board and adjust the code to suit. You will either need to solder an extra pin header in place (it is recommended that this be done at a slight angle to still allow space for a ribbon connector to be used with the main GPIO pins on P1) or solder wires directly to the board.

A P5 header is shown in the following image:

An extra P5 header added

The `RPi.GPIO` library does not have numbering allocated for the P5 header using the GPIO.BOARD references, so we have to use the GPIO.BCM references (the GPIO reference of the Broadcom processor pins) as shown in the following diagram:

GPIO.BCM		P5			GPIO.BCM
<50mA	3V3	2	1	5V	
BCM GPIO29	SCL0	4	3	SDA0	BCM GPIO28
BCM GPIO31		6	5		BCM GPIO30
	GND	8	7	GND	

P5 GPIO pins (Board Revision 2 only)

Change the pin references in the code to reference the P5 pins as follows, and then relocate all the wiring from the P1 header to the P5 header:

```
#HARDWARE SETUP
# P5
# 1[==Lx]7
# 2[=21x]8
#BTN CONFIG - Set GPIO Ports
GPIO_MODE=GPIO.BCM
SHTDWN_BTN = 31 #Pin6 1
LED = 30        #Pin5 L
LAN_SWA = 29    #Pin4 2
```

The GPIO keypad input

We have seen how we can monitor inputs on the GPIO to launch applications and control the Raspberry Pi; however, sometimes we need to control third-party programs. Using the uInput library, we can emulate key presses from a keyboard (or even mouse movement) to control any program using our own custom hardware.

For more information about using uInput, visit `http://tjjr.fi/sw/python-uinput/`.

Getting ready

Perform the following steps to install uInput:

1. First we need to download uInput:

    You will need to download the uInput Python library from Github (~50 KB) using the following commands:

    ```
    wget https://github.com/tuomasjjrasanen/python-uinput/archive/
    master.zip
    ```

    ```
    unzip master.zip
    ```

    The library will unzip to a directory called python-uinput-master.

    Once completed, you can remove the ZIP file using the following command:

    ```
    rm master.zip
    ```

2. Install the required packages (if you have installed them already, the apt-get command will ignore them) using the following commands:

    ```
    sudo apt-get install python3-setuptools python3-dev
    ```

    ```
    sudo apt-get install libudev-dev
    ```

3. Compile and install uInput using the following commands:

    ```
    cd python-uinput-master
    ```

    ```
    sudo python3 setup.py install
    ```

4. Finally, we load the new uinput kernel module using the following command:

    ```
    sudo modprobe uinput
    ```

    To ensure it is loaded on startup, we can add uinput to the modules file using the following command:

    ```
    sudo nano /etc/modules
    ```

    Put uinput on a new line in the file and save it.

5. Create the following circuit using the following equipment:

- ❏ Breadboard (half-sized or larger)
- ❏ 7x Dupont female to male patch wires
- ❏ Six push buttons
- ❏ 6x 470 ohm resistors
- ❏ Breadboarding wire (solid core)

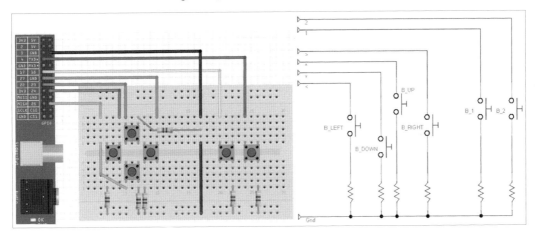

GPIO keypad circuit layout

The keypad circuit can also be built into a permanent circuit by soldering the components into vero prototype board (also known as stripboard), as shown in the following image:

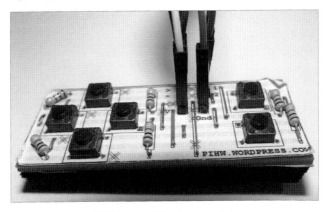

GPIO keypad PiHardware module

 This circuit is available as a solder-yourself kit from
PiHardware.com.

6. Connect the circuit to the Raspberry Pi P1 GPIO pins as follows:

	Button	P1 GPIO Pin
GND		6
v	B_DOWN	22
<	B_LEFT	18
^	B_UP	15
>	B_RIGHT	13
1	B_1	11
2	B_2	7

How to do it...

Create a `gpiokeys.py` script as follows:

```python
#!/usr/bin/python3
#gpiokeys.py
import time
import RPi.GPIO as GPIO
import uinput

#HARDWARE SETUP
# P1
# 2[==G=====<=V==]26
# 1[===2=1>^=====]25
B_DOWN  = 22      #V
B_LEFT  = 18      #<
B_UP    = 15      #^
B_RIGHT = 13      #>
B_1   = 11    #1
B_2   = 7     #2

DEBUG=True
BTN = [B_UP,B_DOWN,B_LEFT,B_RIGHT,B_1,B_2]
MSG = ["UP","DOWN","LEFT","RIGHT","1","2"]

#Setup the DPad module pins and pull-ups
def dpad_setup():
  #Set up the wiring
  GPIO.setmode(GPIO.BOARD)
  # Setup BTN Ports as INPUTS
```

```
    for val in BTN:
      # set up GPIO input with pull-up control
      #(pull_up_down can be:
      #    PUD_OFF, PUD_UP or PUD_DOWN, default PUD_OFF)
      GPIO.setup(val, GPIO.IN, pull_up_down=GPIO.PUD_UP)

def main():
  #Setup uinput
  events = (uinput.KEY_UP,uinput.KEY_DOWN,uinput.KEY_LEFT,
            uinput.KEY_RIGHT,uinput.KEY_ENTER,uinput.KEY_ENTER)
  device = uinput.Device(events)
  time.sleep(2) # seconds
  dpad_setup()
  print("DPad Ready!")

  btn_state=[False,False,False,False,False,False]
  key_state=[False,False,False,False,False,False]
  while True:
    #Catch all the buttons pressed before pressing the related keys
    for idx, val in enumerate(BTN):
      if GPIO.input(val) == False:
        btn_state[idx]=True
      else:
        btn_state[idx]=False

    #Perform the button presses/releases (but only change state once)
    for idx, val in enumerate(btn_state):
      if val == True and key_state[idx] == False:
        if DEBUG:print (str(val) + ":" + MSG[idx])
        device.emit(events[idx], 1) # Press.
        key_state[idx]=True
      elif val == False and key_state[idx] == True:
        if DEBUG:print (str(val) + ":!" + MSG[idx])
        device.emit(events[idx], 0) # Release.
        key_state[idx]=False

    time.sleep(.1)

try:
  main()
finally:
  GPIO.cleanup()
#End
```

How it works...

First, we import `uinput` and define the wiring of the keypad buttons. For each of the buttons in `BTN`, we enable them as inputs with internal pull-ups enabled.

Next, we set up `uinput`, defining the keys we want to emulate and adding them to the `uinput.Device()` function. We wait a few seconds to allow `uinput` to initialize, set the initial button and key states, and start our `main` loop.

The `main` loop is split into two sections: the first part checks through the buttons and records the states in `btn_state`, and the second part compares the `btn_state` with the current `key_state` array. This way, we can detect a change in `btn_state` and call `device.emit()` to toggle the state of the key.

To allow us to run this script in the background, we can run it with `&` as shown in the following command:

```
sudo python3 gpiokeys.py &
```

The `&` character allows the command to run in the background, so we can continue with the command line to run other programs. You can use `fg` to bring it back to the foreground or `%1`, `%2`, and so on if you have several commands running. Use `jobs` to get a list.

You can even put a process/program on hold to get to the command prompt by pressing *Ctrl + Z* and then resume it with `bg` (which will let it run in the background).

You can test the keys using the game created in the *Creating an overhead scrolling game* recipe in *Chapter 4, Creating Games and Graphics*, which you can now control using your GPIO directional pad. Don't forget that if you are connecting to the Raspberry Pi remotely, any key presses will only be active on the locally connected screen.

There's more...

We can do more using `uinput` to provide hardware control for other programs, including those that require mouse input.

Generating other key combinations

You can create several different key mappings in your file to support different programs. For instance, the `events_z80` key mapping would be useful for a Spectrum Emulator such as **fuze** (browse to `http://raspi.tv/2012/how-to-install-fuse-zx-spectrum-emulator-on-raspberry-pi` for details). The `events_omx` key mappings are suitable for controlling video played through the OMX Player using the following command:

```
omxplayer filename.mp4
```

You can get a list of keys supported by omxplayer by using the -k parameter.

Replace the line that defines the events list with a new key mapping, and select different ones by assigning them to events using the following code:

```
events_dpad = (uinput.KEY_UP,uinput.KEY_DOWN,uinput.KEY_LEFT,
               uinput.KEY_RIGHT,uinput.KEY_ENTER,uinput.KEY_ENTER)
events_z80 = (uinput.KEY_Q,uinput.KEY_A,uinput.KEY_O,
               uinput.KEY_P,uinput.KEY_M,uinput.KEY_ENTER)
events_omx = (uinput.KEY_EQUAL,uinput.KEY_MINUS,uinput.KEY_LEFT,
               uinput.KEY_RIGHT,uinput.KEY_P,uinput.KEY_Q)
```

You can find all the KEY definitions in the input.h file; you can view it using the less command (press Q to exit) as shown in the following command:

```
less /usr/include/linux/input.h
```

Emulating mouse events

The uinput library can emulate mouse and joystick events as well as keyboard presses. To use the buttons to simulate a mouse, we can adjust the script to use mouse events (as well as defining mousemove to set the step size of the movement) using the following code:

```
MSG = ["M_UP","M_DOWN","M_LEFT","M_RIGHT","1","Enter"]
events_mouse=(uinput.REL_Y,uinput.REL_Y, uinput.REL_X,
              uinput.REL_X,uinput.BTN_LEFT,uinput.BTN_RIGHT)
mousemove=1
```

We also need to modify the button handling to provide continuous movement, as we don't need to keep track of the state of the keys for the mouse. To do so, use the following code:

```
#Perform the button presses/releases
#(but only change state once)
for idx, val in enumerate(btn_state):
  if MSG[idx] == "M_UP" or MSG[idx] == "M_LEFT":
    state = -mousemove
  else:
    state = mousemove
  if val == True:
    device.emit(events[idx], state) # Press.
  elif val == False:
    device.emit(events[idx], 0) # Release.

time.sleep(0.01)
```

Multiplexed color LEDs

The next example in this chapter demonstrates that some seemingly simple hardware can produce some impressive results if controlled with software. We return to using some RGB LEDs that are wired so that we only need to use eight GPIO pins to control the red, green, and blue elements of five RGB LEDs using a method called **hardware multiplexing** (see the *Hardware multiplexing* subsection in the *There's more...* section of this recipe).

Getting ready

You will need the RGB LED module as shown in the following image:

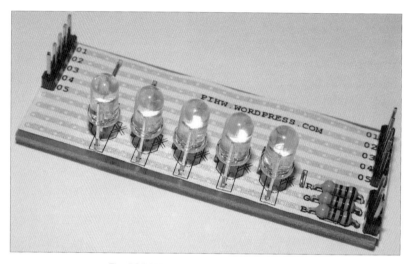

The RGB LED module from PiHardware.com

As you can see in the preceding image, the RGB LED module from `PiHardware.com` comes with GPIO pins and a Dupont female to female cable for connecting it. Although there are two sets of pins labelled 1 to 5, only one side needs to be connected.

Alternatively, you can recreate your own with the following circuit using five common cathode RGB LEDs and 3x 470 ohm resistors and a Vero prototype board (or large breadboard). The circuit will look as shown in the following diagram:

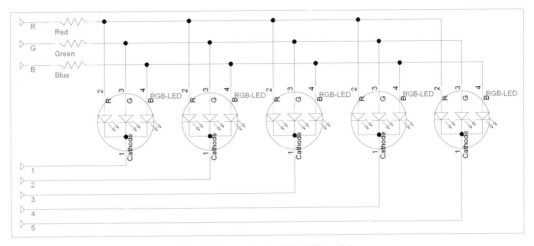

Circuit diagram for the RGB LED module

Strictly speaking, we should use 15 resistors in this circuit (one for each RGB LED element), which will avoid interference from LEDs sharing the same resistor and would also prolong the life of the LEDs themselves if switched on together. However, there is only a slight advantage, particularly since we intend to drive each RGB LED independently of the other four to achieve the multicolor effects.

You will need to connect the circuit to the Raspberry Pi GPIO P1 header as follows:

RGB LED						1		2	3		4		
Rpi GPIO Pin	2	4	6	8	10	12	14	16	18	20	22	24	26
Rpi GPIO Pin	1	3	5	7	9	11	13	15	17	19	21	23	25
RGB LED			5		R	G	B						

How to do it...

Create the `rgbled.py` script and perform the following steps:

1. Import all the required modules and define values to be used with the help of the following code:

```python
#!/usr/bin/python3
#rgbled.py
import time
import RPi.GPIO as GPIO

#Setup Active states
#Common Cathode RGB-LEDs (Cathode=Active Low)
LED_ENABLE = 0; LED_DISABLE = 1
RGB_ENABLE = 1; RGB_DISABLE = 0
#HARDWARE SETUP
# P1
# 2[=====1=23=4==]26
# 1[===5=RGB=====]25
#LED CONFIG - Set GPIO Ports
LED1 = 12; LED2 = 16; LED3 = 18; LED4 = 22; LED5 = 7
LED = [LED1,LED2,LED3,LED4,LED5]
RGB_RED = 11; RGB_GREEN = 13; RGB_BLUE = 15
RGB = [RGB_RED,RGB_GREEN,RGB_BLUE]
#Mixed Colors
RGB_CYAN = [RGB_GREEN,RGB_BLUE]
RGB_MAGENTA = [RGB_RED,RGB_BLUE]
RGB_YELLOW = [RGB_RED,RGB_GREEN]
RGB_WHITE = [RGB_RED,RGB_GREEN,RGB_BLUE]
RGB_LIST = [RGB_RED,RGB_GREEN,RGB_BLUE,RGB_CYAN,
            RGB_MAGENTA,RGB_YELLOW,RGB_WHITE]
```

2. Define functions to set up the GPIO pins using the following code:

```python
def led_setup():
  '''Setup the RGB-LED module pins and state.'''
  #Set up the wiring
  GPIO.setmode(GPIO.BOARD)
  # Setup Ports
  for val in LED:
    GPIO.setup(val, GPIO.OUT)
  for val in RGB:
    GPIO.setup(val, GPIO.OUT)
  led_clear()
```

3. Define various utility functions to help control the LEDs using the following code:

```
def led_gpiocontrol(pins,state):
  '''This function will control the state of
  a single or multiple pins in a list.'''
  #determine if "pins" is a single integer or not
  if isinstance(pins,int):
    #Single integer - reference directly
    GPIO.output(pins,state)
  else:
    #if not, then cycle through the "pins" list
    for i in pins:
      GPIO.output(i,state)

def led_activate(led,color):
  '''Enable the selected led(s) and set the required color(s)
  Will accept single or multiple values'''
  #Enable led
  led_gpiocontrol(led,LED_ENABLE)
  #Enable color
  led_gpiocontrol(color,RGB_ENABLE)

def led_deactivate(led,color):
  '''Deactivate the selected led(s) and set the required
  color(s) will accept single or multiple values'''
  #Disable led
  led_gpiocontrol(led,LED_DISABLE)
  #Disable color
  led_gpiocontrol(color,RGB_DISABLE)

def led_time(led, color, timeon):
  '''Switch on the led and color for the timeon period'''
  led_activate(led,color)
  time.sleep(timeon)
  led_deactivate(led,color)

def led_clear():
  '''Set the pins to default state.'''
  for val in LED:
    GPIO.output(val, LED_DISABLE)
  for val in RGB:
    GPIO.output(val, RGB_DISABLE)

def led_cleanup():
  '''Reset pins to default state and release GPIO'''
  led_clear()
  GPIO.cleanup()
```

4. Create a test function to demonstrate the functionality of the module:

```python
def main():
    '''Directly run test function.
    This function will run if the file is executed directly'''
    led_setup()
    led_time(LED1,RGB_RED,5)
    led_time(LED2,RGB_GREEN,5)
    led_time(LED3,RGB_BLUE,5)
    led_time(LED,RGB_MAGENTA,2)
    led_time(LED,RGB_YELLOW,2)
    led_time(LED,RGB_CYAN,2)

if __name__=='__main__':
    try:
        main()
    finally:
        led_cleanup()
#End
```

How it works...

To start with, we define the hardware setup by defining the states required to **Enable** and **Disable** the LED depending on the type of RGB LED (common cathode) used. If you are using a common anode device, just reverse the Enable/Disable states.

Next, we define the GPIO mapping to the pins to match the wiring we did previously.

We also define some basic color combinations by combining red, green, and/or blue together as shown in the following diagram:

Red Green Blue	000	001	010	011	100	101	110	111
LED State	OFF	Blue	Green	Cyan	Red	Magenta	Yellow	White

LED color combinations

We define a series of useful functions, the first being `led_setup()`, which will set the GPIO numbering to `GPIO.BOARD` and define all the pins used to be outputs. We also call a function named `led_clear()`, which will set the pins to the default state with all the pins disabled.

 This means the LED pins 1-5 (the common cathode on each LED) are set to `HIGH`, while the RGB pins (the separate anodes for each color) are set to `LOW`.

We create a function called `led_gpiocontrol()` that will allow us to set the state of one or more pins. The `isinstance()` function allows us to test a value to see if it matches a particular type (in this case, a single integer); then we can either set the state of that single pin or iterate through the list of pins and set each one.

Next, we define two functions, `led_activate()` and `led_deactivate()`, which will enable and disable the specified LED and color. Finally, we define `led_time()`, which will allow us to specify an LED, color, and time to switch it on for.

We also create `led_cleanup()` to reset the pins (and LEDs) to the default values and call `GPIO.cleanup()` to release the GPIO pins in use.

This script is intended to become a library file, so we will use the `if __name__=='__main__'` check to only run our test code when running the file directly.

> By checking the value of `__name__`, we can determine if the file was run directly (it will equal `__main__`) or if it was imported by another Python script.
>
> This allows us to define special test code that is only executed when we directly load and run the file. If we include this file as a module in another script, then this code will not be executed.
>
> We have used this technique previously in the *There's more...* section in the *Working with text and strings* recipe of *Chapter 2, Starting with Python Strings, Files, and Menus*.

As before, we will use `try/finally` to allow us to always perform clean-up actions, even if we exit early.

To test the script, we will set the LEDs to light up various colors one after another.

There's more...

We can create a few different colors by switching on one or more parts of the RGB LED at a time. However, with some clever programming, we can create a whole spectrum of colors. Also, we can display different colors on each LED, seemingly at the same time.

Hardware multiplexing

An LED requires a high voltage on the anode side and a lower voltage on the cathode side to light up. The RGB LEDs used in the circuit are common cathode, so we must apply a high voltage (3.3V) on the RGB pins and a low voltage (0V) on the cathode pin (wired to pins 1 to 5 for each of the LEDs).

The cathode and RGB pin states are as follows:

RGB-LED	Cathode (1-5)	RGB Pins	Result	Status
	HIGH	HIGH	LED OFF	LED "Disabled"
	HIGH	LOW	LED OFF	
	LOW	HIGH	LED ON	LED "Enabled"
	LOW	LOW	LED OFF	

Cathode and RGB pin states

Therefore, we can enable one or more of the RGB pins but still control which of the LEDs are lit. We enable the pins of the LEDs we want to light up and disable the ones we don't. This allows us to use far fewer pins than we would need to control each of the 15 RGB lines separately.

Displaying random patterns

We can add new functions to our library to produce different effects, such as generating random colors. The following function uses `randint()` to get a value between 1 and the number of colors. We ignore any values that are over the number of the available colors so that we can control how often the LEDs may be switched off. Perform the following steps to add the required functions:

1. Add the `randint()` function from the `random` module to the `rgbled.py` script using the following code:

```
from random import randint
```

2. Now add `led_rgbrandom()` using the following code:

```
def led_rgbrandom(led,period,colors):
    ''' Light up the selected led, for period in seconds,
    in one of the possible colors. The colors can be
    1 to 3 for RGB, or 1-6 for RGB plus combinations,
    1-7 includes white. Anything over 7 will be set as
    OFF (larger the number more chance of OFF).'''
    value = randint(1,colors)
    if value < len(RGB_LIST):
        led_time(led,RGB_LIST[value-1],period)
```

3. Use the following commands in the `main()` function to create a series of flashing LEDs:

```
for i in range(20):
    for j in LED:
        #Select from all, plus OFF
        led_rgbrandom(j,0.1,20)
```

Mixing multiple colors

Until now, we have only displayed a single color at a time on one or more of the LEDs. If you consider how the circuit is wired up, you might wonder how can we get one LED to display one color and another a different one at the same time? The simple answer is that we don't need to—we just do it quickly!

All we need to do is display one single color at a time but change it very quickly back and forth. Fortunately, this is something that computers such as the Raspberry Pi can do very easily, even allowing us to combine the RGB elements to make multiple shades of colors across all the LEDs. Perform the following steps to mix the colors:

1. Add combo color definitions to the top of the `rgbled.py` script, after the definition of the mixed colors, using the following code:

```
#Combo Colors
RGB_AQUA = [RGB_CYAN,RGB_GREEN]
RGB_LBLUE = [RGB_CYAN,RGB_BLUE]
RGB_PINK = [RGB_MAGENTA,RGB_RED]
RGB_PURPLE = [RGB_MAGENTA,RGB_BLUE]
RGB_ORANGE = [RGB_YELLOW,RGB_RED]
RGB_LIME = [RGB_YELLOW,RGB_GREEN]
RGB_COLORS = [RGB_LIME,RGB_YELLOW,RGB_ORANGE,RGB_RED,
              RGB_PINK,RGB_MAGENTA,RGB_PURPLE,RGB_BLUE,
              RGB_LBLUE,RGB_CYAN,RGB_AQUA,RGB_GREEN]
```

The preceding code will provide the combination of colors to create our shades, with `RGB_COLORS` providing a smooth progression through the shades.

2. Next, we need to create a function called `led_combo()` to handle single or multiple colors. The code for the function will be as follows:

```
def led_combo(pins,colors,period):
    #determine if "colors" is a single integer or not
    if isinstance(colors,int):
        #Single integer - reference directly
        led_time(pins,colors,period)
    else:
        #if not, then cycle through the "colors" list
        for i in colors:
            led_time(pins,i,period)
```

3. Now we can create a new script, `rgbledrainbow.py`, to make use of the new functions in our `rgbled.py` module. The `rgbledrainbow.py` script will be as follows:

```python
#!/usr/bin/python3
#rgbledrainbow.py
import time
import rgbled as RGBLED

def next_value(number,max):
  number = number % max
  return number

def main():
  print ("Setup the RGB module")
  RGBLED.led_setup()

  # Multiple LEDs with different Colors
  print ("Switch on Rainbow")
  led_num = 0
  col_num = 0
  for l in range(5):
    print ("Cycle LEDs")
    for k in range(100):
      #Set the starting point for the next set of colors
      col_num = next_value(col_num+1,len(RGBLED.RGB_COLORS))
      for i in range(20):  #cycle time
        for j in range(5): #led cycle
          led_num = next_value(j,len(RGBLED.LED))
          led_color = next_value(col_num+led_num,
                                 len(RGBLED.RGB_COLORS))
          RGBLED.led_combo(RGBLED.LED[led_num],
                           RGBLED.RGB_COLORS[led_color],0.001)

    print ("Cycle COLORs")
    for k in range(100):
      #Set the next color
      col_num = next_value(col_num+1,len(RGBLED.RGB_COLORS))
      for i in range(20): #cycle time
        for j in range(5): #led cycle
          led_num = next_value(j,len(RGBLED.LED))
          RGBLED.led_combo(RGBLED.LED[led_num],
                           RGBLED.RGB_COLORS[col_num],0.001)
  print ("Finished")
```

```
if __name__=='__main__':
  try:
    main()
  finally:
    RGBLED.led_cleanup()
#End
```

The `main()` function will first cycle through the LEDs, setting each color from the `RGB_COLORS` array on all the LEDs. Then, it will cycle through the colors, creating a rainbow effect over the LEDs.

Cycle through multiple colors on the five RGB LEDs

7

Sense and Display Real-world Data

In this chapter, we will cover:

- ▸ Using devices with the I²C bus
- ▸ Reading analog data using an analog-to-digital converter
- ▸ Logging and plotting data
- ▸ Extending the Raspberry Pi GPIO with an I/O expander
- ▸ Sensing and sending data to online services

Introduction

In the previous chapter, we made use of the Raspberry Pi GPIO to directly control and respond to the attached hardware by controlling or reading the GPIO pins. In this chapter, we will learn how to collect analog data from the real world and process it so we can display, log, graph, and share the data and make use of it in our programs.

We will extend the capabilities of the Raspberry Pi by interfacing with **Analog-to-Digital Converters** (**ADCs**), LCD alphanumeric displays, and digital port expanders using Raspberry Pi's GPIO connections.

 Be sure to check out *Appendix, Hardware and Software List*, which lists all the items used in this chapter and places you can obtain them from.

Using devices with the I²C bus

The Raspberry Pi can support several higher-level protocols that a wider range of devices can easily be connected to. In this chapter, we shall focus on the most common bus, called **I²C (I-squared-C)**. It provides a medium speed bus for communicating with devices over two wires. In this section, we shall use I²C to interface with an 8-bit ADC. This device will measure an analog signal, convert it to a relative value between 0 and 255, and send the value as a digital signal (represented by 8 bits) over the I²C bus to Raspberry Pi.

Getting ready

The I²C bus is not enabled in all Raspberry Pi images; therefore, we need to enable the module and install some supporting tools.

In order to make use of the I²C bus, we need to ensure that it is commented out from the `raspi-blacklist.conf` file. You can also comment out the SPI from the list if you wish, which is another type of bus that can be seen in *Chapter 10, Interfacing with Technology*.

Use the following command to edit the file using `nano`:

```
sudo nano /etc/modprobe.d/raspi-blacklist.conf
```

Putting a # at the start of the line, as shown in the following lines, turns it into a comment, enabling the SPI and I²C bus:

```
#blacklist spi-bcm2708
#blacklist i2c-bcm2708
```

Next, we should include the I²C module to be loaded on power up, as follows:

```
sudo nano /etc/modules
```

Add the following on separate lines and save (*Ctrl + X, Y, Enter*):

```
i2c-dev
i2c-bcm2708
```

Next, we will install some tools to use I²C devices directly from the command line, as follows:

```
sudo apt-get update
sudo apt-get install i2c-tools
```

Finally, shut down the Raspberry Pi before attaching the hardware, to allow the changes to be applied, as follows:

```
sudo shutdown -h now
```

You will need a PCF8591 module (retailers of these are listed in *Appendix, Hardware and Software List*) or you can obtain the PCF8591 chip separately and build your own circuit (see the *There's more...* section for details of the circuit).

The PCF8591 ADC and sensor module from dx.com

Connect the **GND**, **VCC**, **SDA**, and **SCL** pins to the Raspberry Pi P1 header as follows:

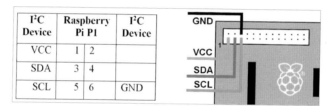

I²C Device	Raspberry Pi P1		I²C Device
VCC	1	2	
SDA	3	4	
SCL	5	6	GND

I²C connections on the Raspberry Pi GPIO P1 Header

 You can use the same I²C tools/code with other I²C devices by studying the datasheet of the device to find out what messages to send/read and which registers are used to control your device.

How to do it...

Detect the I²C device by using `i2cdetect` (the `-y` option skips any warnings about possible interference with other hardware that could be connected to the I²C bus) using the following commands to scan both buses:

```
sudo i2cdetect -y 0
sudo i2cdetect -y 1
```

The PCF8591 address will be displayed on bus 0 or bus 1 (depending on the board revision). The following screenshot shows the output of `i2cdetect`:

```
pi@raspberrypi:~$ sudo i2cdetect -y 0
     0  1  2  3  4  5  6  7  8  9  a  b  c  d  e  f
00:          -- -- -- -- -- -- -- -- -- -- -- -- --
10: -- -- -- -- -- -- -- -- -- -- -- -- -- -- -- --
20: -- -- -- -- -- -- -- -- -- -- -- -- -- -- -- --
30: -- -- -- -- -- -- -- -- -- -- -- -- -- -- -- --
40: -- -- -- -- -- -- -- -- -- -- -- -- -- -- -- --
50: -- -- -- -- -- -- -- -- -- -- -- -- -- -- -- --
60: -- -- -- -- -- -- -- -- -- -- -- -- -- -- -- --
70: -- -- -- -- -- -- -- --
pi@raspberrypi:~$ sudo i2cdetect -y 1
     0  1  2  3  4  5  6  7  8  9  a  b  c  d  e  f
00:          -- -- -- -- -- -- -- -- -- -- -- -- --
10: -- -- -- -- -- -- -- -- -- -- -- -- -- -- -- --
20: -- -- -- -- -- -- -- -- -- -- -- -- -- -- -- --
30: -- -- -- -- -- -- -- -- -- -- -- -- -- -- -- --
40: -- -- -- -- -- -- -- -- 48 -- -- -- -- -- -- --
50: -- -- -- -- -- -- -- -- -- -- -- -- -- -- -- --
60: -- -- -- -- -- -- -- -- -- -- -- -- -- -- -- --
70: -- -- -- -- -- -- -- --
pi@raspberrypi:~$
```

The PCF8591 address (48) is displayed here on bus 1 (on a revision 2 board)

Depending on your Raspberry Pi board revision, the address of the device should be listed on bus 0 (for Model B Rev1 boards) or bus 1 (for Model A and Model B Rev 2). By default, the PCF8591 address is `0x48`.

I²C bus number to use	P1	P5
Model A and Model B Revision 2	1	0
Model B Revision 1	0	n/a

If nothing is listed, shut down and double-check your connections (the module from www.dx.com should have an LED power indicator).

Using the detected bus number (0 or 1) and the device address (0x48) uses `i2cget` to read from the device (after a power up or channel change you will need to read the device twice to see the latest value), as follows:

```
sudo i2cget -y 1 0x48
sudo i2cget -y 1 0x48
```

To read from channel 1 (this is the temperature sensor on the module), we can use `i2cset` to write `0x01` to the PCF8591 control register. Again, use two reads to get a new sample from channel 1, as follows:

```
sudo i2cset -y 1 0x48 0x01
sudo i2cget -y 1 0x48
sudo i2cget -y 1 0x48
```

To cycle through each of the input channels, use `i2cset` to set the control register to `0x04`, as follows:

```
sudo i2cset -y 1 0x48 0x04
```

We can also control the AOUT pin using the following command to set it fully on (lighting up the LED D1):

```
sudo i2cset -y 1 0x48 0x40 0xff
```

Finally, we can use the following command to set it fully off (switching off the LED D1):

```
sudo i2cset -y 1 0x48 0x40 0x00
```

How it works...

The first read from the device after power on will return `0x80` and will also trigger the new sample from channel 0. If you read a second time, it will return the sample previously read and generate a fresh sample. Each reading will be an 8-bit value (ranging from `0` to `255`), representing the voltage 0 to VCC (in this case, 0V to 3.3V). On the `www.dx.com` module, channel 0 is connected to a light sensor, so if you cover up the module with your hand and resend the command, you will observe a change in the values (darker means a higher value and lighter means a lower one). You will find the readings are always one behind; this is because, as it returns the previous sample, it captures the next sample.

We use the following command to specify a particular channel to be read:

```
sudo i2cset -y 1 0x48 0x01
```

This changes the channel that is read to channel 1 (this is marked as **AIN1** on the module). Remember, you will need to perform two reads before you will see data from the newly selected channel. The following table shows the channels and pin names as well as which jumper connectors enable/disable each of the sensors:

Channel	0	1	2	3
Pin Name	AIN0	AIN1	AIN2	AIN3
Sensor	Light Dependent Resistor	Thermistor	None	Potentiometer
Jumper	P5	P4		P6

Next, we control the AOUT pin by setting the analog output enable flag (bit 6) of the control register and using the next value to set the analog voltage (0V-3.3V 0x00-0xFF), as follows:

```
sudo i2cset -y 1 0x48 0x40 0xff
```

Finally, you can set bit 2 (`0x04`) to autoincrement and cycle through the input channels as follows:

```
sudo i2cset -y 1 0x48 0x04
```

Each time you run `i2cget -y 1 0x48`, the next channel will be selected, starting with channel AIN0, then AIN1 through to AIN3, and back to AIN0 again.

To understand how to set a particular bit in a value, it helps to look at the binary representation of a number. The 8-bit value 0x04 can be written as b0000 0100 in binary (0x indicates the value is written in hexadecimal or hex, and b indicates a binary number).

Bits within binary numbers are counted from right to left, starting with 0; that is, MSB 7 6 5 4 3 2 1 0 LSB.

Bit 7 is known as the **Most Significant Bit** (**MSB**) and bit 0 as the **Least Significant Bit** (**LSB**). Therefore, by setting bit 2, we end up with b0000 0100 (which is 0x04).

There's more...

The I²C bus allows us to easily connect multiple devices using only a few wires. The PCF8591 chip can be used to connect your own sensors to the module or just the chip.

Using multiple I²C devices

All commands on the I²C bus are addressed to a specific I²C device (many have the option to set some pins high or low to select additional addresses and allow multiple devices to exist on the same bus). Each device must have a unique address so that only one device will respond at any one time. The PCF8591 starting address is `0x48`, with additional addresses selectable by the three address pins to `0x4F`. This allows up to eight PCF8591 devices to be used on the same bus.

If you decide to use the I²C bus that is located on P5 (on Model A and Rev2 Model B devices), you may need to add 1k8 ohm pull-up resistor between the I²C lines and 3.3V. These resistors are already present on the I²C bus on the P1 connector. However, some I²C modules, including the PCF8591 module, have their own resistors fitted, so it will work without the extra resistors.

I²C bus and level shifting

The I²C bus consists of two wires, one data (SDA) and one clock (SCL). Both are passively pulled to VCC (on the Raspberry Pi, this is 3.3V) with pull-up resistors. The Raspberry Pi will control the clock by pulling it low every cycle and the data line can be pulled low by Raspberry Pi to send commands or by the connected device to respond with data.

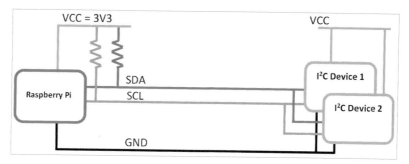

The Raspberry Pi I²C pins include pull-up resistors on SDA and SCL

Since the slave devices can only pull the data line to **GND**, the device may be powered by **3.3V** or even **5V** without the risk of driving the GPIO pins too high (remember that the Raspberry Pi GPIO is not able to handle voltages over 3.3V). This should work as long as the I²C bus of the device will recognize logic high at 3.3V instead of 5V. The I²C device must not have its own pull-up resistors fitted, as this will cause the GPIO pins to be pulled to the supply voltage of the I²C device.

Note the PCF8591 module used in this chapter has resistors fitted, therefore we must only use VCC=3V3. A bidirectional logic level converter can be used to overcome any issues with logic levels. One such device is the **Adafruit** I²C bidirectional logic level translator, shown in the following image:

Adafruit I²C Bi-directional logic level translator module

In addition to ensuring that any logic voltages are at suitable levels for the device you are using, it will allow the bus to be extended over longer wires (the level shifter will also act as a bus repeater).

Using just the PCF8591 chip or adding alternative sensors

The circuit diagram of the PCF8591 module is shown as follows without the sensors attached:

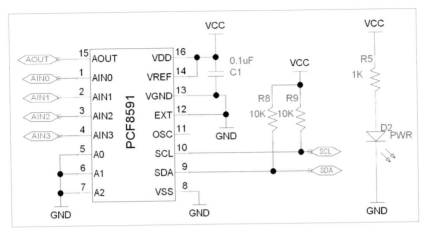

The PCF8591 ADC circuit – VCC, GND, SCL, and SDA are connected to the Raspberry Pi as before

As you can see, excluding the sensors, there are only five additional components. We have a power-filtering capacitor (C1) and the power-indicating LED (D2) with a current-limiting resistor (R5), all of which are optional.

It should be noted that the module includes two 10K pull-up resistors (R8 and R9) for SCL and SDA signals. However, since the P1 I²C connections on the Raspberry Pi also include pull-up resistors, these are not needed on the module (and could be removed). It also means we should only connect this module to VCC=3.3V (if we use 5V, then voltages on SCL and SDA will be around 3.56V, which is too high for the Raspberry Pi GPIO pins).

The sensors on the PCF891 module are all resistive, so the voltage level that is present on analog input will change between GND and VCC as the resistance of the sensor changes.

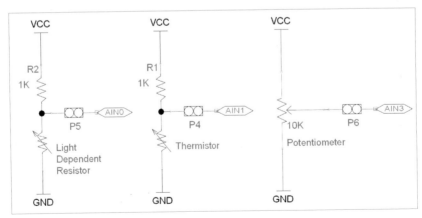

A potential divider circuit is used to provide a voltage proportional to the sensor's resistance

The module uses a circuit known as a potential divider. The resistor at the top balances the resistance provided by the sensor at the bottom to provide a voltage that is somewhere between VCC and GND.

The output voltage (Vout) of the potential divider can be calculated as follows:

$$V_{out} = \frac{R_t}{(R_t + R_b) \times VCC}$$

The R^t and R^b are the resistance values at the top and bottom respectively, and VCC is the supply voltage.

The potentiometer in the module has the 10k ohm resistance split between top and bottom depending on the position of the adjuster. So, halfway, we have 5k ohm on each side and an output voltage of 1.65V; a quarter of the way (clockwise), we have 2.5k ohm and 7.5k ohm, producing 0.825V.

 I've not shown the AOUT circuit, which is a resistor and LED. However, as you will find, an LED isn't suited to indicate an analog output (except to show the on/off states).

For more sensitive circuits, you can use more complex circuits such as a **Wheatstone bridge** (which allows the detection of very small changes in resistance), or you can use dedicated sensors that output an analog voltage based on their readings (such as a **TMP36** temperature sensor). The PCF891 also supports the differential input mode, where one channel can be compared to the input of another (the resultant reading will be the difference between the two).

For more information on the PCF8591 chip, refer to the following datasheet:

```
http://www.nxp.com/documents/data_sheet/PCF8591.pdf
```

Reading analog data using an analog-to-digital converter

The I2CTools (used in the previous section) are very useful for debugging I²C devices on the command line, but they are not practical for use within Python, as they would be slow and require significant overhead to use. Fortunately, there are several Python libraries that provide I²C support, allowing efficient use of I²C to communicate with connected devices and provide easy operation.

We will use such a library to create our own Python module that will allow us to quickly and easily obtain data from the ADC device and use it in our programs. The module is designed in such a way that other hardware or data sources may be put in its place without impacting the remaining examples.

Getting ready

To use the I²C bus using Python 3, we will use Gordon Henderson's wiringPi2 (see `http://wiringpi.com/` for more details).

The easiest way to install wiringPi2 is by using PIP for Python 3. PIP is a package manager for Python that works in a similar way to apt-get. Any packages you wish to install will be automatically downloaded and installed from an online repository.

To install PIP, use the following:

```
sudo apt-get install python3-dev python3-pip
```

Then install wiringPi2 with the following command:

```
sudo pip-3.2 install wiringpi2
```

Once the install has completed, you should see the following, indicating success:

```
ngPi/wiringPi/wiringSerial.o build/temp.linux-armv61-3.2/WiringPi/wiringPi/wirin
gShift.o build/temp.linux-armv61-3.2/wiringpi_wrap.o -o build/lib.linux-armv61-3
.2/_wiringpi2.cpython-32mu.so

Successfully installed wiringpi2
Cleaning up...
pi@raspberrypi:~$
```

Sucessfully installed wiringPi2

You will need the PCF8591 module wired as before to the I²C connections of the Raspberry Pi.

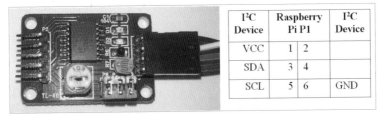

I²C Device	Raspberry Pi P1		I²C Device
VCC	1	2	
SDA	3	4	
SCL	5	6	GND

The PCF8591 module and pin connections to the Raspberry Pi P1 connector (as used in the previous section)

How to do it...

In the next section, we shall write a script to allow us to gather data that we will then use later on in this chapter.

Create the following script, `data_adc.py`, as follows:

1. First import the modules and create the variables we will use, as follows:

```
#!/usr/bin/env python3
#data_adc.py
import wiringpi2
import time

DEBUG=False
LIGHT=0;TEMP=1;EXT=2;POT=3
ADC_CH=[LIGHT,TEMP,EXT,POT]
ADC_ADR=0x48
ADC_CYCLE=0x04
BUS_GAP=0.25
DATANAME=["0:Light","1:Temperature",
          "2:External","3:Potentiometer"]
```

2. Create the class called `device` with a constructor to initialize it, as follows:

```
class device:
  # Constructor:
  def __init__(self,addr=ADC_ADR):
    self.NAME=DATANAME
    self.i2c = wiringpi2.I2C()
    self.devADC=self.i2c.setup(addr)
    pwrup = self.i2c.read(self.devADC) #flush powerup value
    if DEBUG==True and pwrup!=-1:
      print("ADC Ready")
    self.i2c.read(self.devADC) #flush first value
    time.sleep(BUS_GAP)
    self.i2c.write(self.devADC,ADC_CYCLE)
    time.sleep(BUS_GAP)
    self.i2c.read(self.devADC)  #flush first value
```

3. Within the class, define a function to provide a list of channel names as follows:

```
def getName(self):
  return self.NAME
```

4. Define another function (still as part of the class) to return a new set of samples from the ADC channels as follows:

```
def getNew(self):
  data=[]
  for ch in ADC_CH:
    time.sleep(BUS_GAP)
    data.append(self.i2c.read(self.devADC))
  return data
```

5. Finally, after the device class, create a test function to exercise our new `device` class as follows. This is only to be run when the script is executed directly:

```python
def main():
    ADC = device(ADC_ADR)
    print (str(ADC.getName()))
    for i in range(10):
        dataValues = ADC.getNew()
        print (str(dataValues))
        time.sleep(1)

if __name__=='__main__':
    main()
#End
```

You can run the test function of this module using the following command:

```
sudo python3 data_adc.py
```

How it works...

We start by importing `wiringpi2` so we can communicate with our I²C device later on. We will create a class to contain the required functionality to control the ADC. When we create the class, we can initialize wiringPi2 in such a way that it is ready to use the I²C bus (using `wiringpi2.I2C()`), and we set up a generic I²C device with the chip's bus address (using `self.i2c.setup(0x48)`).

> wiringPi2 also has a dedicated class to use with the PCF8591 chip; however, in this case, it is more useful to use the standard I²C functionality to illustrate how any I²C device can be controlled using wiringPi2. By referring to the device datasheet, you can use similar commands to communicate to any connected I²C device (whether it is directly supported or not).

As before, we perform a device read and configure the ADC to cycle through the channels (but instead of `i2cget` and `i2cset`, we use the wiringPi2 read and write functions of the I²C object). Once initialized, the device will be ready to read the analog signals on each of the channels.

The class will also have two member functions. The first function, `getName()`, returns a list of channel names (which we can use to correlate our data to its source) and the second function, `getNew()`, returns a new set of data from all the channels. The data is read from ADC using the `i2c.read()` function and, since we have already put it into cycle mode, each read will be from the next channel.

As we plan to reuse this class later on, we will use the if __name__ test to allow us to define some code to run when we execute the file directly. Within our `main()` function, we create ADC, which is an instance of our new device class. We can choose to select a non-default address if we need to; otherwise, the default address for the chip will be used. We use the `getName()` function to print out the names of the channels and then we can collect data from the ADC (using `getNew()`) and display them.

There's more...

The following allows us to define an alternative version of the device class in `data_adc.py` so it can be used in place of the ADC module. This will allow the remaining sections of the chapter to be tried without needing any specific hardware.

Gathering analog data without hardware

If you don't have an ADC module available, there is a wealth of data available from within Raspberry Pi that you can use instead.

Create the following script, `data_local.py`:

```python
#!/usr/bin/env python3
#data_local.py
import subprocess
from random import randint
import time

MEM_TOTAL=0
MEM_USED=1
MEM_FREE=2
MEM_OFFSET=7
DRIVE_USED=0
DRIVE_FREE=1
DRIVE_OFFSET=9
DEBUG=False
DATANAME=["CPU_Load","System_Temp","CPU_Frequency",
          "Random","RAM_Total","RAM_Used","RAM_Free",
          "Drive_Used","Drive_Free"]

def read_loadavg():
  # function to read 1 minute load average from system uptime
  value = subprocess.check_output(
          ["awk '{print $1}' /proc/loadavg"], shell=True)
  return float(value)
```

```python
def read_systemp():
  # function to read current system temperature
  value = subprocess.check_output(
          ["cat /sys/class/thermal/thermal_zone0/temp"],
          shell=True)
  return int(value)

def read_cpu():
  # function to read current clock frequency
  value = subprocess.check_output(
          ["cat /sys/devices/system/cpu/cpu0/cpufreq/"+
           "scaling_cur_freq"], shell=True)
  return int(value)

def read_rnd():
  return randint(0,255)

def read_mem():
  # function to read RAM info
  value = subprocess.check_output(["free"], shell=True)
  memory=[]
  for val in value.split()[MEM_TOTAL+
                           MEM_OFFSET:MEM_FREE+
                           MEM_OFFSET+1]:
    memory.append(int(val))
  return(memory)

def read_drive():
  # function to read drive info
  value = subprocess.check_output(["df"], shell=True)
  memory=[]
  for val in value.split()[DRIVE_USED+
                           DRIVE_OFFSET:DRIVE_FREE+
                           DRIVE_OFFSET+1]:
    memory.append(int(val))
  return(memory)

class device:
  # Constructor:
  def __init__(self,addr=0):
    self.NAME=DATANAME

  def getName(self):
    return self.NAME
```

```
    def getNew(self):
      data=[]
      data.append(read_loadavg())
      data.append(read_systemp())
      data.append(read_cpu())
      data.append(read_rnd())
      memory_ram = read_mem()
      data.append(memory_ram[MEM_TOTAL])
      data.append(memory_ram[MEM_USED])
      data.append(memory_ram[MEM_FREE])
      memory_drive = read_drive()
      data.append(memory_drive[DRIVE_USED])
      data.append(memory_drive[DRIVE_FREE])
      return data

def main():
  LOCAL = device()
  print (str(LOCAL.getName()))
  for i in range(10):
    dataValues = LOCAL.getNew()
    print (str(dataValues))
    time.sleep(1)

if __name__=='__main__':
  main()
#End
```

The previous script allows us to gather system information from the Raspberry Pi using the following commands (the `subprocess` module allows us to capture the results and process them):

▸ CPU speed:

```
cat /sys/devices/system/cpu/cpu0/cpufreq/scaling_cur_freq
```

▸ CPU load:

```
awk '{print $1}' /proc/loadavg
```

▸ Core temperature (scaled by 1000):

```
cat /sys/class/thermal/thermal_zone0/temp
```

▸ Drive info:

```
df
```

▸ RAM info:

```
free
```

Each data item is sampled using one of the functions. In the case of the drive and RAM information, we split the response into a list (separated by spaces) and select the items that we want to monitor (such as available memory and used drive space).

This is all packaged up to function in the same way as the `data_adc.py` file and the `device` class (so you can choose to use either in the following examples just by swapping the `data_adc` include with `data_local`).

Logging and plotting data

Now that we are able to sample and collect a lot of data, it is important that we can capture and analyze it. We will make use of a Python library called `matplotlib`, which includes lots of useful tools for manipulating, graphing, and analyzing data. We will use `pyplot` (which is a part of `matplotlib`) to produce graphs of our captured data. For more information on `pyplot`, go to `http://matplotlib.org/users/pyplot_tutorial.html`.

Getting ready

To use `pyplot`, we will need to install `matplotlib`.

Due to a problem with the `matplotlib` installer, performing the installation using pip-3.2 doesn't always work correctly. The method that follows will overcome this problem by performing all the steps PIP does manually; however, this can take over 30 minutes to complete.

To save time, you can try the PIP installation, which is much quicker. If it doesn't work, you can install it using this manual method.

Try installing `matplotlib` using PIP with the following commands:

```
sudo apt-get install tk-dev python3-tk libpng-dev
sudo pip-3.2 install numpy
sudo pip-3.2 install matplotlib
```

You can confirm `matplotlib` has installed by running `python3` and trying to import it from the Python terminal, as follows:

```
import matplotlib
```

If the installation failed, it will respond with the following:

```
ImportError: No module named matplotlib
```

Otherwise, there will be no errors.

Use the following steps to install `matplotlib` manually:

1. Install the support packages as follows:

```
sudo apt-get install tk-dev python3-tk python3-dev libpng-dev
sudo pip-3.2 install numpy
sudo pip-3.2 install matplotlib
```

2. Download the source files from the Git repository (the command should be a single line) as follows:

```
wget https://github.com/matplotlib/matplotlib/archive/master.zip
```

3. Unzip and open the `matplotlib-master` folder created, as follows:

```
unzip master.zip
rm master.zip
cd matplotlib-master
```

4. Run the setup file to build (this will take a while) and install it as follows:

```
sudo python3 setup.py build
sudo python3 setup.py install
```

5. Test the installation in the same way as the automated install.

We will either need the PCF8591 ADC module (and wiringPi2 installed as before), or we can use the `data_local.py` module from the previous section (just replace `data_adc` with `data_local` in the import section of the script). We also need to have `data_adc.py` and `data_local.py` in the same directory as the new script, depending on which you use.

How to do it...

Create the following script, `log_adc.py`:

```
#!/usr/bin/python3
#log_adc.c
import time
import datetime
import data_adc as dataDevice

DEBUG=True
FILE=True
VAL0=0;VAL1=1;VAL2=2;VAL3=3 #Set data order
FORMATHEADER="\t%s\t%s\t%s\t%s\t%s"
FORMATBODY="%d\t%s\t%f\t%f\t%f\t%f"
```

```python
if(FILE):f = open("data.log",'w')

def timestamp():
  ts=time.time()
  return datetime.datetime.fromtimestamp(ts).strftime(
                              '%Y-%m-%d %H:%M:%S')

def main():
    counter=0
    myData = dataDevice.device()
    myDataNames=myData.getName()
    header=(FORMATHEADER%("Time",
                        myDataNames[VAL0],myDataNames[VAL1],
                        myDataNames[VAL2],myDataNames[VAL3]))
    if(DEBUG):print (header)
    if(FILE):f.write(header+"\n")
    while(1):
      data=myData.getNew()
      counter+=1
      body=(FORMATBODY%(counter,timestamp(),
                      data[0],data[1],data[2],data[3]))
      if(DEBUG):print (body)
      if(FILE):f.write(body+"\n")
      time.sleep(0.1)

try:
  main()
finally:
  f.close()
#End
```

Create a second script, `log_graph.py`, as follows:

```python
#!/usr/bin/python3
#log_graph.py
import numpy as np
import matplotlib.pyplot as plt

filename = "data.log"
OFFSET=2
with open(filename) as f:
    header = f.readline().split('\t')

data = np.genfromtxt(filename, delimiter='\t', skip_header=1,
                  names=['sample', 'date', 'DATA0',
```

```
                              'DATA1', 'DATA2', 'DATA3'])
fig = plt.figure(1)
ax1 = fig.add_subplot(211)#numrows, numcols, fignum
ax2 = fig.add_subplot(212)
ax1.plot(data['sample'],data['DATA0'],'r',
        label=header[OFFSET+0])
ax2.plot(data['sample'],data['DATA1'],'b',
        label=header[OFFSET+1])
ax1.set_title("ADC Samples")
ax1.set_xlabel('Samples')
ax1.set_ylabel('Reading')
ax2.set_xlabel('Samples')
ax2.set_ylabel('Reading')

leg1 = ax1.legend()
leg2 = ax2.legend()

plt.show()
#End
```

How it works...

The first script, `log_adc.py`, allows us to collect data and write it to a logfile.

We can use the ADC device by importing `data_adc` as `dataDevice` or we can import `data_local` to use the system data. The numbers given to `VAL0` through `VAL3` allow us to change the order of the channels (and if using the `data_local` device, select the other channels). We also define the format string for the header and each line in the logfile (to create a file with data separated by tabs) using `%s`, `%d`, and `%f` to allow us to substitute strings, integers, and float values as shown in the following table:

	Time	0:Light	1:Temperature	2:External	3:Potentiometer
1	2014-02-20 21:24:15	207.00000	216.00000	130.00000	255.00000
2	2014-02-20 21:24:16	207.00000	216.00000	152.00000	255.00000
3	2014-02-20 21:24:17	207.00000	216.00000	145.00000	255.00000
4	2014-02-20 21:24:18	207.00000	216.00000	123.00000	255.00000
5	2014-02-20 21:24:19	207.00000	216.00000	128.00000	255.00000

The table of data captured from the ADC sensor module

If logging to the file (when `FILE=True`), we open `data.log` in the write mode using the `'w'` option (this will overwrite any existing files; to append to a file, use `'a'`).

As part of our data log, we generate `timestamp` using `time` and `datetime` to get the current **Epoch time** (this is the milliseconds since Jan 1, 1970) using the `time.time()` command. We convert the value into a more friendly year-month-day hour:min:sec format using `strftime()`.

The `main()` function starts by creating an instance of our `device` class (we made this in the previous example), which will supply the data. We fetch the channel names from the `data` device and construct the `header` string. If `DEBUG` is set to `True`, the data is printed to screen; if `FILE` is set to `True`, it will be written to file.

In the main loop, we use the `getNew()` function of the device to collect data and format it to display on screen or log to the file. The `main()` function is called using the `try: finally:` command, which will ensure that when the script is aborted the file will be correctly closed.

The second script, `log_graph.py`, allows us to read the logfile and produce a graph of the recorded data, as shown in the following figure:

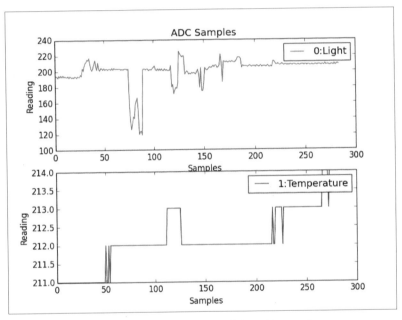

Graphs produced by **log_graph**.py from the light and temperature sensors

We start by opening up the logfile and reading the first line; this contains the header information (which we can then use to identify the data later on). Next, we use `numpy`, a specialist Python library that extends how we can manipulate data and numbers. In this case, we use it to read in the data from the file, split it up based on the tab delimiter, and provide identifiers for each of the data channels.

We define a figure to hold our graphs, adding two subplots (located in a 2 x 1 grid and positions 1 and 2 in the grid – set by the values `211` and `212`). Next, we define the values we want to plot, providing the x values (`data['sample']`), the y values (`data['DATA0']`), the `color` value (`'r'` which is Red or `'b'` for Blue), and `label` (set to the heading text we read previously from the top of the file).

Finally, we set a title, x and y labels for each subplot, enable legends (to show the labels), and display the plot (using `plt.show()`).

There's more...

Now that we have the ability to see the data we have been capturing, we can take things even further by displaying it as we sample it. This will allow us to instantly see how the data reacts to changes in the environment or stimulus. We can also calibrate our data so that we can assign the appropriate scaling to produce measurements in real units.

Plotting live data

Besides plotting data from files, we can use `matplotlib` to plot sensor data as it is sampled. To achieve this, we can use the plot-animation feature, which automatically calls a function to collect new data and update our plot.

Create the following, `live_graph.py`:

```python
#!/usr/bin/python3
#live_graph.py
import numpy as np
import matplotlib.pyplot as plt
import matplotlib.animation as animation
import data_local as dataDevice

PADDING=5
myData = dataDevice.device()
dispdata = []
timeplot=0
fig, ax = plt.subplots()
line, = ax.plot(dispdata)

def update(data):
  global dispdata,timeplot
  timeplot+=1
  dispdata.append(data)
  ax.set_xlim(0, timeplot)
  ymin = min(dispdata)-PADDING
  ymax = max(dispdata)+PADDING
```

```
      ax.set_ylim(ymin, ymax)
      line.set_data(range(timeplot),dispdata)
      return line

  def data_gen():
    while True:
      yield myData.getNew()[1]/1000

  ani = animation.FuncAnimation(fig, update,
                              data_gen, interval=1000)

  plt.show()
  #End
```

We start by defining our `dataDevice` object and creating an empty array, `dispdata[]` that will hold all the data collected. Next, we define our subplot and the line we are going to plot.

The `FuncAnimation()` function allows us to update a figure (`fig`) by defining an update function and a generator function. The generator function (`data_gen()`) will be called every interval (1000ms) and will produce a data value.

This example uses the core temperature reading that, when divided by 1000, gives the actual temperature in degC.

To use the ADC data instead, change the import for `dataDevice` to `data_adc` and adjust the following line to use a channel other than `[1]` and apply a scaling that is different from 1000:

`yield myData.getNew()[1]/1000`

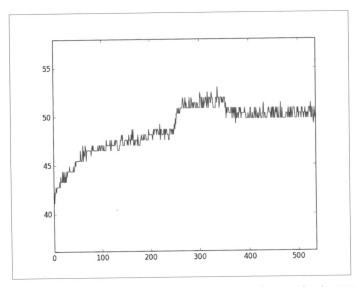

The Raspberry Pi plotting in realtime (core temperature in degC versus time in seconds)

The data value is passed to the `update()` function, which allows us to add it to our `dispdata[]` array that will contain all the data values to be displayed in the plot. We adjust the *x* axis range to be near the `min` and `max` values of the data, as well as adjust the *y* axis to grow as we continue to sample more data.

> The `FuncAnimation()` function requires the `data_gen()` object to be a special type of function called `generator`. A `generator` function produces a continuous series of values each time it is called, and can even use its previous state to calculate the next value if required. This is used to perform continuous calculations for plotting; this is why it is used here. In our case, we just want to run the same sampling function (`new_data()`) continuously, so each time it is called, it will yield a new sample.

Finally, we update the *x* and *y* axes data with our `dispdata[]` array (using the `set_data()` function), which will plot our samples against the number of seconds we are sampling. To use other data, or to plot data from the ADC, adjust the import for `dataDevice` and select the required channel (and scaling) in the `data_gen()` function.

Scaling and calibrating data

You may have noticed that it can sometimes be difficult to interpret data read from an ADC, since the value is just a number. A number isn't much help except to tell you it is slightly hotter or slightly darker than the previous sample. However, if you can use another device to provide comparable values (such as the current room temperature), you can then calibrate your sensor data to provide more useful real-world information.

To obtain a rough calibration, we shall use two samples to create a linear fit model that can then be used to estimate real-world values for other ADC readings (this assumes the sensor itself is mostly linear in its response). The following figure shows a linear fit using two readings at 25 and 30 degrees centigrade, providing estimated ADC values for other temperatures:

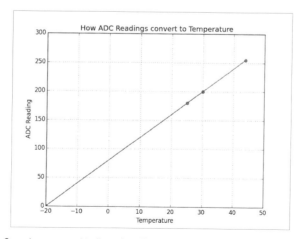

Samples are used to linearly calibrate temperature sensor readings

We can calculate our model using the following function:

```
def linearCal(realVal1,readVal1,realVal2,readVal2):
    #y=Ax+C
    A=(realVal1-realVal2)/(readVal1-readVal2)
    C=realVal1-(readVal1*A)
    cal = (A,C)
    return cal
```

This will return `cal`, which will contain the model slope (`A`) and offset (`C`).

We can then use the following function to calculate the value of any reading by using the calculated `cal` values for that channel:

```
def calValue(readVal,cal=[1,0]):
    realVal=(readVal*cal[0])+cal[1]
    return realVal
```

For more accuracy, you can take several samples and use linear interpolation between the values (or fit the data to other more complex mathematical models), if required.

Extending the Raspberry Pi GPIO with an I/O expander

As we have seen, making use of the higher-level bus protocols allows us to connect to more complex hardware quickly and easily. The I²C can be put to great use by using it to expand the available I/O on the Raspberry Pi as well as providing additional circuit protection (and, in some cases, additional power to drive more hardware).

There are lots of devices available that provide I/O expansion over the I²C bus (and also SPI), but the most commonly used is a 28-pin device, MCP23017, which provides 16 additional digital input/output pins. Being an I²C device, it only requires the 2 signals (SCL and SDA connections plus ground and power) and will happily function with other I²C devices on the same bus.

We shall see how the Adafruit I²C 16x2 RGB LCD Pi Plate makes use of one of these chips to control an LCD alphanumeric display and keypad over the I²C bus (without the I/O expander, this would normally require up to 15 GPIO pins).

Getting ready

You will need the Adafruit I²C 16x2 RGB LCD Pi Plate (which also includes five keypad buttons), and is shown in the following image:

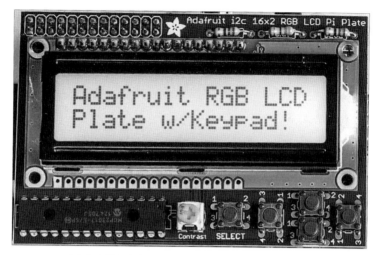

Adafruit I²C 16x2 RGB LCD Pi Plate with keypad buttons

The Adafruit I²C 16x2 RGB LCD Pi Plate directly connects to the GPIO connector of Raspberry Pi.

As before, we can use the PCF8591 ADC module or use the `data_local.py` module from the previous section (use `data_adc` or `data_local` in the import section of the script). The files `data_adc.py` and `data_local.py` should be in the same directory as the new script.

The LCD Pi Plate only requires five pins (SDA, SCL, GND, and 5V); it connects over the whole GPIO header. If we want to use it with other devices, such as the PCF8591 ADC module, then something similar to a TriBorg from PiBorg (which splits the GPIO port into three) can be used.

How to do it...

Create the following script, `lcd_i2c.py`:

```
#!/usr/bin/python3
#lcd_i2c.py
import wiringpi2
import time
```

```python
import datetime
import data_local as dataDevice

AF_BASE=100
AF_E=AF_BASE+13;      AF_RW=AF_BASE+14;     AF_RS=AF_BASE+15
AF_DB4=AF_BASE+12;    AF_DB5=AF_BASE+11;    AF_DB6=AF_BASE+10
AF_DB7=AF_BASE+9

AF_SELECT=AF_BASE+0;  AF_RIGHT=AF_BASE+1;  AF_DOWN=AF_BASE+2
AF_UP=AF_BASE+3;      AF_LEFT=AF_BASE+4;   AF_BACK=AF_BASE+5

AF_GREEN=AF_BASE+6;   AF_BLUE=AF_BASE+7;   AF_RED=AF_BASE+8
BNK=" "*16 #16 spaces

def gpiosetup():
  global lcd
  wiringpi2.wiringPiSetup()
  wiringpi2.mcp23017Setup(AF_BASE,0x20)
  wiringpi2.pinMode(AF_RIGHT,0)
  wiringpi2.pinMode(AF_LEFT,0)
  wiringpi2.pinMode(AF_SELECT,0)
  wiringpi2.pinMode(AF_RW,1)
  wiringpi2.digitalWrite(AF_RW,0)
  lcd=wiringpi2.lcdInit(2,16,4,AF_RS,AF_E,
                      AF_DB4,AF_DB5,AF_DB6,AF_DB7,0,0,0,0)


def printLCD(line0="",line1=""):
  wiringpi2.lcdPosition(lcd,0,0)
  wiringpi2.lcdPrintf(lcd,line0+BNK)
  wiringpi2.lcdPosition(lcd,0,1)
  wiringpi2.lcdPrintf(lcd,line1+BNK)


def checkBtn(idx,size):
  global run
  if wiringpi2.digitalRead(AF_LEFT):
    idx-=1
    printLCD()
  elif wiringpi2.digitalRead(AF_RIGHT):
    idx+=1
    printLCD()
  if wiringpi2.digitalRead(AF_SELECT):
    printLCD("Exit Display")
    run=False
  return idx%size
```

```
def main():
  global run
  gpiosetup()
  myData = dataDevice.device()
  myDataNames=myData.getName()
  run=True
  index=0
  while(run):
    data=myData.getNew()
    printLCD(myDataNames[index],str(data[index]))
    time.sleep(0.2)
    index = checkBtn(index,len(myDataNames))

main()
#End
```

With the LCD module connected, run the script as follows:

```
sudo python3 lcd_i2c.py
```

Select the data channel you want to display using the left and right buttons and press the SELECT button to exit.

How it works...

The wiringPi2 library has excellent support for I/O expander chips, like the one used for the AdaFruit LCD Character module. To use the Adafruit module, we need to set up the pin mapping for all the pins of MCP23017 PortA as shown in the following table (then we set up the I/O expander pins with an offset of `100`):

Name	SELECT	RIGHT	DOWN	UP	LEFT	GREEN	BLUE	RED
MCP23017 PortA	A0	A1	A2	A3	A4	A6	A7	A8
WiringPiPin	100	101	102	103	104	106	107	108

The pin mapping for all the pins of MCP23017 PortB are as follows:

Name	DB7	DB6	DB5	DB4	E	RW	RS
MCP23017 PortB	B1	B2	B3	B4	B5	B6	B7
WiringPiPin	109	110	111	112	113	114	115

To set up the LCD screen, we initialize `wiringPiSetup()` and the I/O expander, `mcp23017Setup()`. We then specify the pin offset and bus address of the I/O expander. Next, we set all the hardware buttons as inputs (using `pinMode(pin number,0)`), and the RW pin of the LCD to an output. The wiringPi2 LCD library expects the RW pin to be set to `LOW` (forcing it into read-only mode), so we set the pin to `LOW` (using `digitalWrite(AF_RW,0)`).

We create an `lcd` object by defining the number of rows and columns of the screen, and if we are using 4- or 8-bit data mode (we are using 4 of the 8 data lines, so it is the 4-bit mode). We also provide the pin mapping of the pins we are using (the last four are set to `0` since we are only using 4 data lines).

Now we create a function called `PrintLCD()` that will allow us to send strings to show on each line of the display. We use `lcdPosition()` to set the cursor position on the `lcd` object for each line and then print the text for each line. We also add some blank spaces at the end of each line to ensure the full line is overwritten.

The next function, `checkBtn()` briefly checks the left/right and select buttons to see if they have been pressed (using the `digitalRead()` function). If the left/right button has been pressed, then the index is set to the previous or next item in the array. If the SELECT button is pressed, then the `run` flag is set to `False` (this will exit the main loop, allowing the script to finish).

The `main()` function calls `gpiosetup()` to create our `lcd` object; then we create our `dataDevice` object and fetch the data names. Within the main loop, we get new data; then we use our `printLCD()` function to display the data name on the top line and the data value on the second line. Finally, we check to see if the buttons have been pressed and set the index to our data as required.

There's more...

Using expander chips such as MCP23017 provide an excellent way to increase the amount of hardware connectivity to the Raspberry Pi while also providing an additional layer of protection (it is cheaper to replace the expander chip Raspberry Pi).

I/O expander voltages and limits

The port expander only uses a small amount of power when in use, but if you are powering it using the 3.3V supply, then you will still only be able to draw a maximum of 50mA in total from all the pins. If you draw too much power, then you may experience system freezes or corrupted read/writes on the SD card.

If you power the expander using the 5V supply, then you can draw up to the maximum the expander can support (around 25mA maximum per pin and 125mA total) as long as your USB power supply is powerful enough.

We must remember that if the expander is powered with 5V, the inputs/outputs and interrupt lines will also be 5V and should never be connected back to the Raspberry Pi (without using level shifters to translate the voltage down to 3.3V).

By changing the wiring of the address pins (A0, A1, and A2) on the expander chip, up to eight modules can be used on the same I²C bus simultaneously. To ensure there is enough current available for each, we would need to use a separate 3.3V supply. A linear regulator such as LM1117-3.3 would be suitable (this would provide up to 800mA at 3.3V, 100mA for each), and only needs the following simple circuit:

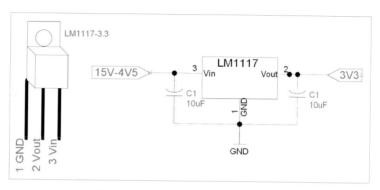

The LM1117 linear voltage regulator circuit

The following diagram shows how a voltage regulator can be connected to the I/O expander (or other device) to provide more current for driving extra hardware:

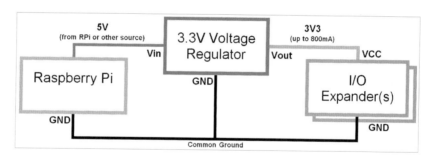

Using a voltage regulator with the Raspberry Pi

The input voltage (Vin) is provided by the Raspberry Pi (for example, from the P1 GPIO pin header, such as 5V pin 2). However, Vin could be provided by any other power supply (or battery pack) as long as it is between 4.5V and 15V and able to provide enough current. The important part is ensuring that the ground connections (GND) of the Raspberry Pi, the power supply (if a separate one is used), the regulator, and the I/O expander are all connected together (as a common ground).

Using your own I/O expander module

You can use one of the I/O expander modules that are available (or just the MCP23017 chip in the following circuit) to control most HD44780-compatible LCD displays:

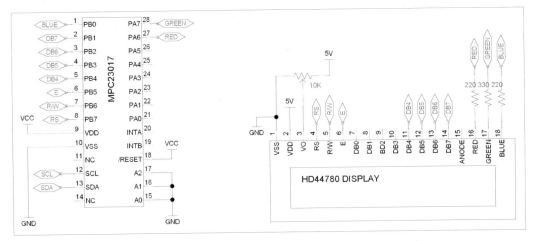

The I/O expander and a HD44780-compatible display

The D-Pad circuit, which is explained in the recipe *The GPIO keypad input* in *Chapter 6, Using Python to Drive Hardware*, can also be connected to the remaining Port A pins of the expander (PA0 to Button 1, PA1 to Right, PA2 to Down, PA3 to Up, PA4 to Left, and PA5 to Button 2). As in the previous example, the buttons will be PA0 to PA4 (WiringPiPin number 100 to 104); apart from these, we have the second button added to PA5 (WiringPiPin number 105).

Directly controlling an LCD alphanumeric display

Alternatively, you can also drive the screen directly from the Raspberry Pi with the following connections:

LCD	VSS	VDD	VO	RS	RW	E	DB4	DB5	DB6	DB7
LCD Pin	1	2	3	4	5	6	11	12	13	14
Raspberry Pi P1	6 (GND)	2 (5V)	Contrast	11	13 (GND)	15	12	16	18	22

The preceding table lists the connections required between the Raspberry Pi and the HD44780-compatible alphanumeric display module.

The contrast pin (V0) can be connected to a variable resistor as before (with one side on 5V and the other on GND); although, depending on the screen, you may find you can connect directly to GND/5V to obtain the maximum contrast.

The wiringPi2 LCD library assumes that the RW pin is connected to GND (read only); this avoids the risk that the LCD will send data back if connected directly to the Raspberry Pi (this would be a problem since the screen is powered by 5V and would send data using 5V logic).

Ensure you update the code with the new `AF_XX` references and refer to the physical pin number by changing the setup within the `gpiosetup()` function. We can also skip the setup of the MCP23017 device.

Have a look at the following commands:

```
wiringpi2.wiringPiSetup()
wiringpi2.mcp23017Setup(AF_BASE,0x20)
```

Replace the preceding commands with the following command:

```
wiringpi.wiringPiSetupPhys()
```

You can see that we only need to change the pin references to switch between using the I/O expander or not using it, which shows how convenient the wiringPi2 implementation is.

Sensing and sending data to online services

In this section, we shall make use of an online service called Xively; the service allows us to connect, transmit, and view data online. Xively makes use of a common protocol that is used for transferring information over HTTP, called REpresentational State Transfer (REST). REST is used by many services such as Facebook and Twitter, using various keys and access tokens to ensure data is transferred securely between authorized applications and the verified sites.

You can perform most REST operations (methods such as POST, GET, SET, and so on) using a Python library called `requests (http://docs.python-requests.org)`, manually.

However, it is often easier to make use of specific libraries available for the service you intend to use. They will handle the authorization process; provide access functions; and, if the service changes, the library can be updated rather than your code.

We will use the `xively-python` library, which provides Python functions to allow us to easily interact with the site.

For details about the `xively-python` library, refer to `http://xively.github.io/xively-python/`.

The data collected by Xively is shown in the following screenshot:

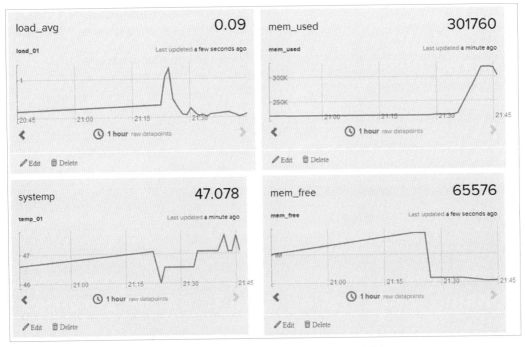

Xively collects and graphs data transferred using REST

Getting ready

You will need to create an account on the site `www.xively.com`, which we will use to receive our data. Go to the site and sign up for a free developer account (via the Login page or the Getting Started section).

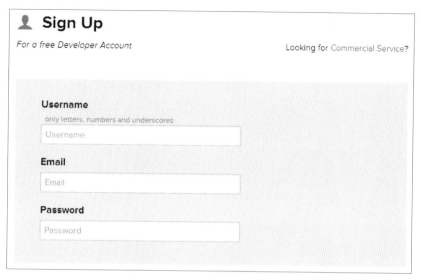

Sign up and create an Xively account

Once you have registered and verified your account, you can follow the instructions that will take you through a test drive example. This will demonstrate linking to data from your smartphone (gyroscopic data, location, and so on), which will give you a taste of what we can do with the Raspberry Pi.

When you log in, you will be taken to the **Development Devices** dashboard (located from the **WebTools** dropdown).

Adding a new device

Select **+Add Device** and fill in the details, giving your device a name and setting **Device** as **Private**.

You will now see the control page for your remote device, which contains all the information you need to connect and also where your data will be displayed.

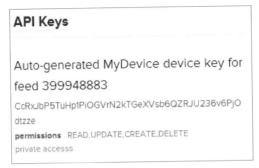

API Keys

Auto-generated MyDevice device key for feed 399948883

CcRxJbP5TuHp1PiOGVrN2kTGeXVsb6QZRJU236v6PjO dtzze

permissions READ,UPDATE,CREATE,DELETE
private accesss

Example API Key and feed number (this will be unique for your device)

Although there is a lot of information on this page, you only need two parts of it.

- The API Key (which is the long code in the API Keys), as follows:

```
API_KEY = CcRxJbP5TuHp1PiOGVrN2kTGeXVsb6QZRJU236v6PjOdtzze
```

- The feed number (referred to in the API Keys section and also listed at the top of the page), as follows:

```
FEED_ID = 399948883
```

Now that we have the details we need to connect with Xively, we can focus on the Raspberry Pi side of things.

We will use pip-3.2 to install Xively, as follows:

```
sudo pip-3.2 install xively-python
```

Ensure that the install reports the following:

```
Successfully installed xively-python requests
```

You are now ready to send some data from your Raspberry Pi.

How to do it...

Create the following script, `xivelyLog.py`. Ensure you set `FEED_ID` and `API_KEY` within the code to match the device you created:

```
#!/usr/bin/env python3
#xivelylog.py
```

```python
import xively
import time
import datetime
import requests
from random import randint
import data_local as dataDevice

# Set the FEED_ID and API_KEY from your account
FEED_ID = 399948883
API_KEY = "CcRxJbP5TuHp1PiOGVrN2kTGeXVsb6QZRJU236v6PjOdtzze"
api = xively.XivelyAPIClient(API_KEY) # initialize api client
DEBUG=True

myData = dataDevice.device()
myDataNames=myData.getName()

def get_datastream(feed,name,tags):
  try:
    datastream = feed.datastreams.get(name)
    if DEBUG:print ("Found existing datastream")
    return datastream
  except:
    if DEBUG:print ("Creating new datastream")
    datastream = feed.datastreams.create(name, tags=tags)
    return datastream

def run():
  print ("Connecting to Xively")
  feed = api.feeds.get(FEED_ID)
  if DEBUG:print ("Got feed" + str(feed))
  datastreams=[]
  for dataName in myDataNames:
    dstream = get_datastream(feed,dataName,dataName)
    if DEBUG:print ("Got %s datastream:%s"%(dataName,dstream))
    datastreams.append(dstream)

  while True:
    data=myData.getNew()
    for idx,dataValue in enumerate(data):
      if DEBUG:
        print ("Updating %s: %s" % (dataName,dataValue))
      datastreams[idx].current_value = dataValue
      datastreams[idx].at = datetime.datetime.utcnow()
    try:
```

```
            for ds in datastreams:
                ds.update()
        except requests.HTTPError as e:
            print ("HTTPError({0}): {1}".format(e.errno, e.strerror))
        time.sleep(60)

    run()
    #End
```

How it works...

First we initialize the Xively API client, to which we supply API_KEY (this authorizes us to send data to the Xively device we created previously). Next, we use the FEED_ID to link us to the specific feed we want to send the data to. Finally, we request datastream to connect to (if it doesn't already exist in the feed, the get_datastream() function will create one for us).

For each datastream in the feed, we supply a name function and tags (these are keywords that help us identify the data; we can use our data names for this).

Once we have defined our datastreams, we enter the main loop; here, we gather our data values from dataDevice. We then set the current_value function and also the timestamp of the data for each data item and apply it to our datastream objects.

Finally, when all the data is ready, we update each of the datastreams and the data is sent to Xively, appearing within a few moments on the dashboard for the device.

We can log in to our Xively account and view data as it comes in, using a standard web browser. This provides the means to send data and remotely monitor it anywhere in the world (perhaps from several Raspberry Pis at once if required). The service even supports the creation of triggers that can send additional messages back if certain items go out of expected ranges, reach specific values, or match set criteria. The triggers can in turn be used to control other devices or raise alerts and so on.

See also

The AirPi Air Quality and Weather project (http://airpi.es) shows you how to add your own sensors or use their AirPi kit to create your own air quality and weather station (with data logging to your own Xively account). The site also allows you to share your Xively data feeds with others from around the world.

8
Creating Projects with the Raspberry Pi Camera Module

In this chapter, we will cover:

 ▸ Getting started with the Raspberry Pi camera module
 ▸ Using the camera with Python
 ▸ Generating a time-lapse video
 ▸ Creating a stop frame animation
 ▸ Making a QR code reader

Introduction

The Raspberry Pi camera module is a special add-on of the Raspberry Pi, which makes use of the **Camera Serial Interface (CSI) connector**. This connects directly to the GPU core of the Raspberry Pi processor, allowing images to be captured directly on the unit.

We shall create a basic **graphical user interface (GUI)** using the tkinter library we used in *Chapter 3, Using Python for Automation and Productivity*, and *Chapter 4, Creating Games and Graphics*. This will form the basis of the remaining examples where we extend the GUI with additional controls so that we can put the camera to various uses for a range of different projects.

This chapter uses the Raspberry Pi camera module, which is available from most retailers listed in the *Makers, hobbyists, and Raspberry Pi specialists* section of the *Appendix, Hardware and Software List*.

Getting started with the Raspberry Pi camera module

We will start by installing and setting up the Raspberry Pi camera module, then we will create a small camera GUI that enables us to preview and take photos. The first GUI we will create is shown in the following image:

A basic camera GUI for the Raspberry Pi camera module

Getting ready

The Raspberry Pi camera module consists of a camera mounted on a small **Printed Circuit Board** (**PCB**) attached to a small ribbon cable. The ribbon cable can be attached directly to the CSI port of the Raspberry Pi board (marked as **S5**, the port is located between the USB and the HDMI port on the Raspberry Pi). The following image shows the Raspberry Pi camera module:

The Raspberry Pi camera module

The Raspberry Pi Foundation provides detailed instructions (and a video) on how to install the camera at `http://www.raspberrypi.org/archives/3890`; carry out the following steps:

1. First, fit the camera as shown in the following image (ensure that you have disconnected the Raspberry Pi from any power sources first):

The ribbon connector for the camera module is located next to the HDMI socket

To fit the ribbon cable into the CSI socket, you need to gently lift up and loosen the tab of the ribbon socket. Insert the ribbon into the slot with the metal contacts facing towards the HDMI port. Take care not to bend or fold the ribbon cable, and ensure that it is seated firmly and level in the socket before pushing the tab back into place.

2. Now, to enable the software, power up the Raspberry Pi and update your distribution with the following commands (while connected to the Internet):

```
sudo apt-get update
sudo apt-get upgrade
```

The previous commands can take some time to execute, but it does not matter whether you execute them with or without the camera connected, so you can do this beforehand. They simply update your system to the latest firmware release (which has support for the camera as a standard).

3. Finally, enable the camera using `raspi-config` (which is also updated in the upgrade process). Use `sudo raspi-config` to run it and find the menu entry for **Enable Camera** and enable it. You will be prompted to reboot afterwards.

How to do it...

You can use two programs that are also installed as part of the upgrade—raspivid and raspistill—to test the camera.

To take a single picture, use the following command (`-t 0` takes the picture immediately):

```
raspistill -o image.jpg -t 0
```

To take a short, 10-second video in the H.264 format, use the following command (the `-t` value is in milliseconds):

```
raspivid -o video.h264 -t 10000
```

How it works...

The full documentation of the camera and the `raspivid` and `raspistill` utilities is available on the Raspberry Pi site at the following link:

```
http://www.raspberrypi.org/wp-content/uploads/2013/07/RaspiCam-
Documentation.pdf
```

To get more information on each of the programs, you can use the `less` command to view the instructions (use q to quit) as shown:

```
raspistill > less
raspivid > less
```

Each command provides full control of the camera settings, such as exposure, white balance, sharpness, contrast, brightness, and so on, and the resolution.

Using the camera with Python

The camera module on the Raspberry Pi is more than just a standard webcam. Since we have full access to the controls and settings from within our own programs, it allows us to take control and create our own camera applications.

In this chapter, we will use the Python module called `picamera` created by Dave Hughes to control the camera module, which performs all the functions `raspivid` and `raspistill` support.

See `http://picamera.readthedocs.org` for additional documentation and lots of useful examples.

Getting ready

The Raspberry Pi camera module should be connected and installed as detailed in the previous section.

In addition, we will also need to install the Python 3 Pillow Library (the details on how to do this have been covered in the *Displaying photo information in an application* recipe in *Chapter 3, Using Python for Automation and Productivity*).

Now, install `picamera` for Python 3 using the following command:

```
sudo apt-get install python3-picamera
```

How to do it...

1. Create the following `cameraGUI.py` script that shall contain the main class for the GUI:

```python
#!/usr/bin/python3
#cameraGUI.py
import tkinter as TK
from PIL import Image
import subprocess
import time
import datetime
import picamera as picam

class SET():
  PV_SIZE=(320,240)
  NORM_SIZE=(2592,1944)
  NO_RESIZE=(0,0)
```

```
        PREVIEW_FILE="PREVIEW.gif"
        TEMP_FILE="PREVIEW.ppm"

    class cameraGUI(TK.Frame):
        def run(cmd):
            print("Run:"+cmd)
            subprocess.call([cmd], shell=True)
        def camCapture(filename,size=SET.NORM_SIZE):
            with picam.PiCamera() as camera:
                camera.resolution = size
                print("Image: %s"%filename)
                camera.capture(filename)
        def getTKImage(filename,previewsize=SET.NO_RESIZE):
            encoding=str.split(filename,".")[1].lower()
            print("Image Encoding: %s"%encoding)
            try:
                if encoding=="gif" and previewsize==SET.NO_RESIZE:
                    theTKImage=TK.PhotoImage(file=filename)
                else:
                    imageview=Image.open(filename)
                    if previewsize!=SET.NO_RESIZE:
                        imageview.thumbnail(previewsize,Image.ANTIALIAS)
                    imageview.save(SET.TEMP_FILE,format="ppm")
                    theTKImage=TK.PhotoImage(file=SET.TEMP_FILE)
            except IOError:
                print("Unable to get: %s"%filename)
            return theTKImage
        def timestamp():
            ts=time.time()
            tstring=datetime.datetime.fromtimestamp(ts)
            return tstring.strftime("%Y%m%d_%H%M%S")

        def __init__(self,parent):
            self.parent=parent
            TK.Frame.__init__(self,self.parent)
            self.parent.title("Camera GUI")
            self.previewUpdate = TK.IntVar()
            self.filename=TK.StringVar()
            self.canvas = TK.Canvas(self.parent,
                                    width=SET.PV_SIZE[0],
                                    height=SET.PV_SIZE[1])
            self.canvas.grid(row=0,columnspan=4)
            self.shutterBtn=TK.Button(self.parent,text="Shutter",
                                      command=self.shutter)
```

```
        self.shutterBtn.grid(row=1,column=0)
        exitBtn=TK.Button(self.parent,text="Exit",
                               command=self.exit)
        exitBtn.grid(row=1,column=3)
        previewChk=TK.Checkbutton(self.parent,text="Preview",
                               variable=self.previewUpdate)
        previewChk.grid(row=1,column=1)
        labelFilename=TK.Label(self.parent,
                          textvariable=self.filename)
        labelFilename.grid(row=2,column=0,columnspan=3)
        self.preview()
    def msg(self,text):
        self.filename.set(text)
        self.update()
    def btnState(self,state):
        self.shutterBtn["state"] = state
    def shutter(self):
        self.btnState("disabled")
        self.msg("Taking photo...")
        self.update()
        if self.previewUpdate.get() == 1:
            self.preview()
        else:
            self.normal()
        self.btnState("active")
    def normal(self):
        name=cameraGUI.timestamp()+".jpg"
        cameraGUI.camCapture(name,SET.NORM_SIZE)
        self.updateDisp(name,previewsize=SET.PV_SIZE)
        self.msg(name)
    def preview(self):
        cameraGUI.camCapture(SET.PREVIEW_FILE,SET.PV_SIZE)
        self.updateDisp(SET.PREVIEW_FILE)
        self.msg(SET.PREVIEW_FILE)
    def updateDisp(self,filename,previewsize=SET.NO_RESIZE):
        self.msg("Loading Preview...")
        self.myImage=cameraGUI.getTKImage(filename,previewsize)
        self.theImage=self.canvas.create_image(0,0,
                               anchor=TK.NW,
                               image=self.myImage)
        self.update()
    def exit(self):
        exit()
#End
```

2. Next, create the following `cameraGUI1normal.py` file to use the GUI:

```python
#!/usr/bin/python3
#cameraGUI1normal.py
import tkinter as TK
import cameraGUI as GUI

root=TK.Tk()
root.title("Camera GUI")
cam=GUI.cameraGUI(root)
TK.mainloop()
#End
```

3. Run the example with the following command:

```
python3 cameraGUI1normal.py
```

How it works...

In the `cameraGUI.py` file, we use a class called `SET` to contain the settings for the application (you will see in the following example why this is particularly helpful and allows us to keep all of the references to the settings in one place).

We will define a base class called `cameraGUI` (so we can attach `Tkinter` objects to it), which inherits a `TK.Frame` class. The `cameraGUI` class will contain all the methods to create the Tkinter application, including laying out the controls and providing all the required functions.

We define the following three utility functions for the class to use:

- ▶ `run()`: This function will allow us to send commands to be run on the command line using `subprocess.call` (we will use `subprocess.call` in the following examples to perform video encoding and other applications).

- ▶ `getTKImage()`: This function will allow us to create a `TK.PhotoImage` object suitable to display on the Tk canvas. The Tkinter canvas is unable to directly display JPG images, so we use the Pillow library (PIL) to resize it for display and convert it into a **PPM** file (the **Portable PixMap** format, which supports more colors than GIF). Since this conversion and resize process can take a few seconds, we will use GIF images to provide a quick camera preview images.

- ▶ `timestamp()`: This function will allow us to generate a timestamp string that we can use to automatically name any images we take.

Within the class initializer (`__init__()`), we define all the control variables, generate all the GUI objects and controls we want to use, and use the `grid()` functions to position the objects. The layout of the GUI is shown in the following image:

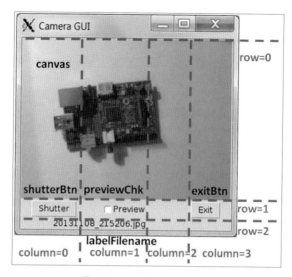

The layout of the camera GUI

We define the following control variables:

- `self.previewUpdate`: This is linked to the status of the **Preview** checkbox (`previewChk`)
- `self.filename`: This is linked to text displayed by the `labelFilename` widget

We also link the **Shutter** button (`shutterBtn`) to `self.shutter()`, which will be called whenever the **Shutter** button is pressed, and the **Exit** button (`exitBtn`) to the `self.exit()` function.

Finally, in the `__init__()` function, we call `self.preview()` that will ensure that **Camera GUI** takes a picture and displays it as soon as the application has started.

When the **Shutter** button is pressed, `self.shutter()` is called. This calls `this.btnState("disabled")` to disable the **Shutter** button while we are taking new pictures. This prevents any pictures being taken while the camera is already in use. When the rest of the actions have been completed, `this.btnState("active")` is used to re-enable the button.

The `self.shutter()` function will call either the `self.normal()` or `self.preview()` function depending on the status of the **Preview** checkbox (by getting the value of `self.previewUpdate`).

The `cameraGUI.camCapture()` function uses `pycamera` to create a camera object, set the resolution, and capture an image using the required filename. The `self.preview()` function takes an image called `PREVIEW_FILE` with a resolution of `PV_SIZE` as defined in the `SET` class.

Next, `self.updateDisp(PREVIEW_FILE)` is called and will use `cameraGUI.getTKImage()` to open the generated `PREVIEW.gif` file as a `TK.PhotoImage` object and apply it to the `Canvas` object in the GUI. We now call `self.update()`, which is a function inherited from the `TK.Frame` class; `self.update()` will allow the Tkinter display to be updated (in this case, with the new image). Finally, the `self.preview()` function will also call `self.msg()` that will update the `self.filename` value with the filename of the image being displayed (`PREVIEW.gif`). Again, this also uses `self.update()` to update the display.

If the **Preview** checkbox is unchecked, then the `self.shutter()` function will call `self.normal()`. However, this time it will take a much larger, 2592 x 1944 (5 megapixel) JPG image with the filename set to the latest `<timestamp>` value obtained from `self.timestamp()`. The resultant image is also resized and converted to a PPM image so it can be loaded as a `TK.PhotoImage` object that will be displayed in the application window.

There's more...

The camera application makes use of class structures to organize the code and make it easy to extend. In the following sections, we explain the types of methods and functions we have defined to allow this.

The Raspberry Pi can also make use of standard USB cameras or webcams. Alternatively, we can use additional Video4Linux drivers to allow the camera module to work like a standard webcam.

Class member and static functions

The `cameraGUI` class has two types of functions defined. First, we define some static methods (`run()`, `getTKImage()`, and `timestamp()`). These methods are tied to the class rather than to a specific instance; this means that we can use them without referring to a particular `cameraGUI` object but to the class itself. This is useful to define utility functions that are related to the class, since they may be useful in other parts of the program as well and may not need to access the data/objects contained within a `cameraGUI` object. The functions can be called using `cameraGUI.run("command")`.

Next, we define the class member functions that, as in the previous classes we have used, include a reference to `self`. This means that they are only accessible to instances of the class (objects of the type `cameraGUI`) and can use the data contained within the object (using the `self` reference).

Using a USB webcam instead

The Raspberry Pi camera module is not the only way you can add a camera to the Raspberry Pi; in most cases, you can use a USB webcam as well. The current Raspberry Pi Raspbian image should detect the most common webcam devices automatically when you plug them in; however, the support can vary.

To determine if your webcam has been detected, check to see if the following device file has been created on your system by running the following command:

```
ls /dev/video*
```

If detected successfully, you will see /dev/video0 or something similar, which is the reference you will use to access your webcam.

Install a suitable image capture program, such as fswebcam, using the following command:

```
sudo apt-get install fswebcam
```

You can test it with the following command:

```
fswebcam -d /dev/video0 -r 320x240 testing.jpg
```

Or alternatively, you can test it using dd as follows:

```
dd if=/dev/video0 of=testing.jpeg bs=11M count=1
```

 Webcams can require additional power from the USB ports of the Raspberry Pi; if you get errors, you may find that using a powered USB hub helps. For a list of supported devices and for troubleshooting, see the Raspberry Pi wiki page at http://elinux.org/RPi_USB_Webcams.

In the previous example, change the following functions in the cameraGUI class as shown:

1. Remove camCapture(), and remove import picamera as picam from the start of the file.

2. Within normal(), replace cameraGUI.camCapture(name,SET.NORM_SIZE) with the following:

   ```
   cameraGUI.run(SET.CAM_PREVIEW+SET.CAM_OUTPUT+
               SET.PREVIEW_FILE)
   ```

3. Within preview(), replace cameraGUI.camCapture(SET.PREVIEW_FILE,SET.PV_SIZE) with the following:

   ```
   cameraGUI.run(SET.CAM_NORMAL+SET.CAM_OUTPUT+name)
   ```

4. Within the `SET` class, define the following variables:

```
CAM_OUTPUT=" "
CAM_PREVIEW="fswebcam -d /dev/video0 -r 320x240"
CAM_NORMAL="fswebcam -d /dev/video0 -r 640x480"
```

By making the previous changes to the `cameraGUI` class, the connected USB webcam will take the images instead.

Additional drivers for the Raspberry Pi camera

Video4Linux drivers are available for the Raspberry Pi camera module. While these additional drivers are not quite official yet (it is likely that they will be included in the Raspbian image when they are). For more details, see `http://www.linux-projects.org/modules/news`.

The driver will allow you to use the camera module like you would a USB webcam, as a `/dev/video*` device, although you will not need this for the examples in this chapter.

Perform the following steps to install the additional drivers:

1. First, download the `apt` keys and add the source to the `apt` sources list. You can do this with the following commands:

```
wget http://www.linux-projects.org/listing/uv4l_repo/lrkey.asc
sudo apt-key add ./lrkey.asc
sudo nano /etc/apt/souces.list
```

2. Add the following into the file (on a single line):

```
deb http://www.linux-projects.org/listing/uv4l_repo/raspbian/
wheezy main
```

3. Install the drivers with the following commands:

```
sudo apt-get update
sudo apt-get install uv4l uv4l-raspicam
```

4. To use the `uv4l` driver, load it using the following command (on a single line):

```
uv4l --driver raspicam --auto-video_nr --width 640 –height480
--encoding jpeg
```

The Raspberry Pi will then be accessible through `/dev/video0` (depending on whether you have other video devices installed). It can be used with standard webcam programs.

See also

For more examples on using the Tkinter library, see *Chapters 3, Using Python for Automation and Productivity*, and *Chapter 4, Creating Games and Graphics*.

Generating a time-lapse video

Having a camera attached to a computer provides us with a great way to take pictures at controlled intervals and automatically process them into a video to create a time-lapse sequence. The `pycamera` Python module has a special `capture_continuous()` function that will create a series of images. For the time-lapse video, we will specify the time between each image and the total number of images that need to be taken. To help the user, we will also calculate the overall duration of the video to provide an indication of how long it will take.

We shall add to our previous GUI interface to provide controls to run time-lapses and also automatically generate a video clip from the results. The GUI will now look similar to the following screenshot:

The time-lapse application

Getting ready

You will need everything set up, as it was for the previous example, including the `cameraGUI.py` file that we created in the same directory and `pycamera` that we installed. We shall also use `mencoder` that will allow us to take the time-lapse images and combine them into a video clip.

To install `mencoder`, use `apt-get` as shown in the following command:

```
sudo apt-get install mencoder
```

An explanation of the command-line options can be found in the man `mencoder` pages.

How to do it...

Create `timelapseGUI.py` in the same directory as `cameraGUI.py` by performing the following steps:

1. Start by importing the supporting modules (including `cameraGUI`) as shown in the following code snippet:

```
#!/usr/bin/python3
#timelapseGUI.py
import tkinter as TK
from tkinter import messagebox
import cameraGUI as camGUI
import time
```

2. Extend the `cameraGUI.SET` class with settings for the time lapse and encoding as follows:

```
class SET(camGUI.SET):
  TL_SIZE=(1920,1080)
  ENC_PROG="mencoder -nosound -ovc lavc -lavcopts"
  ENC_PROG+=" vcodec=mpeg4:aspect=16/9:vbitrate=8000000"
  ENC_PROG+=" -vf scale=%d:%d"%(TL_SIZE[0],TL_SIZE[1])
  ENC_PROG+=" -o %s -mf type=jpeg:fps=24 mf://@%s"
  LIST_FILE="image_list.txt"
```

3. Extend the main `cameraGUI` class with an additional function to perform the time lapse as follows:

```
class cameraGUI(camGUI.cameraGUI):
  def camTimelapse(filename,size=SET.TL_SIZE,
                   timedelay=10,numImages=10):
    with camGUI.picam.PiCamera() as camera:
      camera.resolution = size
      for count, name in \
            enumerate(camera.capture_continuous(filename)):
        print("Timelapse: %s"%name)
        if count == numImages:
          break
        time.sleep(timedelay)
```

4. Add the extra controls for the time-lapse GUI as shown in the following code snippet:

```
    def __init__(self,parent):
      super(cameraGUI,self).__init__(parent)
      self.parent=parent
      TK.Frame.__init__(self,self.parent,background="white")
```

```
self.numImageTL=TK.StringVar()
self.peroidTL=TK.StringVar()
self.totalTimeTL=TK.StringVar()
self.genVideoTL=TK.IntVar()
labelnumImgTK=TK.Label(self.parent,text="TL:#Images")
labelperoidTK=TK.Label(self.parent,text="TL:Delay")
labeltotalTimeTK=TK.Label(self.parent,
                          text="TL:TotalTime")
self.numImgSpn=TK.Spinbox(self.parent,
                  textvariable=self.numImageTL,
                  from_=1,to=99999,
                  width=5,state="readonly",
                  command=self.calcTLTotalTime)
self.peroidSpn=TK.Spinbox(self.parent,
                  textvariable=self.peroidTL,
                  from_=1,to=99999,width=5,
                  command=self.calcTLTotalTime)
self.totalTime=TK.Label(self.parent,
                  textvariable=self.totalTimeTL)
self.TLBtn=TK.Button(self.parent,text="TL GO!",
                  command=self.timelapse)
genChk=TK.Checkbutton(self.parent,text="GenVideo",
                  command=self.genVideoChk,
                  variable=self.genVideoTL)
labelnumImgTK.grid(row=3,column=0)
self.numImgSpn.grid(row=4,column=0)
labelperoidTK.grid(row=3,column=1)
self.peroidSpn.grid(row=4,column=1)
labeltotalTimeTK.grid(row=3,column=2)
self.totalTime.grid(row=4,column=2)
self.TLBtn.grid(row=3,column=3)
genChk.grid(row=4,column=3)
self.numImageTL.set(10)
self.peroidTL.set(5)
self.genVideoTL.set(1)
self.calcTLTotalTime()
```

5. Add supporting functions to calculate the settings and handle the time lapse as follows:

```
def btnState(self,state):
  self.TLBtn["state"] = state
  super(cameraGUI,self).btnState(state)
def calcTLTotalTime(self):
  numImg=float(self.numImageTL.get())-1
```

```
            peroid=float(self.peroidTL.get())
            if numImg<0:
              numImg=1
            self.totalTimeTL.set(numImg*peroid)
        def timelapse(self):
            self.msg("Running Timelapse")
            self.btnState("disabled")
            self.update()
            self.tstamp="TL"+cameraGUI.timestamp()
            cameraGUI.camTimelapse(self.tstamp+'{counter:03d}.jpg',
                                    SET.TL_SIZE,
                                    float(self.peroidTL.get()),
                                    int(self.numImageTL.get()))
            if self.genVideoTL.get() == 1:
              self.genTLVideo()
            self.btnState("active")
            TK.messagebox.showinfo("Timelapse Complete",
                                    "Processing complete")
            self.update()
```

6. Add supporting functions to handle and generate the time-lapse video as follows:

```
        def genTLVideo(self):
            self.msg("Generate video...")
            cameraGUI.run("ls "+self.tstamp+"*.jpg > "
                                    +SET.LIST_FILE)
            cameraGUI.run(SET.ENC_PROG%(self.tstamp+".avi",
                                    SET.LIST_FILE))
            self.msg(self.tstamp+".avi")
    #End
```

Next, create the following `cameraGUI2timelapse.py` script to use the GUI:

```
#!/usr/bin/python3
#cameraGUI2timelapse.py
import tkinter as TK
import timelapseGUI as GUI

root=TK.Tk()
root.title("Camera GUI")
cam=GUI.cameraGUI(root)
TK.mainloop()
#End
```

We import `timelapseGUI` instead of `cameraGUI`; this will add the `timelapseGUI` module to the `cameraGUI` script.

Run the example with the following command:

```
python3 cameraGUI2timelapse.py
```

How it works...

The `timelapseGUI.py` script allows us to take the classes defined in `cameraGUI.py` and extend them. The previous `cameraGUI` class inherits all of the content of the `TK.Frame` class, and using the same technique we can also inherit the `SET` and `cameraGUI` classes in our application.

We add some additional settings to the `SET` class to provide the settings for `mencoder` (to encode the video).

We shall extend the basic `cameraGUI` class by inheriting from `camGUI.cameraGUI` and defining a new version of `__init__()` for the class. Using `super()`, we can include the functionality from the original `__init__()` function and then define the extra controls we want to add to the GUI. The extended GUI is shown in the following screenshot:

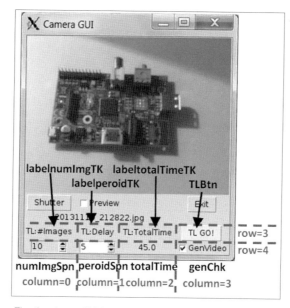

The time-lapse GUI layout that extends the base camera GUI

We define the following control variables:

- `self.numImageTL`: This is linked to the value of the `numImgSpn` spinbox control to specify the number of images we want to take in our time lapse (and also provide the `numimages` value for `camTimelapse`).

- `self.peroidTL`: This is linked to the value of the `peroidSpn` spinbox control; it determines how many seconds there should be between the time-lapse images (and also provides the `timedelay` value for `camTimelapse`).

- `self.totalTimeTL`: This is linked to the `totalTime` label object. It is calculated using the number of images and the `timedelay` time between each to indicate how long the time lapse will run for.

- `self.genVideoTL`: This controls the state of the `genChk` checkbox control. It is used to determine whether the video has been generated after the time-lapse images have been taken.

We link both of the spinbox controls to `self.calcTLTotalTime()` so that when they are changed, the `totalTimeTL` value is also updated (although it is not called if they are edited directly). We link `genChk` to `self.genVideoChk()` and `TLBtn` to `self.timelapse()`.

Finally, we specify the positions of the controls using `grid()` and set some defaults for the time-lapse settings.

The function `self.genVideoChk()` is called when the `genChk` checkbox is ticked or cleared. This allows us to inform the user of the effect that this checkbox has by generating a pop-up message box to say if the video will be generated at the end of the time lapse or if just images will be created.

When the **TL GO!** button is pressed (`TLBtn`), `self.timelapse()` is called; this will disable the **Shutter** and **TL GO!** buttons (since we have also extended the `self.btnState()` function). The `self.timelapse()` function will also set the `self.tstamp` value so the same timestamp can be used for the images and the resulting video file (if generated).

The time lapse is run using the `camTimelapse()` function as shown in the following code:

```
def camTimelapse(filename,size=SET.TL_SIZE,
                   timedelay=10,numImages=10):
  with camGUI.picam.PiCamera() as camera:
    camera.resolution = size
    for count, name in \
          enumerate(camera.capture_continuous(filename)):
      print("Timelapse: %s"%name)
      if count == numImages:
        break
      time.sleep(timedelay)
```

We create a new `PiCamera` object, set the image resolution, and start a for...in loop for `capture_continuous()`. Each time an image is taken, we print the filename and then wait for the required `timedelay` value. Finally, when the required number of images have been taken, we break out of the loop and continue.

Once this is complete, we check the value of `self.genVideoTL` to determine if we want to generate the video (which is handled by `genTLVideo()`).

To generate the video, we first run the following command to create an `image_list.txt` file of the images:

```
ls <self.tstamp>*.jpg > image_list.txt
```

Then we run `mencoder` with the suitable settings (see man `mencoder` pages for what each item does) to create an MPEG4-encoded (8 Mbps) AVI file with 24 frames per second (fps) from the list of time-lapse images. The equivalent command (defined by `ENC_PROG`) is as follows:

```
mencoder -nosound -ovc lavc \
 -lavcopts vcodec=mpeg4:aspect=16/9:vbitrate=8000000 \
 -vf scale=1920:1080 -o <self.tstamp>.avi \
 -mf type=jpeg:fps=24 mf://@image_list.txt
```

> Long commands can be split into several lines on the command terminal by using the \ character. This allows you to continue writing the command on another line, only executing it when you finish a line without the \ character.

There's more...

This chapter uses methods such as class inheritance and function overriding to structure and reuse our code in a number of different ways. When used correctly, these methods could enable us to design complex systems in a logical and flexible way.

Additionally, when generating your own time-lapse sequences, you can opt to switch off the LED on the camera module or make use of the low-light version of the Raspberry Pi camera: the NoIR camera.

Class inheritance and function overriding

In the previous example, we used some clever coding in order to reuse our original `cameraGUI` class and create a plug-in file that extends its features.

The class name does not have to be the same as `cameraGUI` (we just use it in this case so we can swap out the additional GUI components just by changing the file we import). In fact, we could define one basic class that contains several general functions and then extend the class by inheritance into a number of subclasses; here, each subclass defines specific behaviors, functions, and data. The extending and structuring of the subclasses is shown in the following diagram:

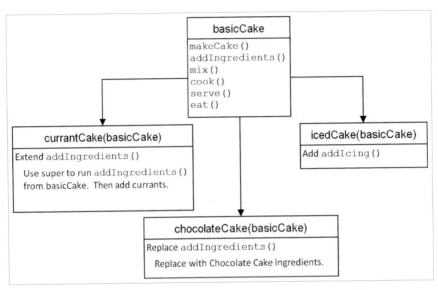

This diagram shows how classes can be extended and structured

To illustrate this, we will take a noncode example where we have written a general recipe for preparing a cake. You can then extend the **basicCake** recipe by inheriting all the **basicCake** elements and add some additional steps (equivalent code functions) to perhaps add icing/frosting on top to make an **icedCake(basicCake)** class. We did this with our SET class by adding additional items to an existing class (we just chose not to change the name).

We can also add in some additional elements to the existing steps (add some currants at the **addIngredients** step and create **currantCake(basicCake)**). We have done this using the `super()` function in our code by adding additional parts to the __init__() function.

You could even override some of the original functions by replacing them with new ones; for instance, you could replace the original recipe for **basicCake** with one to make **chocolateCake(basicCake)** while still using the same instructions to cook and so on. We can do this by defining replacement functions with the same names without using `super()`.

Using structured design in this way can become very powerful since we can easily create many variants of the same sort of object but have all the common elements defined in the same place. This has many advantages when it comes to testing, developing, and maintaining large and complex systems. The key here is to take an overall view of your project and try to identify the common elements before you begin. You will find that the better the structure you have, the easier it is to develop and improve it.

For more information on this, it is worth reading up on object oriented design methods and how to use **Unified Modelling Language** (**UML**) to help you describe and understand your system.

Disabling the camera LED

If you want to create time-lapse videos at night or next to windows, you may notice that the red camera LED (which lights up for every shot) adds unwanted light or reflections. Fortunately, the camera LED can be controlled through the GPIO. The LED is controlled using GPIO.BCM Pin 5; unfortunately, there isn't an equivalent GPIO.BOARD pin number for it.

To add it to a Python script, use the following code:

```
import RPi.GPIO as GPIO

GPIO.cleanup()
GPIO.setmode(GPIO.BCM)
CAMERALED=5 #GPIO using BCM numbering
GPIO.setup(CAMERALED, GPIO.OUT)
GPIO.output(CAMERALED,False)
```

Alternatively, you could use the LED for something else; for example, as an indicator as part of a delay timer that provides a countdown and warning that the camera is about to take an image.

Pi NoIR – taking night shots

There is also a variant of the Raspberry Pi camera module available called **Pi NoIR**. This version of the camera is the same as the original, except that the internal infrared filter has been removed. Among other things, this allows you to use infrared lighting to illuminate areas at night time (just like most night security cameras do) and see everything that is happening in the dark!

The MagPi Issue 18 (www.themagpi.com) has published an excellent feature explaining the other uses of the Pi NoIR camera module.

Creating a stop frame animation

Stop frame (or stop motion) animation is the process of taking a series of still images of items, while making very small movements (typically of an easily moveable object such as a doll or plasticine model) in each frame. When the frames are assembled into a video, the small movements combine to produce an animation.

Multiple images can be combined into an animation

Traditionally, such animations were made by taking hundreds or even thousands of individual photos on a film camera (such as a Cine Super 8 movie camera) and then sending the film off to be developed and playing back the results some weeks later. Despite the inspiring creations by Nick Park at Aardman Animations, including Wallace and Gromit (which are full-length, stop frame animation films), this was a hobby that was a little out of reach for most.

In the modern digital age, we can take multiple images quickly and easily with the luxury of reviewing the results almost instantly. Now anyone can try their hand at their own animated masterpieces with very little cost or effort.

We will extend our original **Camera GUI** with some extra features that will allow us to create our own stop frame animations. It will allow us to take images and try them out in a sequence before generating a finished video for us.

Getting ready

The software setup for this example will be the same as the previous time-lapse example. Again, we will need `mencoder` to be installed and we need the `cameraGUI.py` file in the same directory.

You will also need something to animate, ideally something you can put in different poses, like the two dolls shown in the following image:

Two potential stars for our stop frame animation

How to do it...

Create `animateGUI.py` in the same directory as `cameraGUI.py` by performing the following steps:

1. Start by importing the supporting modules (including `cameraGUI`) as shown in the following code:

```
#!/usr/bin/python3
#animateGUI.py
import tkinter as TK
from tkinter import messagebox
import time
import os
import cameraGUI as camGUI
```

2. Extend the `cameraGUI.SET` class with settings for the image size and encoding as follows:

```
class SET(camGUI.SET):
  TL_SIZE=(1920,1080)
  ENC_PROG="mencoder -nosound -ovc lavc -lavcopts"
  ENC_PROG+=" vcodec=mpeg4:aspect=16/9:vbitrate=8000000"
  ENC_PROG+=" -vf scale=%d:%d"%(TL_SIZE[0],TL_SIZE[1])
  ENC_PROG+=" -o %s -mf type=jpeg:fps=24 mf://@%s"
  LIST_FILE="image_list.txt"
```

3. Extend the main `cameraGUI` class with the functions required for the animation as follows:

```
class cameraGUI(camGUI.cameraGUI):
  def diff(a, b):
    b = set(b)
    return [aa for aa in a if aa not in b]
  def __init__(self,parent):
    super(cameraGUI,self).__init__(parent)
    self.parent=parent
    TK.Frame.__init__(self,self.parent,
                      background="white")
    self.theList = TK.Variable()
    self.imageListbox=TK.Listbox(self.parent,
                  listvariable=self.theList,
                    selectmode=TK.EXTENDED)
    self.imageListbox.grid(row=0, column=4,columnspan=2,
                          sticky=TK.N+TK.S+TK.E+TK.W)
    yscroll = TK.Scrollbar(command=self.imageListbox.yview,
                                   orient=TK.VERTICAL)
    yscroll.grid(row=0, column=6, sticky=TK.N+TK.S)
    self.imageListbox.configure(yscrollcommand=yscroll.set)
    self.trimBtn=TK.Button(self.parent,text="Trim",
                               command=self.trim)
    self.trimBtn.grid(row=1,column=4)
    self.speed = TK.IntVar()
    self.speed.set(20)
    self.speedScale=TK.Scale(self.parent,from_=1,to=30,
                              orient=TK.HORIZONTAL,
                              variable=self.speed,
                              label="Speed (fps)")
    self.speedScale.grid(row=2,column=4)
    self.genBtn=TK.Button(self.parent,text="Generate",
                              command=self.generate)
    self.genBtn.grid(row=2,column=5)
    self.btnAniTxt=TK.StringVar()
    self.btnAniTxt.set("Animate")
    self.animateBtn=TK.Button(self.parent,
              textvariable=self.btnAniTxt,
                  command=self.animate)
    self.animateBtn.grid(row=1,column=5)
    self.animating=False
    self.updateList()
```

4. Add functions to list the images that were taken and remove them from the list using the following code snippet:

```
def shutter(self):
    super(cameraGUI,self).shutter()
    self.updateList()

def updateList(self):
    filelist=[]
    for files in os.listdir("."):
        if files.endswith(".jpg"):
            filelist.append(files)
    filelist.sort()
    self.theList.set(tuple(filelist))
    self.canvas.update()

def generate(self):
    self.msg("Generate video...")
    cameraGUI.run("ls *.jpg > "+SET.LIST_FILE)
    filename=cameraGUI.timestamp()+".avi"
    cameraGUI.run(SET.ENC_PROG%(filename,SET.LIST_FILE))
    self.msg(filename)
    TK.messagebox.showinfo("Encode Complete",
                           "Video: "+filename)
def trim(self):
    print("Trim List")
    selected = map(int,self.imageListbox.curselection())
    trim=cameraGUI.diff(range(self.imageListbox.size()),
                                            selected)
    for item in trim:
        filename=self.theList.get()[item]
        self.msg("Rename file %s"%filename)
        #We could delete os.remove() but os.rename() allows
        #us to change our minds (files are just renamed).
        os.rename(filename,
                  filename.replace(".jpg",".jpg.bak"))
    self.imageListbox.selection_clear(0,
                        last=self.imageListbox.size())
    self.updateList()
```

5. Include functions to perform the test animation using the image list as follows:

```
def animate(self):
  print("Animate Toggle")
  if (self.animating==True):
    self.btnAniTxt.set("Animate")
    self.animating=False
  else:
    self.btnAniTxt.set("STOP")
    self.animating=True
    self.doAnimate()

def doAnimate(self):
  imageList=[]
  selected = self.imageListbox.curselection()
  if len(selected)==0:
    selected=range(self.imageListbox.size())
  print(selected)
  if len(selected)==0:
    TK.messagebox.showinfo("Error",
                    "There are no images to display!")
    self.animate()
  elif len(selected)==1:
    filename=self.theList.get()[int(selected[0])]
    self.updateDisp(filename,SET.PV_SIZE)
    self.animate()
  else:
    for idx,item in enumerate(selected):
      self.msg("Generate Image: %d/%d"%(idx+1,
                                 len(selected)))
      filename=self.theList.get()[int(item)]
      aImage=cameraGUI.getTKImage(filename,SET.PV_SIZE)
      imageList.append(aImage)
    print("Apply Images")
    canvasList=[]
    for idx,aImage in enumerate(imageList):
      self.msg("Apply Image: %d/%d"%(idx+1,
                                 len(imageList)))
      canvasList.append(self.canvas.create_image(0, 0,
                          anchor=TK.NW,
                          image=imageList[idx],
                          state=TK.HIDDEN))
    self.cycleImages(canvasList)
```

```
def cycleImages(self,canvasList):
  while (self.animating==True):
    print("Cycle Images")
    for idx,aImage in enumerate(canvasList):
      self.msg("Cycle Image: %d/%d"%(idx+1,
                            len(canvasList)))
      self.canvas.itemconfigure(canvasList[idx],
                            state=TK.NORMAL)
      if idx>=1:
        self.canvas.itemconfigure(canvasList[idx-1],
                            state=TK.HIDDEN)
      elif len(canvasList)>1:
        self.canvas.itemconfigure(
                    canvasList[len(canvasList)-1],
                            state=TK.HIDDEN)
      self.canvas.update()
      time.sleep(1/self.speed.get())
#End
```

Next, create the following `cameraGUI3animate.py` file to use the GUI:

```
#!/usr/bin/python3
#cameraGUI3animate.py
import tkinter as TK
import animateGUI as GUI

#Define Tkinter App
root=TK.Tk()
root.title("Camera GUI")
cam=GUI.cameraGUI(root)
TK.mainloop()
#End
```

Run the example with the following command:

```
python3 cameraGUI3animate.py
```

How it works...

Once again, we create a new class based on the original `cameraGUI` class. This time, we define the following GUI with six extra controls:

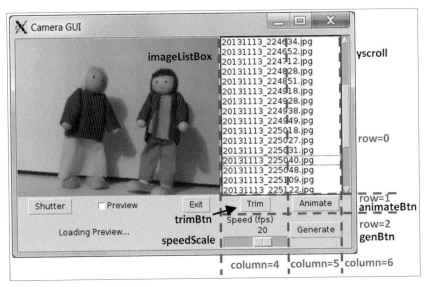

The animation GUI layout

We create a listbox control (`imageListbox`) that will contain a list of the `.jpg` images in the current directory (`self.theList`). This control has a vertical scroll bar (`yscroll`) linked to it to allow easy scrolling of the list, and `selectmode=TK.EXTENDED` is used to allow multiple selections using *Shift* and *Ctrl* (for block and group selections).

Next we add a **Trim** button (`timeBtn`) that will call `self.trim()`. This will remove any items that have not been selected in the list. We use `curselection()` to get a list of the currently selected items from the `imageListbox` control. The `curselection()` function normally returns a list of indexes that are numerical strings, so we use `map(int,...)` to convert the result into a list of integers.

We use this list to get all the indexes that have not been selected using our utility `diff(a,b)` function. The function compares a full list of indexes against the selected ones and returns any that haven't been selected.

The `self.trim()` function uses `os.rename()` to change the filename extensions from `.jpg` to `.jpg.bak` for all the nonselected images. We could delete them using `os.remove()`, but we only really want to rename them to stop them from appearing in the list and final video. The list is repopulated using `self.updateList()`, which updates `self.theList` with a list of all the `.jpg` files available.

We add a scale control (`speedScale`) that is linked to `self.speed` and used to control the playback speed of the animation test. As earlier, we add a **Generate** button (`genBtn`) that calls `self.generate()`.

Finally, we add the **Animate** button (`animateBtn`). The text for the button is linked to `self.btnAniTxt` (making it easy to change within our program), and when pressed, the button calls `self.animate()`.

We override the original `shutter()` function from the original `cameraGUI` script by adding a call to `self.updateList()`. This ensures that after an image has been taken, the list of images is updated with the new image automatically. Again, we use `super()` to ensure that the original functionality is also performed.

The `animate()` function (called by clicking on the **Animate** button) allows us to test a selection of images to see whether they will make a good animation or not. When the button is clicked on, we change the text of the button to **STOP**, the `self.animating` flag to **True** (to indicate that the animation mode is running), and call `doAnimate()`.

The `doAnimate()` function first gets a list of currently selected images in the `imageListbox` control, generates a list of `TK.PhotoImage` objects, and attaches them to the `self.canvas` object in the GUI. Although, if only one image has been selected, we display it directly using `self.updateDisp()`. Alternatively, if no images have been selected, it will try to use them all (unless the list is empty, in which case it will inform the user that there are no images to animate). When we have more than one `TK.PhotoImage` object linked to the canvas, we can loop through them using the `cycleImages()` function.

The `TK.PhotoImage` objects are all created with their states set to `TK.HIDDEN`, which means they are not visible on the canvas. To produce the animation effect, the `cycleImages()` function will set each image to `TK.NORMAL` and then `TK.HIDDEN` again, allowing each frame to be displayed for 1 divided by `self.speed` (the fps value set by the Scale control) before showing the next.

The `cycleImages()` function will perform the animation as long as `self.animating` is **True**, that is, until the `animateBtn` object is clicked on again.

Once the user is happy with their animation, they can generate the video using the **Generate** button (`genBtn`). The `generate()` function will call `mencoder` to generate the final video of all the images in the `imageListbox` control.

If you really want to get into producing animations, you should consider adding some extra features to help you, such as the ability to duplicate and reorder frames. You may want to add some manual adjustments for the camera to avoid white balance and lighting fluctuations caused by the automatic settings of the camera.

There's more...

The camera module is ideal for close-up photography due to its small size and ability to be remotely controlled. By using small lenses or adding hardware controls, you could make a purpose-built animation machine.

Improving the focus

The Raspberry Pi camera lens has been designed mainly for middle to long distance photography, and it therefore has trouble focusing on objects that are closer than 25 cm (10 inches). However, using some basic lenses, we can adjust the effective focal length and make it more suitable for macro photography. You can use add-on lenses that are available for mobile phones or credit card style magnifier lenses to adjust the focus, as shown in the following images:

An add-on macro lens (right) and a credit card magnifier (left) can improve the focus of close-up items

Creating a hardware shutter

Of course, while it is useful to have a display available to review the images taken, it is often useful to be able to simply press a physical button to take an image. Fortunately, this is just a matter of attaching a button (and resistor) to a GPIO pin, as we have done previously (see the *Responding to a button* recipe in *Chapter 6, Using Python to Drive Hardware*), and creating suitable GPIO control code to call our `cameraGUI.camCapture()` function. The code for this is as follows:

```
#!/usr/bin/python3
#shutterCam.py
import RPi.GPIO as GPIO
import cameraGUI as camGUI
import time
```

```
GPIO.setmode(GPIO.BOARD)
CAMERA_BTN=12 #GPIO Pin 12
GPIO.setup(CAMERA_BTN,GPIO.IN,pull_up_down=GPIO.PUD_UP)
count=1
try:
  while True:
    btn_val = GPIO.input(CAMERA_BTN)
    #Take photo when Pin 12 at 0V
    if btn_val==False:
      camGUI.cameraGUI.camCapture("Snap%03d.jpg"%count,
                            camGUI.SET.NORM_SIZE)
      count+=1
    time.sleep(0.1)
finally:
  GPIO.cleanup()
#End
```

The previous code will take a picture when the button is pressed. The following diagram shows the connections and circuit diagram required to achieve this:

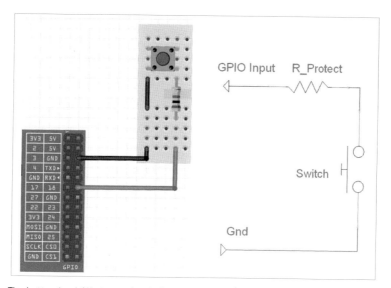

The button (and 1K ohm resistor) should be connected between pins 12 and 6 (GND)

You don't even have to stop here since you can add buttons and switches for any of the controls or settings for the camera if you want to. You can even use other hardware (such as infrared sensors and so on) to trigger the camera to take an image or video.

Making a QR code reader

You have probably seen QR codes in various places, and perhaps even used a few to pick up links from posters or adverts. However, they can be far more useful if you make your own. The following example discusses how we can use the Raspberry Pi to read QR codes and the hidden content (or even link to an audio file or video).

This could be used to create your own personalized Raspberry Pi QR code jukebox, perhaps as an aid for children to provide solutions to math problems or even to play an audio file of you reading your kid's favorite book as they follow along page by page. The following screenshot is an example of a QR code:

You can use QR codes to make magical self-reading books

Getting ready

This example requires a setup similar to the previous examples (except we won't need `mencoder` this time). We will need to install **ZBar**, which is a cross-platform QR code and barcode reader, and **flite** (a text-to-speech utility that we used in *Chapter 6, Using Python to Drive Hardware*).

To install ZBar and flite, use `apt-get` as shown in the following command:

```
sudo apt-get install zbar-tools flite
```

There are Python 2.7 libraries available for Zbar, but they are not currently compatible with Python 3. Zbar also includes a real-time scanner (`zbarcam`) that uses video input to detect barcodes and QR codes automatically. Unfortunately, this isn't compatible with the Raspberry Pi camera either.

This isn't a big problem for us since we can use the `zbarimg` program directly to detect the QR codes from images taken with `picamera`.

Once you have the software installed, you will need some QR codes to scan (see the *There's more...* section in *Generating QR codes*) and some suitably named MP3 files (these could be recordings of you reading the pages of a book or music tracks).

How to do it...

Create the following `qrcodeGUI.py` script in the same directory as `cameraGUI.py`:

```python
#!/usr/bin/python3
#qrcodeGUI.py
import tkinter as TK
from tkinter import messagebox
import subprocess
import cameraGUI as camGUI

class SET(camGUI.SET):
  QR_SIZE=(640,480)
  READ_QR="zbarimg "

class cameraGUI(camGUI.cameraGUI):
  def run_p(cmd):
    print("RunP:"+cmd)
    proc=subprocess.Popen(cmd,shell=True,stdout=subprocess.PIPE)
    result=""
    for line in proc.stdout:
      result=str(line,"utf-8")
    return result
  def __init__(self,parent):
    super(cameraGUI,self).__init__(parent)
    self.parent=parent
    TK.Frame.__init__(self,self.parent,background="white")
    self.qrScan=TK.IntVar()
    self.qrRead=TK.IntVar()
    self.qrStream=TK.IntVar()
    self.resultQR=TK.StringVar()
    self.btnQrTxt=TK.StringVar()
    self.btnQrTxt.set("QR GO!")
    self.QRBtn=TK.Button(self.parent,textvariable=self.btnQrTxt,
                                          command=self.qrGet)
    readChk=TK.Checkbutton(self.parent,text="Read",
                              variable=self.qrRead)
    streamChk=TK.Checkbutton(self.parent,text="Stream",
                                variable=self.qrStream)
    labelQR=TK.Label(self.parent,textvariable=self.resultQR)
    readChk.grid(row=3,column=0)
    streamChk.grid(row=3,column=1)
    self.QRBtn.grid(row=3,column=3)
    labelQR.grid(row=4,columnspan=4)
```

```
          self.scan=False
      def qrGet(self):
        if (self.scan==True):
          self.btnQrTxt.set("QR GO!")
          self.btnState("active")
          self.scan=False
        else:
          self.msg("Get QR Code")
          self.btnQrTxt.set("STOP")
          self.btnState("disabled")
          self.scan=True
          self.qrScanner()
      def qrScanner(self):
        found=False
        while self.scan==True:
          self.resultQR.set("Taking image...")
          self.update()
          cameraGUI.camCapture(SET.PREVIEW_FILE,SET.QR_SIZE)
          self.resultQR.set("Scanning for QRCode...")
          self.update()
          #check for QR code in image
          qrcode=cameraGUI.run_p(SET.READ_QR+SET.PREVIEW_FILE)
          if len(qrcode)>0:
            self.msg("Got barcode: %s"%qrcode)
            qrcode=qrcode.strip("QR-Code:").strip('\n')
            self.resultQR.set(qrcode)
            self.scan=False
            found=True
          else:
            self.resultQR.set("No QRCode Found")
        if found:
          self.qrAction(qrcode)
          self.btnState("active")
          self.btnQrTxt.set("QR GO!")
        self.update()
      def qrAction(self,qrcode):
        if self.qrRead.get() == 1:
          self.msg("Read:"+qrcode)
          cameraGUI.run("sudo flite -t '"+qrcode+"'")
        if self.qrStream.get() == 1:
          self.msg("Stream:"+qrcode)
          cameraGUI.run("omxplayer '"+qrcode+"'")
        if self.qrRead.get() == 0 and self.qrStream.get() == 0:
          TK.messagebox.showinfo("QR Code",self.resultQR.get())
    #End
```

Next, create a copy of `cameraGUItimelapse.py` or `cameraGUIanimate.py` and call it `cameraGUIqrcode.py`. Again, make sure you import the new file for the GUI using the following code:

```
import qrcodeGUI as GUI
```

The GUI with QR code will look as shown in the following screenshot:

The QR code GUI

How it works...

The new `qrcodeGUI.py` file adds the **Read** and **Play** checkbox controls and a button control to start scanning for QR codes. When **QR GO!** is clicked on, `self.qrGet()` will start a cycle of taking images and checking the result with `zbarimg`. If `zbarimg` finds a QR code in the image, then the scanning will stop and the result will be displayed. Otherwise, it will continue to scan until the **STOP** button is clicked on. While the scanning is taking place, the text for `QRBtn` is changed to **STOP**.

In order to capture the output of `zbarimg`, we have to change how we run the command slightly. To do this, we define `run_p()` that uses the following code:

```
proc=subprocess.Popen(cmd,shell=True,stdout=subprocess.PIPE)
```

This returns `stdout` as part of the `proc` object, which contains the output of the `zbarimg` program. We then extract the resulting QR code that was read from the image (if one was found).

When **Read** is selected, `flite` is used to read out the QR code, and if **Play** is selected, `omxplayer` is used to play the file (assuming the QR code contains a suitable link).

For the best results, it is recommended that you take a preview shot first to ensure that you have lined up the target QR code correctly before running the QR scanner.

Example QR code page markers (page001.mp3 and page002.mp3)

The previous QR codes contain `page001.mp3` and `page002.mp3`. These QR codes allow us to play files with the same name if placed in the same directory as our script. You can generate your own QR codes by following the instructions in the *There's more...* section in this recipe.

You could even use the book's ISBN barcode to select a different directory of MP3s based on the barcode read; the barcode allows you to reuse the same set of page-numbered QR codes for any book you like.

There's more...

To make use of the previous example, you can use the example in the next section to generate a range of QR codes to use.

Generating QR codes

You can create QR codes using **PyQRCode** (see `https://pypi.python.org/pypi/PyQRCode` for more information).

You can install PyQRCode using the PIP Python manager as follows (see the *Getting ready* section of the *Displaying photo information in an application* recipe in *Chapter 3, Using Python for Automation and Productivity*):

```
sudo pip-3.2 install pyqrcode
```

To encode QR codes in the PNG format, PyQrCode uses PyPNG (`https://github.com/drj11/pypng`), which can be installed with the following command:

```
sudo pip-3.2 install pypng
```

Use the following `generateQRCodes.py` script to generate QR codes to link to files, such as the `page001.mp3` and `page002.mp3` files that you have recorded:

```python
#!/usr/bin/python3
#generateQRCodes.py
import pyqrcode
valid=False
print("QR-Code generator")
while(valid==False):
    inputpages=input("How many pages?")
    try:
      PAGES=int(inputpages)
      valid=True
    except ValueError:
      print("Enter valid number.")
      pass
print("Creating QR-Codes for "+str(PAGES)+" pages:")
for i in range(PAGES):
  file="page%03d"%(i+1)
  qr_code = pyqrcode.create(file+".mp3")
  qr_code.png(file+".png")
  print("Generated QR-Code for "+file)
print("Completed")
#End
```

Run this code using the following command:

```
python3 generateQRCodes.py
```

The previous code will create a set of QR codes that can be used to activate the required MP3 file and read the page out loud (or play the file that you have linked to it).

See also

The **Open Source Computer Vision** (**OpenCV**) project is a very powerful image and video processing engine; more details are available at `http://opencv.org`.

By combining the camera with OpenCV, the Raspberry Pi is able to recognize and interact with its environment.

An excellent example of this is Samuel Matos's RS4 OpenCV Self-balancing Robot (`http://roboticssamy.blogspot.pt`) that can seek out and respond to various custom signs; the camera module can be used to navigate and control the robot.

9
Building Robots

In this chapter, we will cover:

- ▸ Building a Rover-Pi robot with forward driving motors
- ▸ Using advanced motor control
- ▸ Building a six-legged Pi-Bug robot
- ▸ Avoiding objects and obstacles
- ▸ Getting a sense of direction

Introduction

A little computer with a "brain the size of a planet" (to quote Douglas Adams, the author of *Hitchhikers Guide to the Galaxy*) is perfect to be the brain of your own robotic creation. In reality, the Raspberry Pi probably provides far more processing power than a little robot or rover would need; however, its small size, excellent connectivity, and fairly low-power requirements mean that it is ideally suited.

This chapter will focus on exploring the various ways in which we can combine motors or servos to produce robotic movement and use sensors to gather information and allow our creation to act upon it.

 Be sure to check out the *Appendix, Hardware and Software List*; it lists all the items used in this chapter and the places you can obtain them from.

Building a Rover-Pi robot with forward driving motors

Creating robots does not need to be an expensive hobby. A small, Rover-type robot can be constructed using household items for the chassis (the base everything is attached to), and a couple of small driving motors can be used to move it.

The Rover-Pi robot is a small, buggy-type robot that has just two wheels and a skid or caster at the front to allow it to turn. One such robot is shown in the following image:

A home-built Rover-Pi robot

While it may not be in the same league as a Mars Exploration Rover, however, as you will see, there is plenty for you to experiment with.

You can also purchase many inexpensive robot kits that contain most of what you need in a single package (see the *There's more...* section at the end of this example).

Getting ready

The Rover we are building will need to contain the elements shown in the following diagram:

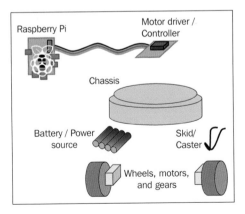

The separate parts of the Rover-Pi robot

The elements are discussed in detail, as follows:

- **Chassis**: This example uses a modified, battery-operated push nightlight (although any suitable platform can be used). Remember that the larger and heavier your robot is, the more powerful the driving motors that will be needed to move it. Alternatively, you can use one of the chassis kits listed in the *There's more...* section. A suitable push nightlight is shown in the following image:

This push nightlight forms the basic chassis of a Rover-Pi robot

- **Front skid or caster**: This can be as simple as a large paper clip (76 mm / 3 inches) bent into shape or a small caster wheel. A skid works best when it is on a smooth surface, but it may get stuck on the carpet. A caster wheel works well on all surfaces, but sometimes, it can have problems turning.

- **Wheels, motors**, and **gears**: The wheel movement of the Rover-Pi robot is a combination of the motor, gears, and wheels. The gears are helpful as they allow a fast-spinning motor to turn the wheels at a slower speed and more force (torque); this will allow better control of our robot. A unit that combines the wheels, motors, and gears in a single unit is shown in the following image:

These wheels with built-in geared motors are ideal for small rovers

▶ **Battery/power source**: The Rover-Pi robot will be powered using 4x AA batteries fitted into the bay of the chassis. Alternatively, a standard battery holder can be used, or even a long wire connected to suitable power supply. It is recommended that you power the motors from a supply independent to the Raspberry Pi. This will help avoid a situation where the Raspberry Pi suddenly loses power when driving the motors, which require a big jump in current to move. Alternatively, you can power the Raspberry Pi with the batteries using a 5V regulator. The following image shows a chassis with 4x AA batteries:

4x AA batteries provide a power source to drive the wheels

▶ **Motor driver/controller**: Motors will require a voltage and current greater than the GPIO can handle. Therefore, we will use a **Darlington array module** (which uses a **ULN2003** chip). See the *There's more...* section at the end of this example for more details on how this particular module works. The following image shows a Darlington array module:

This Darlington array module available at dx.com can be used to drive small motors

- **Small cable ties or wire ties**: This will allow us to attach items such as the motors or controller to the chassis. The following image shows the use of cable ties:

We use cable ties to secure the motors and wheels to the chassis

- **The Raspberry Pi connection**: The easiest setup is to attach the control wires to the Raspberry Pi using long cables, so you can easily control your robot directly using an attached screen and keyboard. Later, you can consider mounting the Raspberry Pi on the robot and controlling it remotely (or even autonomously if you include sensors and intelligence to make sense of them).

In this chapter, we will use the Python library **WiringPi2** to control the GPIO; see *Chapter 7, Sense and Display Real-world Data*, for details on how to install it using PIP (a Python package manager).

How to do it...

Perform the following steps to create a small Rover-Pi robot:

1. At the front of the chassis, you will need to mount the skid by bending the paperclip/wire into a V shape. Attach the paperclip/wire to the front of the chassis by drilling small holes on either side, and thread cable ties through the holes around the wire and pull tight to secure. The fitted wire skid should look similar to the one shown in the following image:

Wire skid fitted to the front of the Rover-Pi robot

2. Before you mount the wheels, you need to work out the approximate center of gravity of the chassis (do this with the batteries fitted in the chassis as they will affect the balance). Get a feel of where the center is by trying to balance the unit on two fingers on either side, and find out how far forward or backward the chassis tilts. For my unit, this was about 1 cm (approximately one-third of an inch) back from the center. You should aim to place the wheel axels slightly behind this so that the Rover will rest slightly forward on the skid. Mark the location of the wheels on the chassis.

3. Drill three holes on each side to mount the wheels using the cable ties. If the cable ties aren't long enough, you can join two together by pulling the end of one through the end of the other (only pull through far enough for the tie to grip so that it extends the tie). The following diagram shows how you can use the cable ties:

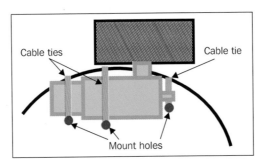

Securely fix the motors to the chassis

4. Next, test the motors by inserting the batteries into the unit; then, disconnect the wires that originally connected to the bulb and touch them to the motor contacts. Determine which connection on the motor should be positive and which should be negative for the motor to move the robot forward (the top of the wheel should move forward when the robot is facing forwards). Connect red and black wires to the motor (on mine, black equals negative at the top and red equals positive at the bottom of the motor), ensuring that the wires are long enough to reach anywhere on the chassis (around 14 cm, that is, approximately 5 and a half inches is enough for the nightlight).

The Rover-Pi robot components should be wired up as shown in the following diagram:

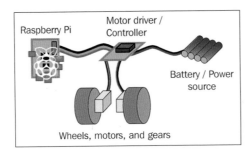

The wiring layout of the Rover-Pi robot

To make the connections, perform the following steps:

1. Connect the black wires of the motors to the **OUT 1** (left) and **OUT 2** (right) output of the Darlington module, and connect the red wires to the last pin (the COM connection).

2. Next, connect the battery wires to the **GND/V-** and **V+** connections at the bottom of the module.

3. Finally, connect the **GND** from the P1 connector (**Pin 6**) to the same **GND** connection.

4. Test the motor control by connecting 3.3V (P1 **Pin 1**) to **IN1** or **IN2** to simulate a GPIO output. When happy, connect GPIO P1 **Pin 16** to **IN1** (for left) and P1 **Pin 18** to **IN2** (for right).

The wiring should now match the details given in the following table:

Raspberry Pi P1	Darlington module
Pin 16: Left	IN1
Pin 18: Right	IN2
Pin 6: GND	GND/V- (marked with "–")
Motor 4x AA battery	
Positive side of battery	V+ (marked with "+")
Negative side of battery	GND/V- (marked with "–")
Motors	
Left motor: black wire	OUT 1 (top pin in white socket)
Right motor: black wire	OUT 2 (second pin in white socket)
Both motors: red wires	COM (last pin in white socket)

Use the following `rover_drivefwd.py` script to test the control:

```
#!/usr/bin/env python3
#rover_drivefwd.py
#HARDWARE SETUP
# P1
# 2[==X====LR====]26
# 1[=============]25
import time
import wiringpi2
ON=1;OFF=0
IN=0;OUT=1
STEP=0.5
PINS=[16,18] # PINS=[L-motor,R-motor]
FWD=[ON,ON]
RIGHT=[ON,OFF]
```

```
LEFT=[OFF,ON]
DEBUG=True

class motor:
  # Constructor
  def __init__(self,pins=PINS,steptime=STEP):
    self.pins = pins
    self.steptime=steptime
    self.GPIOsetup()

  def GPIOsetup(self):
    wiringpi2.wiringPiSetupPhys()
    for gpio in self.pins:
      wiringpi2.pinMode(gpio,OUT)

  def off(self):
    for gpio in self.pins:
      wiringpi2.digitalWrite(gpio,OFF)

  def drive(self,drive,step=STEP):
    for idx,gpio in enumerate(self.pins):
      wiringpi2.digitalWrite(gpio,drive[idx])
      if(DEBUG):print("%s:%s"%(gpio,drive[idx]))
    time.sleep(step)
    self.off()

  def cmd(self,char,step=STEP):
    if char == 'f':
      self.drive(FWD,step)
    elif char == 'r':
      self.drive(RIGHT,step)
    elif char == 'l':
      self.drive(LEFT,step)
    elif char == '#':
      time.sleep(step)

def main():
  import os
  if "CMD" in os.environ:
    CMD=os.environ["CMD"]
    INPUT=False
    print("CMD="+CMD)
  else:
```

```
      INPUT=True
    roverPi=motor()
    if INPUT:
      print("Enter CMDs [f,r,l,#]:")
      CMD=input()
    for idx,char in enumerate(CMD.lower()):
      if(DEBUG):print("Step %s of %s: %s"%(idx+1,len(CMD),char))
      roverPi.cmd(char)

if __name__=='__main__':
  try:
    main()
  finally:
    print ("Finish")
#End
```

 Remember that WiringPi2 should be installed before running the scripts in this chapter (see *Chapter 7, Sense and Display Real-world Data*).

Run the previous code using the following command:

```
sudo python3 rover_drivefwd.py
```

The script will prompt you with following message:

```
Enter CMDs [f,r,l,#]:
```

You can enter a series of commands to follow, for example:

```
ffrr#ff#llff
```

The previous command will instruct the Rover-Pi robot to perform a series of movements— forward (f), right (r), pause (#), and left (l).

How it works...

Once you have built the robot and wired up the wheels to the motor controller, you can discover how to control it.

Start by importing time (which will allow you to put pauses in the motor control) and wiringpi2 to allow control of the GPIO pins. Use wiringpi2 here since it makes it much easier to make use of IO expanders and other I²C devices if you want to later on.

Define values to use for setting the pins ON/OFF, for the direction IN/OUT, as well as the duration of each motor STEP. Also define which PINS are wired to the motor controls and our movements FWD, RIGHT, and LEFT. The movement is defined in such a way that by switching both motors ON, you will move forward; or, by switching just one motor ON, you will turn. By setting these values at the start of the file using variables, our code is easier to maintain and understand.

We define a `motor` class that will allow us to reuse it in other code or easily swap it with alternative `motor` classes so we can use other hardware if we want to. We set the default pins we are using and our `steptime` value (the `steptime` object defines how long we drive the motor(s) for each step). However, both can still be specified when initializing the object if desired.

Next, we call `GPIOsetup()`; it selects the physical pin numbering mode (so we can refer to the pins as they are located on the board). We also set all of the pins we are using to output.

Finally, for the `motor` class, we define the following three functions:

- The first function we define (called `off()`) will allow us to switch off the motors, so we cycle through the pins list and set each GPIO pin to low (and therefore, switch the motors off).

- The `drive()` function allows us to provide a list of drive actions (a combination of ON and OFF for each of the GPOI pins). Again, we cycle through each of the pins and set them to the corresponding drive action, wait for the step time, and then switch off the motors using the `off()` function.

- The last function we define (called `cmd()`) simply allows us to send char (a single character) and use it to select the set of drive actions we want to use (FWD, RIGHT, or LEFT), or wait (#).

For testing, `main()` allows us to specify a list of actions that need to be performed from the command line using the following command:

```
sudo CMD=f#lrr##fff python3 rover_drivefwd.py
```

Using `os.environ` (by importing the `os` module so we can use it), we can check for CMD in the command and use it as our list of drive actions. If no CMD command has been provided, we can use the `input()` function to prompt for a list of drive actions directly. To use the `motor` class, we set `roverPi=motor()`; this allows us to call the `cmd()` function (of the motor class) with each character from the list of drive actions.

There's more...

Your robot should only be limited by your own creativity. There are lots of suitable chassis you can use, other motors, wheels, and ways to control and drive the wheels. You should experiment and test things to determine which combinations work best together. That is all part of the fun!

Darlington array circuits

Darlington transistors are a low-cost way to drive higher powered devices, such as motors or even relays. They consist of two transistors arranged in a series, where one feeds the other (allowing the gain in the current to be multiplied). That is, if the first transistor has a gain of 20, and the second also has a gain of 20, together they will provide an overall gain of 400. This means that 1 mA on the base pin (1) will allow you to drive up to 400 mA through the Darlington transistor. The Darlington transistor's electrical symbol is shown in the following diagram:

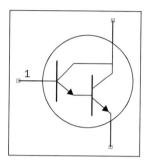

The electrical symbol for a Darlington transistor shows how two transistors are packaged together

The ULN2003 chip is used in the previous module and provides 7 NPN Darlington transistors (an 8-way version ULN2803 is also available if more output is required or to use with two stepper motors). The following diagram shows how a Darlington array can be used to drive motors:

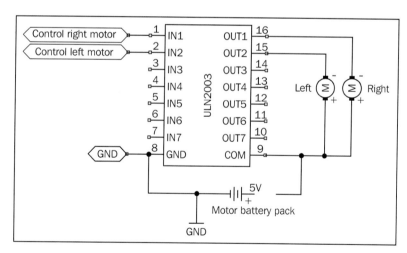

A Darlington array being used to drive two small motors

Each output from the chip can supply a maximum of 500 mA at up to 50V (enough to power most small motors). However, with extended use, the chip may overheat, so a heat sink is recommended when driving larger motors. An internal diode connected across each Darlington for protection is built into the chip. This is needed because when the motor moves without being driven (this can occur due to the natural momentum of the motor), it will act like a generator. A reverse voltage called **back EMF** is created, which would destroy the transistor if it wasn't dissipated back through the diode.

One disadvantage of the chip is that the positive supply voltage must always be connected to the common pin (COM), so each output is only able to sink current. That is, it will only drive the motor in one direction, with the positive voltage on COM and the negative voltage on the OUT pins. Therefore, we will need a different solution if we wish to drive our Rover-Pi robot in different directions (see the next example in the *Using advanced motor control* recipe).

These chips can also be used to drive certain types of stepper motors. One of the modules from dx.com includes a stepper motor as a part of the kit. Although the gearing is for very slow movement at around 12 seconds per rotation (too slow for a Rover), it is still interesting to use (for a clock perhaps).

Transistor and relay circuits

Relays are able to handle much higher powered motors since they are mechanical switches controlled by an electromagnetic coil that physically moves the contacts together. However, they require a reasonable amount of current to be turned on and usually more than 3.3 volts. To switch even small relays, we need around 60 mA at 5V (more than is available from the GPIO), so we will still need to use some additional components to switch it.

We can use the Darlington array (as used previously) or a small transistor (any small transistor like the 2N2222 will be fine) to provide the current and voltage required to switch it. The following circuit will allow us to do this:

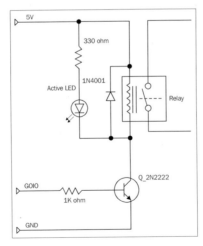

The transistor and relay circuit used to drive external circuits

Much like a motor, a relay can also generate EMF spikes, so a protection diode is also needed to avoid any reverse voltage on the transistor.

This is a very useful circuit, not just for driving motors but for any external circuit as well; the physical switch allows it to be independent and electrically isolated from the Raspberry Pi controlling it.

As long as the relay is rated correctly, you can drive DC or AC devices through it.

> You can also use some relays to control items powered by mains. However, this should be done only with extreme caution and proper electrical training. Electricity from mains can kill or cause serious harm.

PiBorg has a readymade module named the **PicoBorg** that will allow the switching of up to four relays. It uses devices called **MOSFETs** that are essentially high-power versions of transistors that function with the same principle as discussed previously.

Tethered or untethered robots

An important choice when designing your own Rover-Pi robot is to decide if you want to make it fully self-contained or if you are happy to have a tether (a long control/power cable connected to the Rover-Pi). Using a tether, you can keep the weight of the Rover-Pi robot down, which means the small motors will be able to move the unit with ease. This will allow you to keep the Raspberry Pi separate from the main unit so it can remain connected to a screen and keyboard for easy programming and debugging. The main disadvantage is that you will need a long, umbilical-like connection to your Rover-Pi robot (with a wire for each control signal) that may impede its movement. However, as we will see later, you may only need three or four wires to provide all the control you need (see the *Using I/O expanders* section in the next recipe).

If you intend to mount the Raspberry Pi directly on the Rover-Pi robot, you will need a suitable power supply, such as a phone charger battery pack. If the battery pack has two USB ports, then you may be able to use it as a power source to drive both the Raspberry Pi and the motors. The unit must be able to maintain the supplies independently as any power spike caused by driving the motors could reset the Raspberry Pi.

Remember that if the Raspberry Pi is now attached to the robot, you will need a means to control it. This can be a USB Wi-Fi dongle that will allow a remote connection via SSH and so on, or a wireless keyboard (that uses RF/Bluetooth), or even the GPIO D-Pad from *Chapter 6*, *Using Python to Drive Hardware*, can be used for direct control.

However, the more you mount on the chassis, the harder the motors will need to work to move. You may find that stronger motors are required, rather than the little ones used here. A Rover-Pi robot powered by a USB battery pack is shown in the following image:

A battery-powered Raspberry Rover-Pi robot being controlled via Wi-Fi (cable management is optional)

Rover kits

If you don't fancy making your own chassis, there are also a number of pre-made Rover chassis available that can be used. They are as follows:

- 2WD Magician Robot Chassis from SparkFun
- 4 Motor Smart Car Chassis from DX.com
- 2 Wheel Smart Car Model DX.com

 Be sure to check out the *Appendix, Hardware and Software List*; it lists all the items used in this chapter and the places you can obtain them from.

Using advanced motor control

The previous driving circuits are not suitable for driving motors in more than one direction (as they only switch the motor on or off). However, using a circuit named an H-bridge, you can switch and control the motor's direction too. The switch combinations are shown in the following diagram:

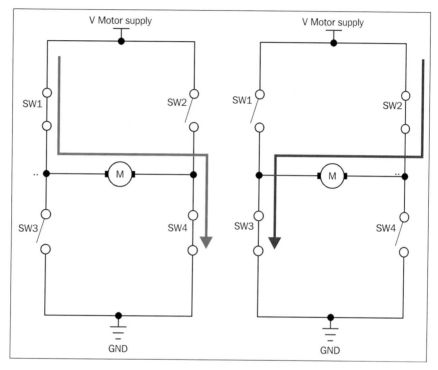

The direction of the motor can be controlled by different switch combinations

Using a different combination of switching, we can change the direction of the motor by switching the positive and negative supply to the motor (**SW1** and **SW4** activate the motor, and **SW2** and **SW3** reverse the motor). However, not only do we need four switching devices for each motor, but since the ULN2X03 devices and PiBorg's PicoBorg module can only sink current, equivalent devices would be required to source current (to make up the top section of switches).

Fortunately, there are purpose-built H-bridge chips, such as L298N, that contain the previous circuit inside them to provide a powerful and convenient solution for controlling motors.

Getting ready

We shall replace the previous Darlington array module with the H-bridge motor controller shown in the following image:

The H-bridge motor controller allows directional control of motors

There is some detailed information about this unit available at `http://www.geekonfire.com/wiki/index.php?title=Dual_H-Bridge_Motor_Driver`.

Or the datasheet of L298N is available at `http://www.st.com/st-web-ui/static/active/en/resource/technical/ document/datasheet/CD00000240.pdf`.

How to do it...

The unit will need to be wired as follows (this will be similar for other H-bridge type controllers, but check with the relevant datasheet if unsure).

The following table shows how the motors and motor power supply connect to the H-bridge controller module:

The motor side of the module						
Motor A		**VMS**	**GND**	**5V OUT**	**Motor B**	
Left motor Red wire	Left motor Black wire	Battery positive	Battery GND	None	Right motor Red wire	Right motor Black wire

The following table shows how the H-bridge controller module connects to the Raspberry Pi:

Control side of the module							
ENA	**IN1**	**IN2**	**IN3**	**IN4**	**ENB**	**GND**	**5V**
None	P1 Pin 15	P1 Pin 16	P1 Pin 18	P1 Pin 22	None	P1 Pin 6	None

It is recommended that you keep the pull-up resistor jumpers on (UR1-UR4) and allow the motor supply to power the onboard voltage regulator, which in turn will power the L298N controller (jumper 5V_EN). The on-board regulator (the 78M05 device) can supply up to 500 mA, enough for the L298N controller plus any additional circuits such as an IO expander (see the *There's more...* section for more information). Both the ENA and ENB pins should be disconnected (the motor output will stay enabled by default).

You will need to make the following changes to the previous rover_drivefwd.py script (you can save it as rover_drive.py).

At the top of the file, redefine PINS as follows:

```
PINS=[15,16,18,22]    # PINS=[L_FWD,L_BWD,R_FWD,R_BWD]
```

And, update the control patterns as follows:

```
FWD=[ON,OFF,ON,OFF]
BWD=[OFF,ON,OFF,ON]
RIGHT=[OFF,ON,ON,OFF]
LEFT=[ON,OFF,OFF,ON]
```

Next, we need to add the backwards command to cmd() as follows:

```
def cmd(self,char,step=STEP):
  if char == 'f':
    self.drive(FWD,step)
  elif char == 'b':
    self.drive(BWD,step)
  elif char == 'r':
    self.drive(RIGHT,step)
  elif char == 'l':
    self.drive(LEFT,step)
  elif char == '#':
    time.sleep(step)
```

Finally, we can update the prompt that we have within the main() function to include b (backwards) as an option, as follows:

```
print("Enter CMDs [f,b,r,l,#]:")
```

How it works...

The H-bridge motor controller recreates the previous switching circuit with additional circuitry to ensure that the electronic switches cannot create a short circuit (by not allowing **SW1** and **SW3** or **SW2** and **SW4** to be enabled at the same time). The H-bridge motor controller's switching circuit is as shown in the following diagram:

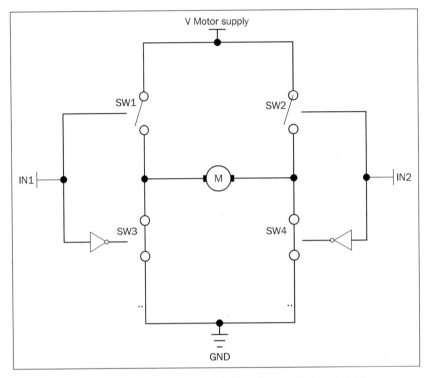

An approximation of the H-bridge switching circuit (in Motor off state)

The input (**IN1** and **IN2**) will produce the following action on the motors:

IN1	0	1
IN2		
0	Motor off	Motor backwards
1	Motor forwards	Motor off

As we did in the previous recipe, we can move forward by driving both motors forward; however, now we can drive them both backwards (to move backwards) as well as in opposite directions (allowing us to turn the Rover-Pi robot on the spot).

There's more...

We can achieve finer control of the motors using a **pulse width modulated** (**PWM**) signal and expand the available input/output using an IO expander.

Motor speed control using PWM control

Currently, the Rover-Pi robot motors are controlled by being switched on and off; however, if the robot is moving too fast (for example, if you have fitted bigger motors or used higher gearing), we could make use of the **ENA** and **ENB** input on the controller. If these are set low, the motor output is disabled, and if set high, it is enabled again. Therefore, by driving them with a PWM signal, we can control the speed of the motors. We could even set slightly different PWM rates (if required) to compensate for any differences in the motors/wheels or surface to drive them at slightly different speeds, as shown in the following diagram:

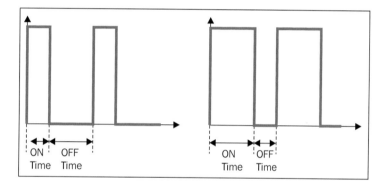

A pulse width modulated signal controls the ratio of the ON and OFF times

A PWM signal is a digital on/off signal that has different amounts of **ON** time compared to **OFF** time. A motor driven with a 50:50, ON:OFF signal would drive a motor with half the power of an ON signal at 100 percent and would therefore run slower. Using different ratios, we can drive the motors at different speeds.

We can use the hardware PWM of the Raspberry Pi (P1 Pin 12 can use the PWM driver).

 The PWM driver normally provides one of the audio channels of the analog audio output. Sometimes, this generates interference; therefore, it is suggested that you disconnect any devices connected to the analog audio socket.

The hardware PWM function is enabled in `wiringpi2` by setting the pin mode to `2` (which is the value of `PWM`) and specifying the on time (represented as `ON_TIME`) as follows:

```
PWM_PIN=12; PWM=2; ON_TIME=512   #0-1024 Off-On

  def GPIOsetup(self):
    wiringpi2.wiringPiSetupPhys()
    wiringpi2.pinMode(PWM_PIN,PWM)
    wiringpi2.pwmWrite(PWM_PIN,ON_TIME)
    for gpio in self.pins:
      wiringpi2.pinMode(gpio,OUT)
```

However, this is only suitable for joint PWM motor control (as it is connected to both ENA and ENB) since there is only the one available hardware PWM output.

Another alternative is to use the software PWM function of `wiringpi2`. This creates a crude PWM signal using software; depending on your requirements, this may acceptable. The code for generating a software PWM signal on P1 Pin 7 and P1 Pin 11 is as follows:

```
PWM_PIN_ENA=7;PWM_PIN_ENA=11;RANGE=100 #0-100  (100Hz Max)
ON_TIME1=20; ON_TIME2=75 #0-100
ON_TIME1=20   #0-100
  def GPIOsetup(self):
    wiringpi2.wiringPiSetupPhys()
    wiringpi2.softPwmCreate(PWM_PIN_ENA,ON_TIME1,RANGE)
    wiringpi2.softPwmCreate(PWM_PIN_ENB,ON_TIME2,RANGE)
    for gpio in self.pins:
      wiringpi2.pinMode(gpio,OUT)
```

The previous code sets both pins to 100 Hz, with P1 Pin 7 set to an on time of 2 ms (and an off time of 8 ms) and P1 Pin 11 set to 7.5 ms / 2.5 ms.

To adjust the PWM timings, use `wiringpi2.softPwmWrite(PWM_PIN_ENA,ON_TIME2)`.

The accuracy of the PWM signal may be interrupted by other system processes, but it can control a small micro servo, even if slightly jittery.

Using I/O expanders

As we have seen previously, `wiringpi2` allows us to easily adjust our code to make use of I/O expanders using I²C. In this case, it can be useful to add additional circuits, such as sensors and LED status indicators, perhaps even displays and control buttons to assist with debugging and controlling the Rover-Pi robot as you develop it.

It can be particularly helpful if you intend to use it as a tethered device, since you will only require three wires to connect back to the Raspberry Pi (I²C Data P1 Pin 3, I²C Clock P1 Pin 5, and Ground P1 Pin 6), with I²C VCC being provided by the motor controller 5V output.

As done earlier, add defines for the I²C address and pin base as follows:

```
IO_ADDR=0x20
AF_BASE=100
```

Then, in `gpiosetup()`, set up the MCP23017 device using the following code:

```
wiringpi2.mcp23017Setup(AF_BASE,IO_ADDR)
```

Ensure that any pin references you make are numbered 100-115 (to refer to the I/O expander pins A0-7 and B0-7) with `AF_BASE` added (which is the pin offset for the I/O expander).

Building a six-legged Pi-Bug robot

Controlling motors is very useful to create vehicle-like robots, but creating more naturally behaving robot components such as servos can provide excellent results. There are many creative designs of insect-like robots, or even biped designs (with humanoid-like legs), that use servos to provide natural joint movements. The design in this example uses three servos, but these principles and concepts can easily be applied to far more complex designs, to control legs/arms that use multiple servos. The Pi-Bug robot is shown in the following image:

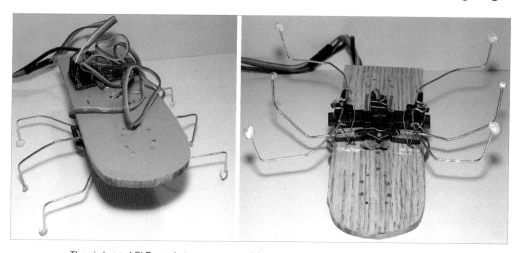

The six-legged Pi-Bug robot uses a servo driver to control three servos to scuttle around

Getting ready

You will need the following hardware:

- **A PWM driver module**: A driver module such as the Adafruit 16-Channel 12-bit PWM/ Servo Driver will be needed. This uses a PCA9685 device; see the datasheet at `http://www.adafruit.com/datasheets/PCA9685.pdf` for details.

- **3x micro servos**: The MG90S 9g Metal Gear Servos provide a reasonable amount of torque at a low cost.

- **A heavy gauge wire**: This will form the legs; three giant paper clips (76 mm / 3 inches) are ideal for this.

- **A light gauge wire / cable ties**: These will be used to connect the legs to the servos and to mount the servos to the main board.

- **A small section of plywood or fiberboard**: Holes can be drilled into this, and the servos can be mounted on it.

You will need to have wiringPi2 installed to control the PWM module, and it will be useful to install the I²C tools for debugging. See *Chapter 7, Sense and Display Real-world Data*, for details on how to install WiringPi2 and the I²C tools. The I²C connections are as shown in the following diagram:

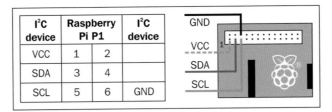

I²C device	Raspberry Pi P1		I²C device
VCC	1	2	
SDA	3	4	
SCL	5	6	GND

I²C connections on the Raspberry Pi GPIO P1 header

How to do it...

The Pi-Bug robot uses three servos, one on either side and one in the middle one. Mount each servo by drilling a hole on either side of the servo body, loop a wire or cable ties through it, and pull to hold the servo tightly.

Bend the paper clip wire into a suitable shape to form the Pi-Bug robot's legs, and add a small kink that will allow you to wire the legs securely to the servo arms. It is recommended that you run the program first, with the Pi-Bug robot set to the home position h before you screw the servo arms in place. This will ensure that the legs are located in the middle.

The following diagram shows the components on the Pi-Bug robot:

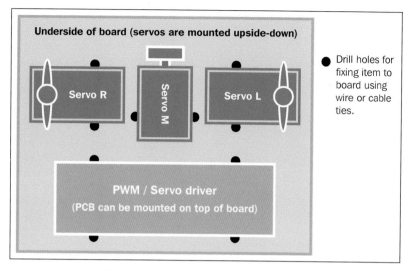

Underside of board (servos are mounted upside-down)

Servo R

Servo M

Servo L

Drill holes for fixing item to board using wire or cable ties.

PWM / Servo driver
(PCB can be mounted on top of board)

The layout of components on the Pi-Bug robot

Create the following `servoAdafruit.py` script to control the servos:

```python
#!/usr/bin/env python3
#servoAdafruit.py
import wiringpi2
import time

#PWM Registers
MODE1=0x00
PRESCALE=0xFE
LED0_ON_L=0x06
LED0_ON_H=0x07
LED0_OFF_L=0x08
LED0_OFF_H=0x09

PWMHZ=50
PWMADR=0x40

class servo:
  # Constructor
  def __init__(self,pwmFreq=PWMHZ,addr=PWMADR):
    self.i2c = wiringpi2.I2C()
    self.devPWM=self.i2c.setup(addr)
    self.GPIOsetup(pwmFreq,addr)
```

```
    def GPIOsetup(self,pwmFreq,addr):
      self.i2c.read(self.devPWM)
      self.pwmInit(pwmFreq)

    def pwmInit(self,pwmFreq):
      prescale = 25000000.0 / 4096.0    # 25MHz / 12-bit
      prescale /= float(pwmFreq)
      prescale = prescale - 0.5 #-1 then +0.5 to round to
                                # nearest value
      prescale = int(prescale)
      self.i2c.writeReg8(self.devPWM,MODE1,0x00) #RESET
      mode=self.i2c.read(self.devPWM)
      self.i2c.writeReg8(self.devPWM,MODE1,
                      (mode & 0x7F)|0x10) #SLEEP
      self.i2c.writeReg8(self.devPWM,PRESCALE,prescale)
      self.i2c.writeReg8(self.devPWM,MODE1,mode) #restore mode
      time.sleep(0.005)
      self.i2c.writeReg8(self.devPWM,MODE1,mode|0x80) #restart

   def setPWM(self,channel, on, off):
     on=int(on)
     off=int(off)
     self.i2c.writeReg8(self.devPWM,
                     LED0_ON_L+4*channel,on & 0xFF)
     self.i2c.writeReg8(self.devPWM,LED0_ON_H+4*channel,on>>8)
     self.i2c.writeReg8(self.devPWM,
                     LED0_OFF_L+4*channel,off & 0xFF)
     self.i2c.writeReg8(self.devPWM,LED0_OFF_H+4*channel,off>>8)

def main():
   servoMin = 205  # Min pulse 1ms 204.8 (50Hz)
   servoMax = 410  # Max pulse 2ms 409.6 (50Hz)
   myServo=servo()
   myServo.setPWM(0,0,servoMin)
   time.sleep(2)
   myServo.setPWM(0,0,servoMax)

if __name__=='__main__':
   try:
     main()
   finally:
     print ("Finish")
 #End
```

Create the following `bug_drive.py` script to control the Pi-Bug robot:

```python
#!/usr/bin/env python3
#bug_drive.py
import time
import servoAdafruit as servoCon

servoMin = 205  # Min pulse 1000us 204.8 (50Hz)
servoMax = 410  # Max pulse 2000us 409.6 (50Hz)

servoL=0; servoM=1; servoR=2
TILT=10
MOVE=30
MID=((servoMax-servoMin)/2)+servoMin
CW=MID+MOVE; ACW=MID-MOVE
TR=MID+TILT; TL=MID-TILT
FWD=[TL,ACW,ACW,TR,CW,CW] #[midL,fwd,fwd,midR,bwd,bwd]
BWD=[TR,ACW,ACW,TL,CW,CW] #[midR,fwd,fwd,midL,bwd,bwd]
LEFT=[TR,ACW,CW,TL,CW,ACW] #[midR,fwd,bwd,midL,bwd,fwd]
RIGHT=[TL,ACW,CW,TR,CW,ACW] #[midL,fwd,bwd,midR,bwd,fwd]
HOME=[MID,MID,MID,MID,MID,MID]
PINS=[servoM,servoL,servoR,servoM,servoL,servoR]
STEP=0.2
global DEBUG
DEBUG=False

class motor:
  # Constructor
  def __init__(self,pins=PINS,steptime=STEP):
    self.pins = pins
    self.steptime=steptime
    self.theServo=servoCon.servo()

  def off(self):
    #Home position
    self.drive(HOME,step)

  def drive(self,drive,step=STEP):
    for idx,servo in enumerate(self.pins):
      if(drive[idx]==servoM):
        time.sleep(step)
      self.theServo.setPWM(servo,0,drive[idx])
      if(drive[idx]==servoM):
        time.sleep(step)
      if(DEBUG):print("%s:%s"%(gpio,drive[idx]))
```

```
      def cmd(self,char,step=STEP):
        if char == 'f':
          self.drive(FWD,step)
        elif char == 'b':
          self.drive(BWD,step)
        elif char == 'r':
          self.drive(RIGHT,step)
        elif char == 'l':
          self.drive(LEFT,step)
        elif char == 'h':
          self.drive(HOME,step)
        elif char == '#':
          time.sleep(step)

  def main():
    import os
    DEBUG=True
    if "CMD" in os.environ:
      CMD=os.environ["CMD"]
      INPUT=False
      print("CMD="+CMD)
    else:
      INPUT=True
    bugPi=motor()
    if INPUT:
      print("Enter CMDs [f,b,r,l,h,#]:")
      CMD=input()
    for idx,char in enumerate(CMD.lower()):
      if(DEBUG):print("Step %s of %s: %s"%(idx+1,len(CMD),char))
      bugPi.cmd(char)

  if __name__ == '__main__':
    try:
      main()
    except KeyboardInterrupt:
      print ("Finish")
  #End
```

How it works...

We explain how the previous script functions by exploring how the servos are controlled using a PWM. Next, we see how the servo class provides the methods to control the PCA9685 device. Finally, we look at how the movements of the three servos combine to produce forward and turning motions for the Pi-Bug robot itself.

Controlling the servos

To control the servos used for the Pi-Bug robot, we require a special control signal that will determine the angle that the servo is required to move to. We will send the servo a PWM signal where the duration of the on time will allow us to control the angle of the servo arm (and thereby allow us to control the Pi-Bug robot's legs). The following diagram shows how a PWM signal can be used to control the angle of the servo:

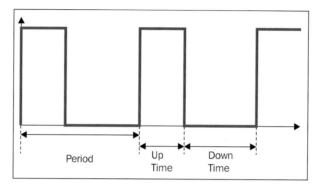

The angle of the servo is controlled by the duration of the Up Time of the PWM signal

Most servos will have an angular range of approximately 180 degrees and the mid-position of 90 degrees. A PWM frequency of 50 Hz will have a period of 20 ms, and the mid-position of 90 degrees typically corresponds to an **Up Time** of 1.5 ms, with a range of +/- 0.5 ms to 0.4 ms for near 0 degrees and near 180 degrees. Each type of servo will be slightly different, but you should be able to adjust the code to suit if required. The following diagram shows how you can control the servo angle using different PWM up-times:

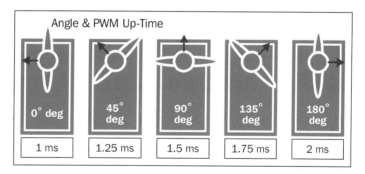

The servo angle is controlled by sending a PWM Up-Time between 1ms and 2ms

Another type of servo is called a **continuous servo** (not used here). It allows you to control the rotation speed instead of the angle, and will rotate at a constant speed, depending on the PWM signal that has been applied. Both servo types have internal feedback loops that will continuously drive the servo until the required angle or speed is reached.

Although it is theoretically possible to generate these signals using software, you will find that any tiny interruption by other processes on the system will interfere with the signal timing; this, in turn, will produce an erratic response from the servo. This is why we use a hardware PWM controller, which only needs to be set with a specific up and down time, to then generate the required signal automatically for us.

The servo class

The servo code is based on the PWM driver that Adafruit uses for their module; however, it is not Python 3 friendly, so we need to create our own version. We will use Wiringpi2's I²C driver to initialize and control the I²C PWM controller. We define the registers that we will need to use (see the datasheet for the PCA9685 device) as well as its default bus address `0x40` (PWMADR) and the PWM frequency of 50 Hz (PWMHZ).

Within our servo class, we initialize the I²C driver in `wiringpi2` and set up our `devPWM` device on the bus. Next, we initialize the PWM device itself (using `pwmInit()`). We have to calculate the **prescaler** required for the device to convert the onboard 25 MHz clock to a 50 Hz signal to generate the PWM frequency we need; we will use the following formula:

$$\text{prescale} = \left(\frac{25\text{MHz}}{12\text{-bit} \times \text{pwmFreq}} \right) + 0.5$$

The prescale register value sets the PWM frequency using a 12-bit value to scale the 25 MHz clock

The prescale value is loaded into the device, and a device reset is triggered to enable it.

Next, we create a function to allow the PWM ON and OFF times to be controlled. The `ON` and `OFF` times are 12-bit values (0-4096), so each value is split into upper and lower bytes (8 bits each) that need to be loaded into two registers. For the `L` (low) registers, we mask off the upper 8 bits using `&0xFF`, and for the `H` (high) registers, we shift down by 8 bits to provide the higher 8 bits. Each PWM channel will have two registers for the on time and two for the off time, so we can multiply the addresses of the first PWM channel registers by 4 and the channel number to get the addresses of any of the others.

To test our `servo` class, we define the minimum and maximum ranges of the servos, which we calculate as follows:

- The PWM frequency of 50 Hz has a 20 ms period (*T=1/f*)
- The ON/OFF times range from 0-4096 (so 0 ms to 20 ms)

Now, we can calculate the control values for 0 degrees (1 ms) and 180 degrees (2 ms) as follows:

- ▸ 1 ms (servo min) is equal to 4096/20 ms, which is 204.8
- ▸ 2 ms (servo max) is equal to 4096/10 ms, which is 409.6

We round the values to the nearest whole number.

Learning to walk

The Pi-Bug robot uses a common design that allows three servos to be used to create a small, six-legged robot. The servos at the two ends provide forward and backward movement, while the servo in the middle provides the control. The following image shows the mounted servos:

The servos are mounted upside down on the underside of the board

The following table assumes that the left and right servos are mounted upside down on the underside of the board, with the middle servo fitted vertically. You shall have to adjust the code if mounted differently.

The following table shows the servo movements used to walk forward:

Direction	Middle (servoM)	Left (servoL)	Right (servoR)
home	MID/Middle	MID/Middle	MID/Middle
fwdStep1	TR / Right side up	ACW / Legs forward	ACW / Legs backward
fwdStep2	TL / Left side up	CW / Legs backward	CW / Legs forward

The following diagram shows how the movement makes the Pi-Bug robot step forward:

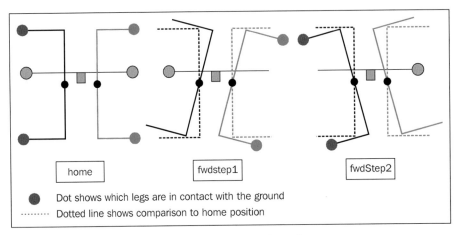

The Pi-Bug robot moving forward

While it may seem a little confusing at first, when you see the robot moving, it should make more sense.

For the first forward step, we move the middle servo (servoM) clockwise so that the left side of the Pi-Bug robot is lifted off the ground by the movement of the remaining middle leg. We can then move the left servo (servoL) to move the legs on the left side forward (ready for movement later, they are not touching the ground at this point). Now by moving the right servo (servoR), we can move the legs on the right backwards (allowing the Pi-Bug robot to be pushed forward on that side).

The second forward step is the same, except that we use the middle servo (servoM) to lift the right side off the ground. Again, we move the legs that are off the ground forward (ready for next time) and then move the legs on the other side backward (allowing that side of the Pi-Bug robot to move forward). By repeating the forward steps, the Pi-Bug robot will move forward, or by swapping the sides that are being lifted up by the middle servo (servoM), it will move backward. The result is a rather bug-like scuttle!

To make the Pi-Bug robot turn, we perform a similar action, except that just like the advanced motor control for the Rover-Pi robot, we move one side of the robot forward and the other side backward. The following table shows the servo movements used to turn right:

Direction	Middle (servoM)	Left (servoL)	Right (servoR)
home	MID/Middle	MID/Middle	MID/Middle
rightStep1	TL / Left side up	CW / Legs backward	ACW / Legs backward
rightStep2	TR / Right side up	ACW / Legs forward	CW / Legs forward

The steps to turn the Pi-Bug robot to the right are shown in the following diagram:

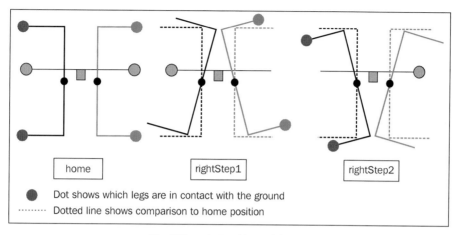

The Pi-Bug robot making a right turn

To turn right, we lift the left side of the Pi-Bug robot off the ground, but this time, we move the legs on both sides backward. This allows the right side of the Pi-Bug robot to move forward. The second half of the step lifts the right side off the ground, and we move the legs forward (which will push the left side of the Pi-Bug robot backward). In this manner, the bug will turn as it steps; again, just by swapping the sides that are being lifted, we can change the direction that the Pi-Bug robot will turn in.

The Pi-Bug code for walking

The code for the Pi-Bug robot has been designed to provide the same interface as the Rover-Pi robot so that they can be interchanged easily. You should notice that each class consists of the same four functions (`__init__()`, `off()`, `drive()`, and `cmd()`). The `__init__()` function defines the set of pins we will control, the `steptime` value of the walking action (this time, the gap between movements), and the previously defined servo module.

Once again, we have an `off()` function that provides a function that can be called to set the servos in their middle positions (which is very useful for when you need to fit the legs in position, as described previously in the home position). The `off()` function uses the `drive()` function to set each servo to the `MID` position. The `MID` value is half way between `servoMin` and `servoMax` (1.5 ms to give a position of 90 degrees).

The `drive()` function is just like the previous motor control version; it cycles through each of the actions required for each servo as defined in the various movement patterns (`FWD`, `BWD`, `LEFT`, and `RIGHT`) we discussed previously. However, to reproduce the required pattern of movement, we cycle through each servo twice, while inserting a small delay whenever we move the middle servo (`servoM`). This allows time for the servo to move and provide the necessary tilt to lift the other legs off the ground before allowing them to move.

We define each of the servo commands as a clockwise (CW) or anticlockwise/counterclockwise (ACW) movement of the servo arm. Since the servos are mounted upside down, an anticlockwise (clockwise if viewed from above) movement of the left servo (servoL) will bring the legs forwards, while the same direction of movement on the right servo (servoR) will move the legs backward (which is **fwdStep1** in the previous diagram). In this way, each of the patterns can be defined.

Once again, we provide a test function using the following command that allows a list of instructions to either be defined from the command line or directly entered at the prompt:

```
sudo CMD=fffll##rr##bb##h python3 bug_drive.py
```

This includes the addition of h to return to the **home** position, if desired.

Avoiding objects and obstacles

To avoid obstacles, you can place sensors around the robot perimeter to activate whenever an object is encountered. Depending on how you want your robot to behave, one avoidance strategy is to just reverse any action (with an additional turn for forward/backward actions) that was last taken that caused one of the sensors to be activated.

Getting ready

You need some micro switches to be triggered when there is an impact with objects. Depending on the type you have, you need to place enough switches to detect any object around the outside (if required, you can use an additional length of wire to extend the reach of the switch). Shown in the following image are two possible sensors that will cause the switch to activate when the spring or the metal arm hits an object. You need to determine which contacts of the switch open or close the circuit (this will depend on the device).

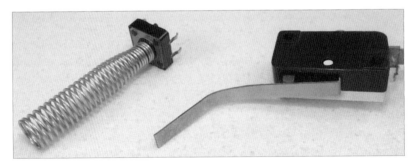

Small micro switches can be used as collision sensors

How to do it...

Connect the switches to the GPIO using a method similar to the one we used previously in *Chapter 6, Using Python to Drive Hardware*, for the D-Pad controller. A circuit diagram of the switches is as follows:

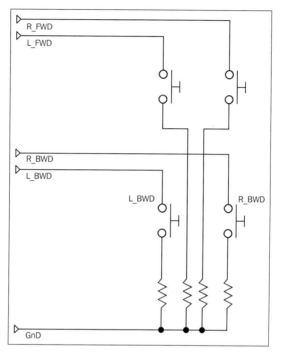

The switches should include current limiting resistors (1K ohm is ideal)

How you connect to the Raspberry Pi's GPIO will depend on how your motor/servo drive is wired up. For example, a Rover-Pi robot with the H-bridge motor controller can be wired up as follows:

Motor control							
ENA	**IN1**	**IN2**	**IN3**	**IN4**	**ENB**	**GND**	**5V**
None	P1 Pin 15	P1 Pin 16	P1 Pin 18	P1 Pin 22	None	P1 Pin 6	None

Four additional proximity/collision sensors can be connected to the Raspberry Pi GPIO as follows:

Proximity/collision sensors				
R_FWD	**L_FWD**	**R_BWD**	**L_BWD**	**GND**
P1 Pin 7	P1 Pin 11	P1 Pin 12	P1 Pin 13	P1 Pin 6

If you wired it differently, you can adjust the pin numbers within the code as required. If you require additional pins, then any of the multipurpose pins, such as RS232 RX/TX (pins 8 and 10) or the SPI/I²C, can be used as normal GPIO pins too; just set them as input or output as normal. Normally, we just avoid using them as they are often more useful for expansion and other things, so it is sometimes useful to keep them available.

You can even use a single GPIO pin for all your sensors if you are just using the following example code, since the action is the same, regardless of which sensor is triggered. However, by wiring each one separately, you can adjust your strategy based on where the obstacle is around the robot or provide additional debug information about which sensor has been triggered.

Create the following `avoidance.py` script:

```python
#!/usr/bin/env python3
#avoidance.py
import rover_drive as drive
import wiringpi2
import time

opCmds={'f':'bl','b':'fr','r':'ll','l':'rr','#':'#'}
PINS=[7,11,12,13]    # PINS=[L_FWD,L_BWD,R_FWD,R_BWD]
ON=1;OFF=0
IN=0;OUT=1
PULL_UP=2;PULL_DOWN=1

class sensor:
  # Constructor
  def __init__(self,pins=PINS):
    self.pins = pins
    self.GPIOsetup()

  def GPIOsetup(self):
    wiringpi2.wiringPiSetupPhys()
    for gpio in self.pins:
      wiringpi2.pinMode(gpio,IN)
      wiringpi2.pullUpDnControl(gpio,PULL_UP)

  def checkSensor(self):
    hit = False
    for gpio in self.pins:
      if wiringpi2.digitalRead(gpio)==False:
        hit = True
    return hit
```

```
def main():
  myBot=drive.motor()
  mySensors=sensor()
  while(True):
    print("Enter CMDs [f,b,r,l,#]:")
    CMD=input()
    for idx,char in enumerate(CMD.lower()):
      print("Step %s of %s: %s"%(idx+1,len(CMD),char))
      myBot.cmd(char,step=0.01)#small steps
      hit = mySensors.checkSensor()
      if hit:
        print("We hit something on move: %s Go: %s"%(char,
                                         opCmds[char]))
        for charcmd in opCmds[char]:
          myBot.cmd(charcmd,step=0.02)#larger step

if __name__ == '__main__':
  try:
    main()
  except KeyboardInterrupt:
    print ("Finish")
#End
```

How it works...

We import `rover_drive` to control the robot (if we are using a Pi-Bug robot, `bug_drive` can be used) and `wiringpi2` so that we can use the GPIO to read the sensors (defined as `PINS`). We define `opCmds`, which uses a Python dictionary to allocate new commands in response to the original command (using `opCmds[char]`, where `char` is the original command).

We create a new class called `sensor` and set up each of the switches as GPIO input (each with an internal pull-ups set). Now, whenever we make a movement (as earlier, from the list of requested commands in the `main()` function), we check to see if any of the switches have been triggered (by calling `mySensor.checkSensor()`).

If a switch was tripped, we stop the current movement and then move in the opposite direction. However, if we are moving forward when one of the sensors is triggered, we move backward and then turn. This allows the robot to gradually turn away from the object that is blocking its path and continue its movement in another direction. Similarly, if we are moving backwards and a sensor is triggered, we move forward and then turn. By combining simple object avoidance with directional information, the robot can be commanded to navigate around as desired.

There's more...

There are also ways to detect objects that are near the robot without actually making physical contact with it. One such way is to use ultrasonic sensors, commonly used for vehicle reversing/parking sensors.

Ultrasonic reversing sensors

Ultrasonic sensors provide an excellent way to measure the distance of the robot from obstacles (providing a measurement of between 2 cm and 20 cm) and are available at most electrical hobby stores (see the *Appendix, Hardware and Software List*). The ultrasonic module functions by sending a short burst of ultrasonic pulses and then measures the time it takes for the receiver to detect the echo. The module then produces a pulse on the echo output that is equal to the time measured. This time is equal to the distance travelled divided by the speed of sound (340.29 m/sec or 34,029 cm/s), which is the distance from the sensor to the object and back again. An ultrasonic module is shown in the following image:

The HC-SR04 ultrasonic sensor module

The sensor requires 5V to power it; it has an input that will receive the trigger pulse and an output that the echo pulse will be sent on. While the module works with a 3.3V trigger pulse, it responds with a 5V signal on the echo line; so, it requires some extra resistors to protect the Raspberry Pi's GPIO.

The following circuit diagram shows the connection of the sensor output:

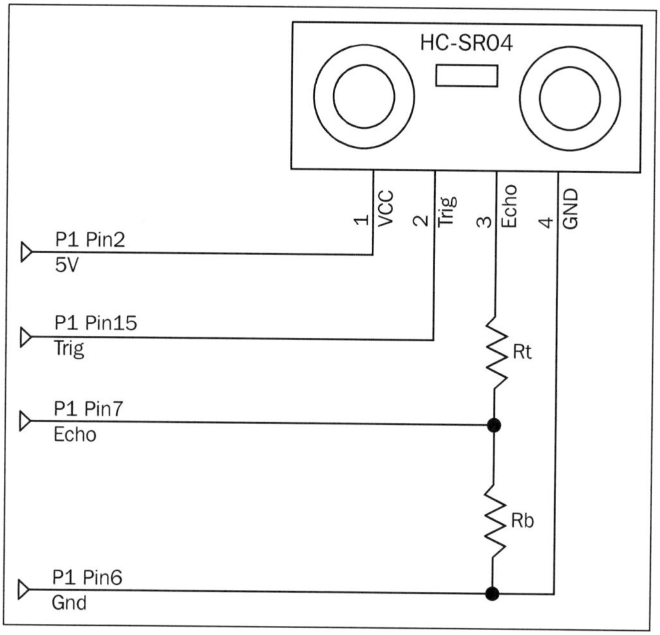

The sensor echo output must be connected to the Raspberry Pi via a potential divider

The resistors **Rt** and **Rb** create a potential divider; the aim is to drop the echo voltage from 5V to around 3V (but not less than 2.5V). Use the following equation from *Chapter 7, Sense and Display Real-world Data*, to obtain the output voltage:

$$V_{out} = \frac{R_t}{(R_t + R_b) \text{ x VCC}}$$

The output voltage (Vout) of the potential divider is calculated using this equation

This means that we should aim for an **Rt** to **Rb** ratio of 2:3 to give 3V (and not aim lower than 1:1, which would give 2.5V); that is, **Rt** equals 2K ohm and **Rb** equals 3K ohm, or 330 ohm and 470 ohm will be fine.

If you have a voltage meter, you can check it (with everything else disconnected). Connect the top of the potential divider to P1 Pin 2 (5V), the bottom to P1 Pin 6 (GND), and measure the voltage from the middle (it should be around 3V).

Create the following `sonic.py` script:

```python
#!/usr/bin/python3
#sonic.py
import wiringpi2
import time
import datetime

ON=1;OFF=0; IN=0;OUT=1
TRIGGER=15; ECHO=7
PULSE=0.00001 #10us pulse

SPEEDOFSOUND=34029 #34029 cm/s

def gpiosetup():
  wiringpi2.wiringPiSetupPhys()
  wiringpi2.pinMode(TRIGGER,OUT)
  wiringpi2.pinMode(ECHO,IN)
  wiringpi2.digitalWrite(TRIGGER,OFF)
  time.sleep(0.5)

def pulse():
  wiringpi2.digitalWrite(TRIGGER,ON)
  time.sleep(PULSE)
  wiringpi2.digitalWrite(TRIGGER,OFF)
  starttime=time.time()
  stop=starttime
  start=starttime
  while wiringpi2.digitalRead(ECHO)==0 and start<starttime+2:
    start=time.time()
  while wiringpi2.digitalRead(ECHO)==1 and stop<starttime+2:
    stop=time.time()
  delta=stop-start
  print("Start:%f Stop:%f Delta:%f"%(start,stop,delta))
  distance=delta*SPEEDOFSOUND
  return distance/2.0

def main():
  global run
  gpiosetup()
  while(True):
    print("Sample")
    print("Distance:%.1f"%pulse())
    time.sleep(2)
```

```
if __name__ == '__main__':
  try:
    main()
  except KeyboardInterrupt:
    print ("Finish")
#End
```

First, we define the pins `TRIGGER` and `ECHO`, the length of the trigger pulse, and also the speed of sound (340.29 m/s). The `TRIGGER` pin is set as an output and the `ECHO` as an input (we will not need a pull-up or pull-down resistor since the module already has one).

The `pulse()` function will send a short trigger pulse (10 microseconds), then it will time the duration of the echo pulse. We then calculate the total distance travelled by dividing the duration by the speed of sound (the distance to the object is just half of this value).

Unfortunately, the sensor can get confused with certain types of objects; it will either detect echoes that bounce off a nearby object before being reflected back or not pick up narrow items such as chair legs. However, combined with localized collision sensors, the ultrasonic sensor can aid with the general navigation and avoidance of the larger objects.

An improvement to this setup would be to mount the sonic sensor on top of a servo, thereby allowing you to make a sensor sweep of the robot's surroundings. By making multiple sweeps, taking distance measurements, and tracking the angle of the servo, you could build an internal map of the robot's surroundings.

Getting a sense of direction

In order to navigate your robot around the environment, you will need to keep track of which way your robot is facing. You can estimate the angle that your robot turns at by measuring the angle that it turned at in a fixed time period. For wheeled robots, you can also measure the rotation of each wheel using a rotary encoder (a device that provides a count of the wheel's rotations). However, as you make the robot take multiple turns, the direction the robot is facing becomes more and more uncertain as differences in the surfaces and the grip of the wheels or legs cause differences in the angles that the robot is turning at.

Fortunately, we can use an electronic version of a compass; it allows us to determine the direction that the robot is facing by providing an angle from the magnetic North. If we know which direction the robot is facing, we can receive commands requesting a particular angle and ensure that the robot moves towards it. This allows the robot to perform controlled movements and navigate as required.

When given a target angle, we can determine which direction we need to turn towards, until we reach it.

Getting ready

You need a magnetometer device such as the PiBorg's **XLoBorg** module (which is a combined I^2C magnetometer and accelerometer). In this example, we focus on the magnetometer (the smaller chip on the left) output only. The XLoBorg module looks as shown in the following image:

The PiBorg XLoBorg module contains a 3-axis magnetometer and accelerometer

This device can be used with both types of robots, and the angle information received from the module can be used to determine which direction the robot needs to move in.

The module is designed to connect directly to the P1 header, which will block all the remaining pins. So in order to use other GPIO devices, a GPIO splitter (such as the PiBorg **TriBorg**) can be used. Alternatively, you can use Dupont female to male patch wires to connect just the I^2C pins. The connections to be made are shown in the following diagram:

I^2C Device	Raspberry Pi P1		I^2C Device
VCC	1	2	
SDA	3	4	
SCL	5	6	GND

I^2C Device	PiBorg TriBorg		I^2C Device
	2	1	VCC
	4	3	SDA
GND	6	5	SCL

Connections to manually wire the XLoBorg module to the Raspberry Pi (using standard I^2C connections)

When viewed from the underside, the PiBorg XLoBorg pins are mirrored compared to the Raspberry Pi P1 header.

How to do it...

Create a Python 3 friendly version of the XLoBorg library (XLoBorg3.py) using wiringpi2 as follows:

```python
#!/usr/bin/env python3
#XLoBorg3.py
import wiringpi2
import struct
import time

def readBlockData(bus,device,register,words):
  magData=[]
  for i in range(words):
    magData.append(bus.readReg16(device,register+i))
  return magData

class compass:
  def __init__(self):
    addr = 0x0E #compass
    self.i2c = wiringpi2.I2C()
    self.devMAG=self.i2c.setup(addr)
    self.initCompass()

  def initCompass(self):
    # Acquisition mode
    register = 0x11    # CTRL_REG2
    data  = (1 << 7)   # Reset before each acquisition
    data |= (1 << 5)   # Raw mode, do not apply user offsets
    data |= (0 << 5)   # Disable reset cycle
    self.i2c.writeReg8(self.devMAG,register,data)
    # System operation
    register = 0x10    # CTRL_REG1
    data  = (0 << 5)   # Output data rate
                       # (10 Hz when paired with 128 oversample)
    data |= (3 << 3)   # Oversample of 128
    data |= (0 << 2)   # Disable fast read
    data |= (0 << 1)   # Continuous measurement
    data |= (1 << 0)   # Active mode
    self.i2c.writeReg8(self.devMAG,register,data)

  def readCompassRaw(self):
    #x, y, z = readCompassRaw()
    self.i2c.write(self.devMAG,0x00)
```

```
        [status, xh, xl, yh, yl,
          zh, zl, who, sm, oxh, oxl,
          oyh, oyl, ozh, ozl,
          temp, c1, c2] = readBlockData(self.i2c,self.devMAG, 0, 18)
        # Convert from unsigned to correctly signed values
        bytes = struct.pack('BBBBBB', xl, xh, yl, yh, zl, zh)
        x, y, z = struct.unpack('hhh', bytes)
        return x, y, z


if __name__ == '__main__':
  myCompass=compass()
  try:
    while True:
      # Read the MAG Data
      mx, my, mz = myCompass.readCompassRaw()
      print ("mX = %+06d, mY = %+06d, mZ = %+06d" % (mx, my, mz))
      time.sleep(0.1)
  except KeyboardInterrupt:
    print("Finished")
#End
```

How it works...

The script is based on the XLoBorg library available for the XLoBorg module, except that we use WiringPi2, which is Python 3 friendly, to perform the I²C actions. Just like our motor/servo drivers, we also define it as a class so that we can drop it into our code and easily replace it with alternative devices if required.

We import `wiringpi2`, `time`, and also a library called `struct` (which allows us to quickly unpack a block of data read from the device into separate items).

We create the `compass` class, which will include the `__init__()`, `initCompass()`, and `readCompassRaw()` functions. The `readCompassRaw()` function is the equivalent of the standard XLoBorg `ReadCompassRaw()` function provided by their library.

The `__init__()` function sets up the I²C bus with `wiringpi2` and registers the degMAG device on the bus address `0x0E`. The `initCompass()` function sets the `CTRL_REG1` and `CTRL_REG2` registers of the device with the settings required to quickly get raw readings from the device.

More details on the MAG3110 registers are available from `http://www.freescale.com/files/sensors/doc/data_sheet/MAG3110.pdf`.

The `readCompassRaw()` function reads the data registers of the device in a single block (using the custom function `readBlockData()`). It reads all the 18 registers of the device (`0x00` through to `0x11`). The sensor readings we need are contained within the registers `0x01` to `0x06`, which contain the x, y, and z readings split into upper and lower bytes (8-bit values). The `struct.pack()` and `struct.unpack()` functions provide an easy way to package them together and resplit them as separate words (16-bit values).

We can test our script by creating a `myCompass` object from the `compass` class and reading the sensor values using `myCompass.readCompassRaw()`. You will see the raw x, y, and z values from the device, just as you would from the standard XLoBorg library.

As you will find, these values aren't much use on their own since they are uncalibrated and only give you RAW readings from the magnetometer. What we need is a far more useful angle relative to the relative to magnetic North (see the following *There's more...* section for details on how to do this).

There's more...

So far, the basic library allows us to see the strength of the magnetic field on each of the three axes around the sensor (up/down, left/right, and forward/backward). While we can see that these values will change as we move the sensor around, this is not enough to steer our robot. First, we need to calibrate the sensor and then determine the direction of the robot from the readings of the *x* and *y* axes.

Calibrating the compass

The compass needs to be calibrated in order to report values that are centered and equalized. This is needed because there are magnetic fields all around, so by calibrating the sensor, we can cancel out the effect of any localized fields.

By measuring the readings of the compass on all axes, we can determine the minimum and maximum values for each axis. This will allow us to calculate both the midpoint of the readings and also the scaling so that each axis will read the same value whenever it is facing the same way.

Add the following code at the top of the file (after the `import` statements):

```
CAL=100 #take CAL samples
```

Add the following code to `__init__(self)` of the `compass` class:

```
self.offset,self.scaling=self. calibrateCompass ()
if DEBUG:print("offset:%s scaling:%s"%(str(self.offset),
                                str(self.scaling)))
```

Add a new function named `calibrateCompass()` within the `compass` class as follows:

```
def calibrateCompass(self,samples=CAL):
  MAXS16=32768
  SCALE=1000.0
  avg=[0,0,0]
  min=[MAXS16,MAXS16,MAXS16];max=[-MAXS16,-MAXS16,-MAXS16]
  print("Rotate sensor around axis (start in 5 sec)")
  time.sleep(5)
  for calibrate in range(samples):
    for idx,value in enumerate(self.readCompassRaw()):
      avg[idx]+=value
      avg[idx]/=2
      if(value>max[idx]):
        max[idx]=value
      if(value<min[idx]):
        min[idx]=value
    time.sleep(0.1)
    if DEBUG:print("#%d min=[%+06d,%+06d,%+06d] "
                   %(calibrate,min[0],min[1],min[2])
                   +" avg[%+06d,%+06d,%+06d] "
                   %(avg[0],avg[1],avg[2])
                   +" max=[%+06d,%+06d,%+06d] "
                   %(max[0],max[1],max[2]))
  offset=[]
  scaling=[]
  for idx, value in enumerate(min):
    magRange=max[idx]-min[idx]
    offset.append((magRange/2)+min[idx])
    scaling.append(SCALE/magRange)
  return offset,scaling
```

Add another new function named `readCompass()` in the `compass` class as follows:

```
def readCompass(self):
  raw = self.readCompassRaw()
  if DEBUG:print("mX = %+06d, mY = %+06d, mZ = %+06d"
                 % (raw[0],raw[1],raw[2]))
  read=[]
  for idx,value in enumerate(raw):
    adj=value-self.offset[idx]
    read.append(adj*self.scaling[idx])
  return read
```

If you look closely at the readings (if you use `readCompass()`), you will now find that all the readings have the same range and are centered around the same values.

Calculating the compass bearing

The XLoBorg library only provides access to the RAW values of the MAG3110 device, which provides a measure of how strong the magnetic field is on each of the axes. To determine the direction of the sensor, we can use the readings from the x and y axes (assuming we have mounted and calibrated the sensor horizontally). The readings of the x and y axes are proportional to the magnetic field in each direction around the sensor, as shown in the following diagram:

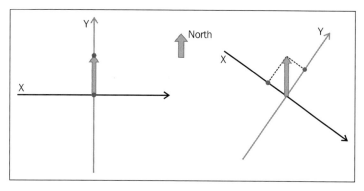

The magnetometer measures the strength of the magnetic field on each axis

The angle at which we turned away from the north can be calculated with the formula shown in the following diagram:

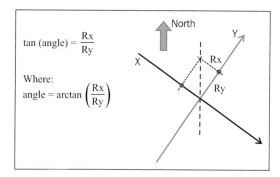

The angle we are pointing towards that is relative to the magnetic north can be calculated using the measurements Rx and Ry

We can now obtain the `compass` angle by adding the following `readCompassAngle()` function to our `compass` class, as follows:

```
def readCompassAngle(self,cal=True):
  if cal==True:
    read = self.readCompass()
  else:
    read = self.readCompassRaw()
```

```
angle = math.atan2 (read[1],read[0]) # cal angle in radians
if (angle < 0):
   angle += (2 * math.pi) # ensure positive
angle = (angle * 360)/(2*math.pi); #report in degrees
return angle
```

We also need to add the following import with the other `import` statements:

```
import math
```

We use the math function, `math.atan2()`, to calculate our angle (`atan2` will return with the angle relative to the x axis of the coordinates `read[1]` and `read[2]`—the angle we want). The angle is in radians, which means one full turn is defined as 2Pi rather than 360 degrees. We convert it back to degrees by multiplying it by 360 and dividing by 2Pi. Since we wish to have our angle between the range of 0 to 360 degrees (rather than -180 to 180 degrees), we must ensure that it is positive by adding the equivalent of a full circle (2Pi) to any negative values.

With the sensor calibrated and the angle calculated, we should now have proper compass bearing to use on our robot. To compare, you can see the result of using the uncalibrated value in our calculation by calling the function with `readCompassAngle (cal=False)`.

Saving the calibration

Having calibrated the sensor once in its current position, it would be inconvenient to have to calibrate it each and every time that you run the robot. Therefore, you can add the following code to your library to automatically save your calibration and read it from a file the next time you run your robot. To create a new calibration, either delete or rename `mag.cal` (which is created in the same folder as your script) or create your `compass` object with `compass(newCal=True)`.

Add the following code near the top of the file (after the `imports` statements):

```
FILENAME="mag.cal"
```

Change `__init__(self)` to `__init__(self,newCal=False)`.

Also, consider the following line:

```
self.offset,self.scaling=self.calibrateCompass()
```

Change the previous line to the following line:

```
self.offset,self.scaling=self.readCal(newCal)
```

Add `readCal()` to the `compass` class as follows:

```python
def readCal(self,newCal=False,filename=FILENAME):
    if newCal==False:
        try:
            with open(FILENAME,'r') as magCalFile:
                line=magCalFile.readline()
                offset=line.split()
                line=magCalFile.readline()
                scaling=line.split()
                if len(offset)==0 or len(scaling)==0:
                    raise ValueError()
                else:
                    offset=list(map(float, offset))
                    scaling=list(map(float, scaling))
        except (OSError,IOError,TypeError,ValueError) as e:
            print("No Cal Data")
            newCal=True
            pass
    if newCal==True:
        print("Perform New Calibration")
        offset,scaling=self.calibrateCompass()
        self.writeCal(offset,scaling)
    return offset,scaling
```

Add `writeCal()` to the `compass` class as follows:

```python
def writeCal(self,offset,scaling):
    if DEBUG:print("Write Calibration")
    if DEBUG:print("offset:"+str(offset))
    if DEBUG:print("scaling:"+str(scaling))
    with open(FILENAME,'w') as magCalFile:
        for value in offset:
            magCalFile.write(str(value)+" ")
        magCalFile.write("\n")
        for value in scaling:
            magCalFile.write(str(value)+" ")
        magCalFile.write("\n")
```

Driving the robot using the compass

All that remains for us to do now is to use the compass bearing to steer our robot to the desired angle.

Create the following `compassDrive.py` script:

```python
#!/usr/bin/env python3
#compassDrive.py
import XLoBorg3 as XLoBorg
import rover_drive as drive
import time

MARGIN=10 #turn until within 10degs
LEFT="l"; RIGHT="r"; DONE="#"

def calDir(target, current, margin=MARGIN):
  target=target%360
  current=current%360
  delta=(target-current)%360
  print("Target=%f Current=%f Delta=%f"%(target,current,delta))

  if delta <= margin:
    CMD=DONE
  else:
    if delta>180:
      CMD=LEFT
    else:
      CMD=RIGHT
  return CMD

def main():
  myCompass=XLoBorg.compass()
  myBot=drive.motor()
  while(True):
    print("Enter target angle:")
    ANGLE=input()
    try:
      angleTarget=float(ANGLE)
      CMD=LEFT
      while (CMD!=DONE):
        angleCompass=myCompass.readCompassAngle()
        CMD=calDir(angleTarget,angleCompass)
        print("CMD: %s"%CMD)
        time.sleep(1)
```

```
        myBot.cmd(CMD)
      print("Angle Reached!")
    except ValueError:
      print("Enter valid angle!")
      pass

  if __name__ == '__main__':
    try:
      main()
    except KeyboardInterrupt:
      print ("Finish")
  #End
```

We import the modules that we previously created: XLoBorg3, rover_drive (for the Rover-Pi robot or the alternative bug_drive, as required), and time. Next, we create a function that will return LEFT, RIGHT, or DONE based on the given target angle (requested by the user) and the current angle (read from the compass class). If the compass angle is within 180 degrees less than the target angle, then we turn LEFT. Similarly, if it is within 180 degrees, we turn RIGHT. Finally, if the compass angle is within the margin (+10 degrees / -10 degrees), then we are DONE. By using angle%360 (which gives us the remainder from dividing the angle by 360), we ensure the angles are all 0-360 (that is, -90 becomes 270).

For the main() function, we create myCompass (an XLoBorg.compass object) and myBot (a drive.motor() object); these allow us to determine the direction we are facing in and provide us with a way to drive in the desired direction. Within the main loop, we prompt for a target angle, find the current angle that our robot is facing at, and then continue to turn towards the required angle until we reach it (or reach somewhere near enough).

10
Interfacing with Technology

In this chapter, we will cover:

- ▸ Automating your home with remote sockets
- ▸ Using SPI to control an LED matrix
- ▸ Communicating using a serial interface
- ▸ Controlling the Raspberry Pi over Bluetooth
- ▸ Controlling USB devices

Introduction

One of the key aspects of the Raspberry Pi that differentiates it from an average computer is its ability to interface with and control hardware. In this chapter, we use the Raspberry Pi to control remotely activated mains sockets, send commands over serial connections from another computer, and control the GPIO remotely. We make use of SPI (another useful protocol) to drive an 8 x 8 LED matrix display.

We also use a Bluetooth module to connect with a smartphone, allowing information to be transferred wirelessly between devices. Finally, we take control of USB devices by tapping into the commands sent over USB.

 Be sure to check out the *Hardware list* section in the *Appendix, Hardware and Software List*; it lists all the items used in this chapter and the places you can obtain them from.

Automating your home with remote sockets

The Raspberry Pi can make an excellent tool for home automation by providing accurate timing, control, and the ability to respond to commands, button inputs, environmental sensors, or messages from the Internet.

Getting ready

Great care must be taken when controlling devices that use electricity from the mains since high voltages and currents are often involved.

Never attempt to modify or alter devices that are connected to mains electricity without proper training. You must never directly connect any homemade devices to the mains supply. All electronics must undergo rigorous safety testing to ensure that there will be no risk or harm to people or property in the event of a failure.

In this example, we will use remote controlled radio frequency (RF) plug-in sockets; these use a separate remote unit to send a specific RF signal to switch any electrical device that is plugged into it on or off. This allows us to modify the remote control and use the Raspberry Pi to activate the switches safely, without interfering with dangerous voltages.

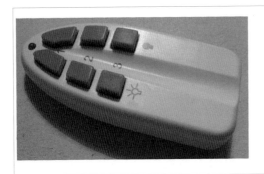

Remote control and remote mains socket

The particular remote control used in this example has six buttons on it to directly switch three different sockets on or off and is powered by a 12-volt battery. It can be switched into four different channels, which would allow you to control a total of 12 sockets (each socket has a similar selector that will be used to set the signal it will respond to).

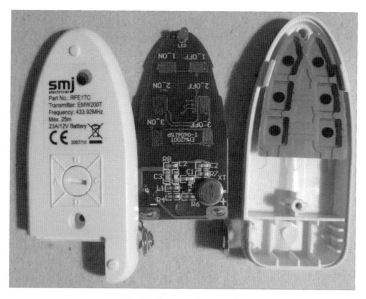

Inside the remote control

The remote buttons, when pressed, will broadcast a specific RF signal (this one uses a transmission frequency of 433.92 MHz). This will trigger any socket(s) that is set to the corresponding channel (A, B, C, or D) and number (1, 2, or 3).

Internally, each of the buttons connects two separate signals to ground, the number (1, 2, or 3), and state (on or off). This triggers the correct broadcast that is to be made by the remote control.

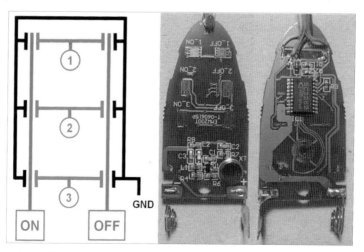

Connect the wires to ON, OFF, 1, 2, 3, and GND at suitable points on the remote's PCB (only ON, OFF, 1, and GND are connected in the image)

It is recommended that you do not connect anything to your sockets that could cause a hazard if switched on or off. The signals sent by the remote are not unique (there are only 4 different channels available). This therefore makes it possible for someone else nearby who has a similar set of sockets to unknowingly activate/deactivate one of your sockets. It is recommended that you select a channel other than the default, A, which will slightly reduce the chance of someone else accidentally using the same channel.

To allow the Raspberry Pi to simulate the button presses of the remote, we will need five relays to allow us to select the number (1, 2, or 3) and state (on or off).

A prebuilt Relay Module can be used to switch the signals

Alternatively, the transistor and relay circuit from *Chapter 9, Building Robots*, can be used to simulate the button presses.

Wire the relay control pins to the Raspberry Pi GPIO and connect the socket remote control to each relay output as follows:

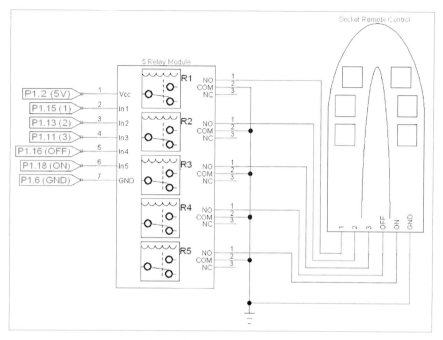

The socket remote control circuit

 Although the remote socket requires both the number (1, 2, or 3) and the state (on or off) to activate a socket, it is the state signal that activates the RF transmission. To avoid draining the remote's battery, we must ensure that we have turned off the state signal.

How to do it...

Create the following socketControl.py script:

```python
#!/usr/bin/python3
# socketControl.py
import time
import RPi.GPIO as GPIO
#HARDWARE SETUP
# P1
# 2[V=G====XI====]26
# 1[=====321=====]25
#V=5V  G=Gnd
```

```python
sw_num=[15,13,11]#Pins for Switch 1,2,3
sw_state=[16,18]#Pins for State X=Off,I=On
MSGOFF=0; MSGON=1
SW_ACTIVE=0; SW_INACTIVE=1

class Switch():
  def __init__(self):
    self.setup()
  def __enter__(self):
    return self
  def setup(self):
    print("Do init")
    #Setup the wiring
    GPIO.setmode(GPIO.BOARD)
    for pin in sw_num:
      GPIO.setup(pin,GPIO.OUT)
    for pin in sw_state:
      GPIO.setup(pin,GPIO.OUT)
    self.clear()
  def message(self,number,state):
    print ("SEND SW_CMD: %s %d" % (number,state))
    if state==MSGON:
      self.on(number)
    else:
      self.off(number)
  def on(self,number):
    print ("ON: %d"% number)
    GPIO.output(sw_num[number-1],SW_ACTIVE)
    GPIO.output(sw_state[MSGON],SW_ACTIVE)
    GPIO.output(sw_state[MSGOFF],SW_INACTIVE)
    time.sleep(0.5)
    self.clear()
  def off(self,number):
    print ("OFF: %d"% number)
    GPIO.output(sw_num[number-1],SW_ACTIVE)
    GPIO.output(sw_state[MSGON],SW_INACTIVE)
    GPIO.output(sw_state[MSGOFF],SW_ACTIVE)
    time.sleep(0.5)
    self.clear()
  def clear(self):
    for pin in sw_num:
      GPIO.output(pin,SW_INACTIVE)
    for pin in sw_state:
      GPIO.output(pin,SW_INACTIVE)
  def __exit__(self, type, value, traceback):
    self.clear()
    GPIO.cleanup()
```

```
def main():
  with Switch() as mySwitches:
    mySwitches.on(1)
    time.sleep(5)
    mySwitches.off(1)

if __name__ == "__main__":
    main()
#End
```

The socket control script performs a quick test by switching the first socket on for 5 seconds and then turning it off again.

To control the rest of the sockets, create a GUI menu as follows:

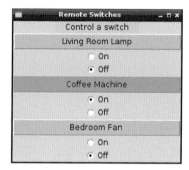

Remote Switches GUI

Create the following `socketMenu.py` script:

```
#!/usr/bin/python3
#socketMenu.py
import tkinter as TK
import socketControl as SC

#Define Switches ["Switch name","Switch number"]
switch1 = ["Living Room Lamp",1]
switch2 = ["Coffee Machine",2]
switch3 = ["Bedroom Fan",3]
sw_list = [switch1,switch2,switch3]
SW_NAME = 0; SW_CMD  = 1
SW_COLOR=["gray","green"]

class swButtons:
  def __init__(self,gui,sw_index,switchCtrl):
    #Add the buttons to window
    self.msgType=TK.IntVar()
    self.msgType.set(SC.MSGOFF)
```

```
            self.btn = TK.Button(gui,
                        text=sw_list[sw_index][SW_NAME],
                        width=30, command=self.sendMsg,
                        bg=SW_COLOR[self.msgType.get()])
            self.btn.pack()
            msgOn = TK.Radiobutton(gui,text="On",
                    variable=self.msgType, value=SC.MSGON)
            msgOn.pack()
            msgOff = TK.Radiobutton(gui,text="Off",
                    variable=self.msgType,value=SC.MSGOFF)
            msgOff.pack()
            self.sw_num=sw_list[sw_index][SW_CMD]
            self.sw_ctrl=switchCtrl
        def sendMsg(self):
            print ("SW_CMD: %s %d" % (self.sw_num,
                                        self.msgType.get()))
            self.btn.configure(bg=SW_COLOR[self.msgType.get()])
            self.sw_ctrl.message(self.sw_num,
                                self.msgType.get())


root = TK.Tk()
root.title("Remote Switches")
prompt = "Control a switch"
label1 = TK.Label(root, text=prompt, width=len(prompt),
                    justify=TK.CENTER, bg='lightblue')
label1.pack()
#Create the switch
with SC.Switch() as mySwitches:
    #Create menu buttons from sw_list
    for index, app in enumerate(sw_list):
        swButtons(root,index,mySwitches)
    root.mainloop()
#End
```

How it works...

The first script defines a class called Switch; it sets up the GPIO pins required to control the five relays (within the setup function). It also defines the __enter__ and __exit__ functions, which are special functions used by the with..as statement. When a class is created using with..as, it uses __enter__ to perform any extra initialization or setup (if required), and then it performs any cleanup by calling __exit__. When the Switch class has been executed, all the relays are switched off to preserve the remote's battery and GPIO. cleanup() is called to release the GPIO pins. The parameters of the __exit__ function (type, value, traceback) allow for the handling of any specific exceptions that may have occurred when the class was being executed within the with..as statement (if required).

To control the sockets, create two functions that will switch the relevant relays on or off to activate the remote control to send the required signal to the sockets. Then, shortly after, turn the relays off again using `clear()`. To make controlling the switches even easier, create a `message` function that will allow a switch number and state to be specified.

We make use of the `socketControl.py` script by creating a Tkinter GUI menu. The menu is made up of three sets of controls (one for each of the switches) that are defined by the `swButtons` class.

The `swButtons` class creates a `Tkinter` button and two `Radiobutton` controls. Each `swButtons` object is given an index and a reference to the `mySwitches` object. This allows us to set a name for the button and control a particular switch when it is pressed. The socket is activated/deactivated by calling `message()`, with the required switch number and state set by the `Radiobutton` controls.

There's more...

The previous example allows you to rewire the remotes of most remote controlled sockets, but another option is to emulate the signals to control it directly.

Sending RF control signals directly

Instead of rewiring the remote control, you can replicate the remote's RF signals using a transmitter that uses the same frequency as your sockets (these particular units use 433.94 MHz). This will depend on the particular sockets and sometimes your location—some countries prohibit the use of certain frequencies—as you may require certification before making your own transmissions.

The 433.94 MHz RF transmitter (left) and receiver (right)

Issue 8 of *The MagPi* covers how to do this in detail in the *Santa Trap* article at `http://www.themagpi.com/issue/issue-8/article/home-automation-the-santa-trap`; it shows how to sample and replicate the required signals. Overall, this can provide a much neater solution; however, it relies on the sockets using a simple transmission method and the availability of a compatible transmitter.

You could even set up the Raspberry Pi to use the receiver module to detect signals from the remote (on an unused channel) and act upon them (to start processes, control other hardware, or perhaps trigger a software shutdown/reboot).

Using SPI to control an LED matrix

In *Chapter 7*, *Sense and Display Real-world Data*, we connected to devices using a bus protocol called I²C. The Raspberry Pi also supports another chip-to-chip protocol called **SPI** (**Serial Peripheral Interface**). The SPI bus differs from I²C because it uses two single direction data lines (where I²C uses one bidirectional data line). Although SPI requires more wires (I²C uses two bus signals, SDA and SCL), it supports the simultaneous sending and receiving of data and much higher clock speeds than I²C.

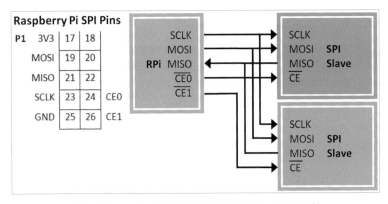

General connections of SPI devices with the Raspberry Pi

The SPI bus consists of the following four signals:

- **SCLK**: This provides the clock edges to read/write data on the input/output lines; it is driven by the master device. As the clock signal changes from one state to another, the SPI device will check the state of the MOSI signal to read a single bit. Similarly, if the SPI device is sending data, it will use the clock signal edges to synchronize when it sets the state of the MISO signal.

- **CE**: This refers to Chip Enable (typically, a separate Chip Enable is used for each slave device on the bus). The master device will set the Chip Enable signal to low for the device that it wants to communicate with. When the Chip Enable signal is set to high, it ignores any other signals on the bus. This signal is sometimes called **Chip Select** (**CS**) or **Slave Select** (**SS**).

- **MOSI**: This stands for Master Output, Slave Input (it connects to Data Out of the master device and Data In of the slave device).
- **MISO**: This stands for Master Input, Slave Output (it provides a response from the slave).

The following diagram shows each of the signals:

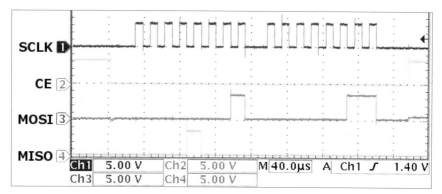

The SPI signals: SCLK (1), CE(2), MOSI(3), and MISO(4)

The previous scope trace shows two bytes being sent over SPI. Each byte is clocked into the SPI device using the **SCLK (1)** signal. A byte is signified by a burst of eight clock cycles (a low and then high period on the **SCLK (1)** signal), where the value of a specific bit is read when the clock state changes. The exact sample point is determined by the clock mode; in the following diagram, it is when the clock goes from low to high:

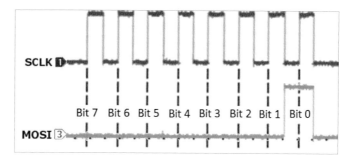

The first data byte sent by the Raspberry Pi to the SPI device on the MOSI(3) signal

The first byte sent is 0x01 (all the bits are low, except **Bit 0**) and the second sent is 0x03 (only **Bit 1** and **Bit 0** are high). At the same time, the **MOSI (4)** signal returns data from the SPI device—in this case, 0x08 (**Bit 3** is high) and 0x00 (all the bits are low). The **SCLK (1)** signal is used to sync everything, even the data being sent from the SPI device.

The **CE (2)** signal is held low while the data is being sent to instruct that particular SPI device to listen to the **MOSI (4)** signal. When the **CE (2)** signal is set to high again, it indicates to the SPI device that the transfer has been completed.

The following is an image of an 8 x 8 LED matrix that is controlled via the **SPI Bus**:

An 8 x 8 LED module displaying the letter K

Getting ready

The wiringPi2 library that we used previously for I²C also supports SPI. Ensure that wiringPi2 is installed (see *Chapter 7, Sense and Display Real-world Data*, for details) so that we can use it here.

Next, we need to enable SPI (if we didn't do so when we enabled I²C previously).

```
sudo nano /etc/modprobe.d/raspi-blacklist.conf
```

Add # before `spi-bcm2708` to comment it out. When done, save and reboot it using `sudo reboot` to apply the change.

You can confirm that the SPI is active by listing all the running modules using the following command:

```
lsmod
```

You can test the SPI with the following `spiTest.py` script:

```python
#!/usr/bin/python3
# spiTest.py
import wiringpi2
```

```
print("Add SPI Loopback - connect P1-Pin19 and P1-Pin21")
print("[Press Enter to continue]")
input()
wiringpi2.wiringPiSPISetup(1,500000)
buffer=str.encode("HELLO")
print("Buffer sent %s" % buffer)
wiringpi2.wiringPiSPIDataRW(1,buffer)
print("Buffer received %s" % buffer)
print("Remove the SPI Loopback")
print("[Press Enter to continue]")
input()
buffer=str.encode("HELLO")
print("Buffer sent %s" % buffer)
wiringpi2.wiringPiSPIDataRW(1,buffer)
print("Buffer received %s" % buffer)
#End
```

Connect inputs 19 and 21 to create an SPI loopback for testing.

The SPI loopback test

You should get the following result:

```
Buffer sent b'HELLO'
Buffer received b'HELLO'
Remove the SPI Loopback
[Press Enter to continue]

Buffer sent b'HELLO'
Buffer received b'\x00\x00\x00\x00\x00'
```

The example that follows uses an LED 8 x 8 matrix display that is being driven by an SPI-controlled **MAX7219 LED driver**:

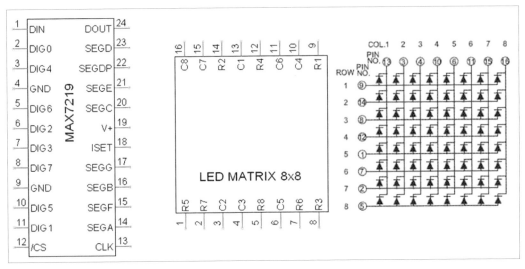

An LED Controller MAX7219 pin-out, LED matrix pin-out, and LED matrix internal wiring (left to right)

Although the device has been designed to control eight separate 7-segment LED digits, we can use it for our LED matrix display. When used for digits, each of the 7 segments (plus a decimal place) is wired to one of the SEG pins, and the COM connection of each of the digits is wired to the DIG pins. The controller then switches each of the segments on as required, while setting the relevant digit COM low to enable it. The controller can quickly cycle through each of the digits using the DIG pin fast enough that all eight appear to be lit at the same time.

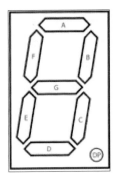

A 7-segment LED digit uses segments A to G, plus DP (decimal place)

We use the controller in a similar way, except each SEG pin will connect to a column in the matrix and the DIG pins will enable/disable a row.

We use an 8 x 8 module connected to the MAX7219 chip as follows:

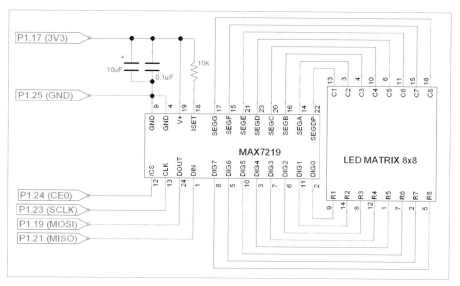

The MAX7219 LED controller driving an 8 x 8 LED matrix display

How to do it...

To control an LED matrix connected to an SPI MAX7219 chip, create the following `matrixControl.py` script:

```python
#!/usr/bin/python3
# matrixControl.py
import wiringpi2
import time

MAX7219_NOOP        = 0x00
DIG0=0x01; DIG1=0x02; DIG2=0x03; DIG3=0x04
DIG4=0x05; DIG5=0x06; DIG6=0x07; DIG7=0x08
MAX7219_DIGIT=[DIG0,DIG1,DIG2,DIG3,DIG4,DIG5,DIG6,DIG7]
MAX7219_DECODEMODE   = 0x09
MAX7219_INTENSITY    = 0x0A
MAX7219_SCANLIMIT    = 0x0B
MAX7219_SHUTDOWN     = 0x0C
MAX7219_DISPLAYTEST  = 0x0F
SPI_CS=1
SPI_SPEED=100000
```

```
class matrix():
  def __init__(self,DEBUG=False):
    self.DEBUG=DEBUG
    wiringpi2.wiringPiSPISetup(SPI_CS,SPI_SPEED)
    self.sendCmd(MAX7219_SCANLIMIT, 8)    # enable outputs
    self.sendCmd(MAX7219_DECODEMODE, 0)   # no digit decode
    self.sendCmd(MAX7219_DISPLAYTEST, 0)  # display test off
    self.clear()
    self.brightness(7)                    # brightness 0-15
    self.sendCmd(MAX7219_SHUTDOWN, 1)     # start display
  def sendCmd(self, register, data):
    buffer=(register<<8)+data
    buffer=buffer.to_bytes(2, byteorder='big')
    if self.DEBUG:print("Send byte: 0x%04x"%
                         int.from_bytes(buffer,'big'))
    wiringpi2.wiringPiSPIDataRW(SPI_CS,buffer)
    if self.DEBUG:print("Response:  0x%04x"%
                         int.from_bytes(buffer,'big'))
    return buffer
  def clear(self):
    if self.DEBUG:print("Clear")
    for row in MAX7219_DIGIT:
      self.sendCmd(row + 1, 0)
  def brightness(self,intensity):
    self.sendCmd(MAX7219_INTENSITY, intensity % 16)

def letterK(matrix):
    print("K")
    K=(0x0066763e1e366646).to_bytes(8, byteorder='big')
    for idx,value in enumerate(K):
        matrix.sendCmd(idx+1,value)

def main():
    myMatrix=matrix(DEBUG=True)
    letterK(myMatrix)
    while(1):
      time.sleep(5)
      myMatrix.clear()
      time.sleep(5)
      letterK(myMatrix)

if __name__ == '__main__':
    main()
#End
```

Running the script (`sudo python3 matrixControl.py`) displays the letter K.

We can use a GUI to control the output of the LED matrix using `matrixMenu.py`:

```python
#!/usr/bin/python3
#matrixMenu.py
import tkinter as TK
import time
import matrixControl as MC

#Enable/Disable DEBUG
DEBUG = True
#Set display sizes
BUTTON_SIZE = 10
NUM_BUTTON = 8
NUM_LIGHTS=NUM_BUTTON*NUM_BUTTON
MAX_VALUE=0xFFFFFFFFFFFFFFFF
MARGIN = 2
WINDOW_H = MARGIN+((BUTTON_SIZE+MARGIN)*NUM_BUTTON)
WINDOW_W = WINDOW_H
TEXT_WIDTH=int(2+((NUM_BUTTON*NUM_BUTTON)/4))
LIGHTOFFON=["red4","red"]
OFF = 0; ON = 1
colBg = "black"

def isBitSet(value,bit):
  return (value>>bit & 1)

def setBit(value,bit,state=1):
  mask=1<<bit
  if state==1:
    value|=mask
  else:
    value&=~mask
  return value

def toggleBit(value,bit):
  state=isBitSet(value,bit)
  value=setBit(value,bit,not state)
  return value

class matrixGUI(TK.Frame):
  def __init__(self,parent,matrix):
    self.parent = parent
    self.matrix=matrix
```

```
    #Light Status
    self.lightStatus=0
    #Add a canvas area ready for drawing on
    self.canvas = TK.Canvas(parent, width=WINDOW_W,
                        height=WINDOW_H, background=colBg)
    self.canvas.pack()
    #Add some "lights" to the canvas
    self.light = []
    for iy in range(NUM_BUTTON):
      for ix in range(NUM_BUTTON):
        x = MARGIN+MARGIN+((MARGIN+BUTTON_SIZE)*ix)
        y = MARGIN+MARGIN+((MARGIN+BUTTON_SIZE)*iy)
        self.light.append(self.canvas.create_rectangle(x,y,
                            x+BUTTON_SIZE,y+BUTTON_SIZE,
                            fill=LIGHTOFFON[OFF]))
    #Add other items
    self.codeText=TK.StringVar()
    self.codeText.trace("w", self.changedCode)
    self.generateCode()
    code=TK.Entry(parent,textvariable=self.codeText,
                justify=TK.CENTER,width=TEXT_WIDTH)
    code.pack()
    #Bind to canvas not tk (only respond to lights)
    self.canvas.bind('<Button-1>', self.mouseClick)

def mouseClick(self,event):
    itemsClicked=self.canvas.find_overlapping(event.x,
                        event.y,event.x+1,event.y+1)
    for item in itemsClicked:
      self.toggleLight(item)

def setLight(self,num):
    state=isBitSet(self.lightStatus,num)
    self.canvas.itemconfig(self.light[num],
                        fill=LIGHTOFFON[state])

def toggleLight(self,num):
    if num != 0:
      self.lightStatus=toggleBit(self.lightStatus,num-1)
      self.setLight(num-1)
      self.generateCode()
```

```python
    def generateCode(self):
      self.codeText.set("0x%016x"%self.lightStatus)

    def changedCode(self,*args):
      updated=False
      try:
        codeValue=int(self.codeText.get(),16)
        if(codeValue>MAX_VALUE):
          codeValue=codeValue>>4
        self.updateLight(codeValue)
        updated=True
      except:
        self.generateCode()
        updated=False
      return updated

    def updateLight(self,lightsetting):
      self.lightStatus=lightsetting
      for num in range(NUM_LIGHTS):
        self.setLight(num)
      self.generateCode()
      self.updateHardware()

    def updateHardware(self):
      sendBytes=self.lightStatus.to_bytes(NUM_BUTTON,
                                          byteorder='big')
      print(sendBytes)
      for idx,row in enumerate(MC.MAX7219_DIGIT):
        response = self.matrix.sendCmd(row,sendBytes[idx])
        print(response)

def main():
  global root
  root=TK.Tk()
  root.title("Matrix GUI")
  myMatrixHW=MC.matrix(DEBUG)
  myMatrixGUI=matrixGUI(root,myMatrixHW)
  TK.mainloop()

if __name__ == '__main__':
    main()
#End
```

The Matrix GUI allows us to switch each of the LEDs on/off by clicking on each of the squares (or by directly entering the hexadecimal value) to create the required pattern.

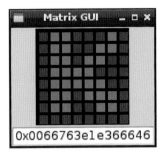

The Matrix GUI to control the 8 x 8 LED matrix

How it works...

Initially, we defined addresses for each of the control registers used by the MAX7219 device. View the datasheet at http://datasheets.maximintegrated.com/en/ds/MAX7219-MAX7221.pdf for more information.

We create a class called matrix that will allow us to control the module. The __init__() function sets up the SPI of the Raspberry Pi (using SPI_CS as pin 26 CS1 and SPI_SPEED as 100 kHz).

The key function in our matrix class is the sendCmd() function; it uses wiringpi2.wiringPiSPIDataRW(SPI_CS,buff) to send buffer (which is the raw byte data that we want to send) over the SPI bus (while also setting the SPI_CS pin low when the transfer occurs). Each command consists of two bytes: the first specifies the address of the register and the second sets the data that needs to be put into it. To display a row of lights, we send the address of one of the ROW registers (MC.MAX7219_DIGIT) and the bit-pattern we want to display (as a byte).

After the wiringpi2.wiringPiSPIDataRW() function is called, buffer contains the result of whatever is received on the MISO pin (which is read simultaneously as the data is sent via the MOSI pin). If connected, this will be the output of the LED module (a delayed copy of the data that was sent). Refer to the following *There's more...* section regarding daisy-chained SPI configurations to learn how the chip output can be used.

To initialize the MAX7219, we need to ensure that it is configured in the correct mode. First, we set the **Scan Limit** field to 7 (which enables all the DIG0 - DIG7 outputs). Next, we disable the built-in digit decoding since we are using the raw output for the display (and don't want it to try to display digits). We also want to ensure that the MAX7219_DISPLAYTEST register is disabled (if enabled, it would turn on all the LEDs).

We ensure the display is cleared by calling our own `clear()` function, which sends 0 to each of the `MAX7219_DIGIT` registers to clear each of the rows. Finally, we use the `MAX7219_INTENSITY` register to set the brightness of the LEDs. The brightness is controlled using a PWM output to make the LEDs appear brighter or darker according to the brightness that is required.

Within the `main()` function, we perform a quick test to display the letter K on the grid by sending a set of 8 bytes (`0x0066763e1e366646`).

	Bits LSB to MSB								
	0	1	2	3	4	5	6	7	
DIG7	0	1	1	0	0	0	1	0	0x46
DIG6	0	1	1	0	0	1	1	0	0x66
DIG5	0	1	1	0	1	1	0	0	0x36
DIG4	0	1	1	1	1	0	0	0	0x1e
DIG3	0	1	1	1	1	1	0	0	0x3e
DIG2	0	1	1	0	1	1	1	0	0x76
DIG1	0	1	1	0	0	1	1	0	0x66
DIG0	0	0	0	0	0	0	0	0	0x00

Each 8 x 8 pattern consists of 8 bits in 8 bytes (one bit for each column, making each byte a row in the display)

The `matrixGUI` class creates a canvas object that is populated with a grid of rectangle objects to represent the 8 x 8 grid of LEDs we want to control (these are kept in `self.light`). We also add a text entry box to display the resulting bytes that we will send to the LED matrix module. We then bind the mouse `<Button-1>` event to the canvas so that `mouseClick` is called whenever a mouse click occurs within the area of the canvas.

We attach a function called `changedCode()` to the `codeText` variable using `trace`, a special Python function, which allows us to monitor specific variables or functions. If we use the `'w'` value with the `trace` function, the Python system will call the callback function whenever the value is written to.

When the `mouseClick()` function is called, we use the `event.x` and `event.y` coordinates to identify the object that is located there. If an item is detected, then the ID of the item is used (via `toggleLight()`) to toggle the corresponding bit in the `self.lightStatus` value, and the color of the light in the display changes accordingly (via `setLight()`). The `codeText` variable is also updated with the new hexadecimal representation of the `lightStatus` value.

The changeCode() function allows us to use the codeText variable and translate it into an integer. This allows us to check whether it is a valid value. Since it is possible to enter text here freely, we must validate it. If we are unable to convert it to an integer, the codeValue text is refreshed using the lightStatus value. Otherwise, we check if it is too large, in which case we perform a bit-shift by 4 to divide it by 16 until it is within a valid range. We update the lightStatus value, the GUI lights, the codeText variable, and also the hardware (by calling updateHardware()).

The updateHardware() function makes use of the myMatrixHW object that was created using the MC.matrix class. We send the bytes that we want to display to the matrix hardware one byte at a time (along with the corresponding MAX7219_DIGIT value to specify the row).

There's more...

The SPI bus allows us to control multiple devices on the same bus, by using the Chip Enable signal. Some devices, such as the MAX7219 also allow what is known as a daisy-chain SPI configuration.

Daisy-chain SPI configuration

You may have noticed that the matrix class also returns a byte when we send the data on the MOSI line. This is the data output from the MAX7219 controller on the DOUT connection. The MAX7219 controller actually passes all the DIN data through to DOUT, which is one set of instructions behind the DIN data. In this way, the MAX7219 can be daisy-chained (with each DOUT feeding into the next DIN). By holding the CE signal low, multiple controllers can be loaded with data by being passed though one another. The data is ignored while CE is set to low, the outputs will only be changed when we set it high again. In this way, you can clock in all the data for each of the modules in the chain and then set CE to high to update them.

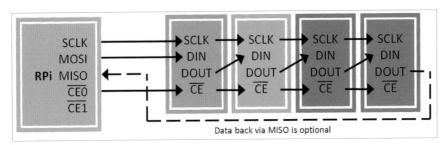

The daisy-chain SPI configuration

We need to do this for each row that we wish to update (or use MAX7219_NOOP if we want to keep the current row the same). This is known as a daisy-chain SPI configuration, supported by some SPI devices, where data is passed through each device on the SPI bus to the next one, which allows the use of three bus control signals for multiple devices.

Communicating using a serial interface

Traditionally, serial protocols such as RS232 are a common way to connect devices such as printers and scanners as well as joysticks and mouse devices to computers. Now, despite being superseded by USB, many peripherals still make use of this protocol for internal communication between components, to transfer data, and to update firmware. For electronics hobbyists, RS232 is a very useful protocol for debugging and controlling other devices while avoiding the complexities of USB.

The two scripts in this example allow for the control of the GPIO pins to illustrate how we can remotely control the Raspberry Pi through the serial port. The serial port could be connected to a PC, another Raspberry Pi, or even an embedded microcontroller (such as Arduino, PIC, or similar).

Getting ready

The easiest way to connect to the Raspberry Pi via a serial protocol will depend on whether your computer has a built-in serial port or not. The serial connection, software, and test setup are described in the following three steps:

1. Create an RS232 serial connection between your computer and the Raspberry Pi. For this, you need one of the following setups:

    ❑   If your computer has a built-in serial port available, you can use a Null-Modem cable with an RS232 to USB adaptor to connect to the Raspberry Pi.

USB for an RS232 adaptor

A Null-Modem is a serial cable/adaptor that has the TX and RX wires crossed over so that one side is connected to the TX pin of the serial port whereas the other side is connected to the RX pin.

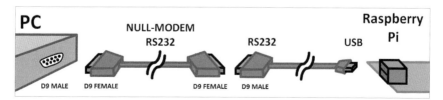

A PC serial port connected to the Raspberry Pi via a Null-Modem cable and an RS232 to USB adaptor

A list of supported USB to RS232 devices is available at the following link:

```
http://elinux.org/RPi_VerifiedPeripherals#USB_
UART_and_USB_to_Serial_.28RS-232.29_adapters
```

Refer to the *There's more...* section for details on how to set them up.

- ❏ If you do not have a serial port built into your computer, you can use another USB to RS232 adaptor to connect to the PC/laptop, converting the RS232 to the more common USB connection.

- ❏ If you do not have any available USB ports on the Raspberry Pi, you can use the GPIO serial pins directly with either a Serial Console Cable or a Bluetooth serial module (refer to the *There's more...* section for details). Both of these will require some additional setup.

 For all cases, you can use an RS232 loopback to confirm that everything is working and set up correctly (again, refer to the *There's more...* section).

2. Next, prepare the software you need for this example.

   You will need to install pySerial so we can use the serial port with Python 3. Install pySerial with the following command (you will also need PIP installed; refer to *Chapter 3, Using Python for Automation and Productivity*, for details):

   ```
   sudo pip-3.2 install pyserial
   ```

   Refer to the pySerial site for further documentation:
   http://pyserial.sourceforge.net.

3. In order to demonstrate the RS232 serial control, you will require some example hardware, attached to the Raspberry Pi's GPIO pins.

   The serialMenu.py script allows the GPIO pins to be controlled through commands sent through the serial port. To fully test this, you can connect suitable output devices (such as LEDs) to each of the GPIO pins. You can ensure that the total current is kept low using 470 ohm resistors for each of the LEDs so that the maximum GPIO current that the Raspberry Pi can supply is not exceeded.

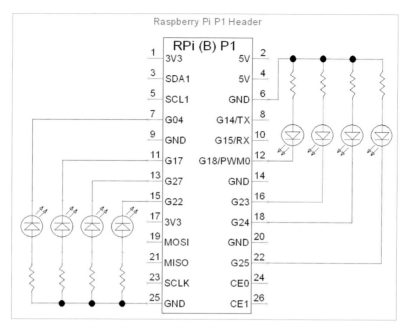

A test circuit to test the GPIO output via serial control

How to do it...

Create the following `serialControl.py` script:

```python
#!/usr/bin/python3
#serialControl.py
import serial
import time

#Serial Port settings
SERNAME="/dev/ttyUSB0"
#default setting is 9600,8,N,1
IDLE=0; SEND=1; RECEIVE=1

def b2s(message):
  '''Byte to String'''
  return bytes.decode(message)
def s2b(message):
  '''String to Byte'''
  return bytearray(message,"ascii")

class serPort():
  def __init__(self,serName="/dev/ttyAMA0"):
```

```python
        self.ser = serial.Serial(serName)
        print (self.ser.name)
        print (self.ser)
        self.state=IDLE
    def __enter__(self):
        return self
    def send(self,message):
        if self.state==IDLE and self.ser.isOpen():
            self.state=SEND
            self.ser.write(s2b(message))
            self.state=IDLE

    def receive(self, chars=1, timeout=5, echo=True,
                terminate="\r"):
        message=""
        if self.state==IDLE and self.ser.isOpen():
            self.state=RECEIVE
            self.ser.timeout=timeout
            while self.state==RECEIVE:
                echovalue=""
                while self.ser.inWaiting() > 0:
                    echovalue += b2s(self.ser.read(chars))
                if echo==True:
                    self.ser.write(s2b(echovalue))
                message+=echovalue
                if terminate in message:
                    self.state=IDLE
        return message
    def __exit__(self,type,value,traceback):
        self.ser.close()

def main():
    try:
        with serPort(serName=SERNAME) as mySerialPort:
            mySerialPort.send("Send some data to me!\r\n")
            while True:
                print ("Waiting for input:")
                print (mySerialPort.receive())
    except OSError:
        print ("Check selected port is valid: %s" %serName)
    except KeyboardInterrupt:
        print ("Finished")

if __name__=="__main__":
    main()
#End
```

Ensure that the `serName` element is correct for the serial port we want to use (such as `/dev/ttyAMA0` for the GPIO pins or `/dev/ttyUSB0` for a USB RS232 adaptor).

Connect the other end to a serial port on your laptop or computer (the serial port can be another USB to RS232 adaptor).

Monitor the serial port on your computer using a serial program such as HyperTerminal or RealTerm (`http://realterm.sourceforge.net`) for Windows or Serial Tools for OS X. You will need to ensure that you have the correct COM port set and a baud rate of 9600 bps (`Parity=None`, `Data Bits=8`, `Stop Bits=1`, and `Hardware Flow Control=None`).

The script will send a request for data from the user and wait for a response.

To send data to the Raspberry Pi, write some text on the other computer and press *Enter* to send it over to the Raspberry Pi.

You will see output similar to the following on the Raspberry Pi terminal:

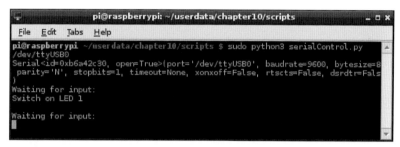

The text "Switch on LED 1" has been sent via a USB to RS232 cable from a connected computer

You will also see output similar to the following on the serial monitoring program:

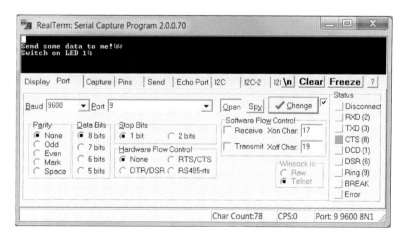

RealTerm displaying typical output from the connected serial port

Press *Ctrl* + *C* on the Raspberry Pi to stop the script.

Now, create a GPIO control menu. Create `serialMenu.py`:

```python
#!/usr/bin/python3
#serialMenu.py
import time
import RPi.GPIO as GPIO
import serialControl as SC
SERNAME = "/dev/ttyUSB0"
running=True

CMD=0;PIN=1;STATE=2;OFF=0;ON=1
GPIO_PINS=[7,11,12,13,15,16,18,22]
GPIO_STATE=["OFF","ON"]
EXIT="EXIT"

def gpioSetup():
  GPIO.setmode(GPIO.BOARD)
  for pin in GPIO_PINS:
    GPIO.setup(pin,GPIO.OUT)

def handleCmd(cmd):
  global running
  commands=cmd.upper()
  commands=commands.split()
  valid=False
  print ("Received: "+ str(commands))
  if len(commands)==3:
    if commands[CMD]=="GPIO":
      for pin in GPIO_PINS:
        if str(pin)==commands[PIN]:
          print ("GPIO pin is valid")
          if GPIO_STATE[OFF]==commands[STATE]:
            print ("Switch GPIO %s %s"% (commands[PIN],
                                         commands[STATE]))
            GPIO.output(pin,OFF)
            valid=True
          elif GPIO_STATE[ON]==commands[STATE]:
            print ("Switch GPIO %s %s"% (commands[PIN],
                                         commands[STATE]))
            GPIO.output(pin,ON)
            valid=True
```

```
      elif commands[CMD]==EXIT:
        print("Exit")
        valid=True
        running=False
      if valid==False:
        print ("Received command is invalid")
        response="  Invalid:GPIO Pin#(%s) %s\r\n"% (
                        str(GPIO_PINS), str(GPIO_STATE))
      else:
        response="  OK\r\n"
      return (response)

def main():
  try:
    gpioSetup()
    with SC.serPort(serName=SERNAME) as mySerialPort:
      mySerialPort.send("\r\n")
      mySerialPort.send("  GPIO Serial Control\r\n")
      mySerialPort.send("  -------------------\r\n")
      mySerialPort.send("  CMD PIN STATE "+
                        "[GPIO Pin# ON]\r\n")
      while running==True:
        print ("Waiting for command...")
        mySerialPort.send(">>")
        cmd = mySerialPort.receive(terminate="\r\n")
        response=handleCmd(cmd)
        mySerialPort.send(response)
      mySerialPort.send("  Finished!\r\n")
  except OSError:
    print ("Check selected port is valid: %s" %serName)
  except KeyboardInterrupt:
    print ("Finished")
  finally:
    GPIO.cleanup()

main()
#End
```

When you run the script (`sudo python3 serialMenu.py`), type the control messages within the serial monitoring program:

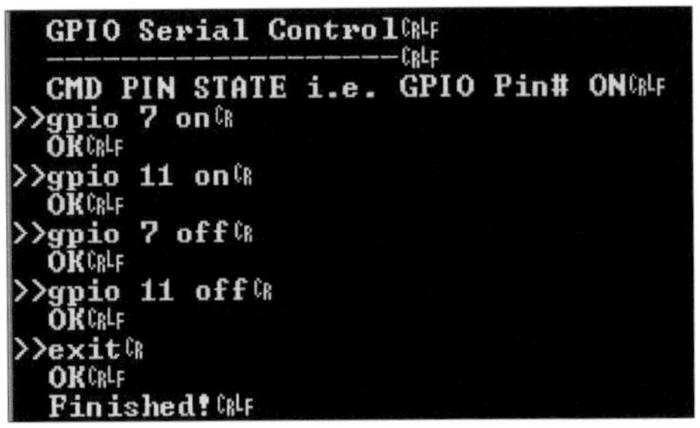

The GPIO Serial Control menu

The terminal output on the Raspberry Pi will be similar to the following screenshot, and the LEDs should respond accordingly:

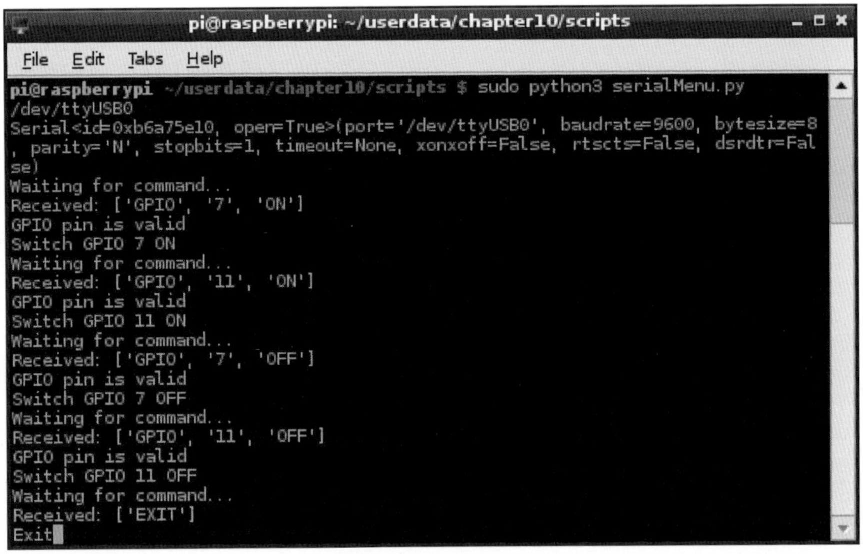

The GPIO Serial Control menu

The Raspberry Pi validates the commands received from the serial connection and switches the LEDs connected to the GPIO pins 7 and 11 on and then off.

How it works...

The first script, `serialControl.py`, provides us with a `serPort` class. We define the class with the following functions:

- ▸ `__init__(self,serName="/dev/ttyAMA0")`: This function will create a new serial device using `serName`—the default of `"/dev/ttyAMA0"` is the ID for the GPIO serial pins (see the *There's more...* section). After it is initialized, information about the device is displayed.

- ▸ `__enter__(self)`: This is a dummy function that allows us to use the `with`...`as` method.

- ▸ `send(self,message)`: This is used to check that the serial port is open and not in use; if so, it will then send a message (after converting it to raw bytes using the `s2b()` function).

- ▸ `receive(self, chars=1, echo=True, terminate="\r")`: After checking whether the serial port is open and not in use, this function then waits for data through the serial port. The function will collect data until the terminate characters are detected, and then the full message is returned.

- ▸ `__exit__(self,type,value,traceback)`: This function is called when the `serPort` object is no longer required by the `with`...`as` method, so we can close the port at this point.

The `main()` function in the script performs a quick test of the class by sending a prompt for data through the serial port to a connected computer and then waiting for input that will be followed by the terminate character(s).

The next script, `serialMenu.py`, allows us to make use of the `serPort` class.

The `main()` function sets up the GPIO pins as outputs (via `gpioSetup()`), creates a new `serPort` object, and finally, waits for commands through the serial port. Whenever a new command is received, the `handleCmd()` function is used to parse the message to ensure that it is correct before acting on it.

The script will switch a particular GPIO pin on or off as commanded through the serial port using the GPIO command keyword. We could add any number of command keywords and control (or read) whatever device (or devices) we attached to the Raspberry Pi. We now have a very effective way to control the Raspberry Pi using any devices connected via a serial link.

There's more...

In addition to the serial transmit and receive, the RS232 serial standard includes several other control signals. To test it, you can use a serial loopback to confirm if the serial ports are set up correctly.

Configuring a USB to RS232 device for the Raspberry Pi

Once you have connected the USB to RS232 device to the Raspberry Pi, check to see if a new serial device is listed by typing the following command:

```
dmesg | grep tty
```

The `dmesg` command lists events that occur on the system; using `grep`, we can filter any messages that mention `tty`, as shown in the following code:

```
[ 2409.195407] usb 1-1.2: pl2303 converter now attached to ttyUSB0
```

This shows that a PL2303-based USB-RS232 device was attached (at 2,409 seconds after startup) and allocated the `ttyUSB0` identity. You will see that a new serial device has been added within the `/dev/` directory (usually `/dev/ttyUSB0` or something similar).

If the device has not been detected, you can try steps similar to the ones used in *Chapter 1, Getting Started with a Raspberry Pi Computer*, to locate and install suitable drivers (if they are available).

RS232 signals and connections

The RS232 serial standard has lots of variants and includes six additional control signals.

The Raspberry Pi GPIO serial drivers (and the Bluetooth TTL module used in the following example) only support RX and TX signals. If you require support for other signals, such as DTR that is often used for a reset prior to the programming of AVR/Arduino devices, then alternative GPIO serial drivers may be needed to set these signals via other GPIO pins. Most RS232 to USB adaptors should support the standard signals; however, ensure that anything you connect is able to handle standard RS232 voltages.

Pin	Signal			Pin	Signal	
1	Carrier Detector (DCD)	DCD		6	Data Set Ready	DSR
2	Receive Data (Rx)	RXD		7	Request to Send	RTS
3	Transmit Data (Tx)	TXD		8	Clear to Send	CTS
4	Data Terminal Ready	DTR		9	Ring Indicator	RI
5	Signal Ground (SG)	GND				

PIN 1 → ● ● ● ● ● ← PIN 5
PIN 6 → ● ● ● ● ← PIN 9
RS232 D9

The RS232 9-Way D Connector pin-out and signals

For more details on the RS232 serial protocol and to know how these signals are used, visit the following link:

```
http://en.wikipedia.org/wiki/Serial_port
```

Using the GPIO built-in serial pins

Standard RS232 signals can range from -15V to +15V, so you must never directly connect any RS232 device to the GPIO serial pins. You must use an RS232 to TTL voltage-level converter (such as a MAX232 chip) or a device that uses TTL-level signals (such as another microcontroller or a TTL serial console cable).

A USB to TTL serial console cable

The Raspberry Pi has TTL-level serial pins on the P1 GPIO header that allow the connection of a TTL serial USB cable. The wires will connect to the Raspberry Pi GPIO pins, and the USB will plug in to your computer and be detected like a standard RS232 to USB cable.

				Serial Console Cable
3V3	1	2	5V	
RPi GPIO	3	4	5V	5V Red (optional)
P1	5	6	GND	GND Black
	7	8	TX	RXD White
	9	10	RX	TXD Green

Connection of a USB to TTL serial console cable to the Raspberry Pi GPIO

It is possible to provide power from the USB port to the 5V pin; however, this will bypass the built-in polyfuse, so it is not recommended for general use (just leave the 5V wire disconnected and power as normal through the micro-USB).

By default, these pins are set up to allow remote terminal access, allowing you to connect to the COM port via PuTTY and create a serial SSH session.

A serial SSH session can be helpful if you want to use the Raspberry Pi without a display attached to it.

However, a serial SSH session is limited to text-only terminal access since it does not support X10 Forwarding, as used in the *Connecting remotely to Raspberry Pi over the network using SSH (and X11 Forwarding)* section of Chapter 1, *Getting Started with a Raspberry Pi Computer*.

In order to use it as a standard serial connection, we have to disable the serial console so it is available for us to use.

First, we need to edit `/boot/cmdline.txt` to remove the first `console` and `kgboc` options (do not remove the other `console=tty1` option, which is the default terminal when you switch on).

```
sudo nano /boot/cmdline.txt
dwc_otg.lpm_enable=0 console=ttyAMA0,115200 kgdboc=ttyAMA0,115200
console=tty1 root=/dev/mmcblk0p2 rootfstype=ext4 elevator=deadline
rootwait
```

The previous command line becomes the following (ensure that this is still a single command line):

```
dwc_otg.lpm_enable=0 console=tty1 root=/dev/mmcblk0p2 rootfstype=ext4
elevator=deadline rootwait
```

We also have to remove the task that runs the `getty` command (the program that handles the text terminal for the serial connection) by commenting it out with #. This is set in `/etc/inittab` as follows:

```
sudo nano /etc/inittab
T0:23:respawn:/sbin/getty -L ttyAMA0 115200 vt100
```

The previous command line becomes the following:

```
#T0:23:respawn:/sbin/getty -L ttyAMA0 115200 vt100
```

To reference the GPIO serial port in our script, we use its name, `/dev/ttyAMA0`.

The RS232 loopback

You can check whether the serial port connections are working correctly using a serial loopback.

A simple loopback consists of connecting RXD and TXD together. These are pins 8 and 10 on the Raspberry Pi GPIO P1 header or pins 2 and 3 on the standard RS232 D9 connector on the USB-RS232 adaptor.

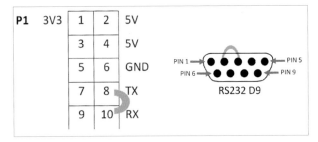

Serial loopback connections to test the Raspberry Pi GPIO (left) and RS232 9-Way D Connector (right)

An RS232 full loopback cable also connects pin 4 (DTR) and pin 6 (DSR) as well as pin 7 (RTS) and pin 8 (CTS) on the RS232 adaptor. However, this is not required for most situations, unless these signals are used. By default, no pins are allocated on the Raspberry Pi specifically for these additional signals.

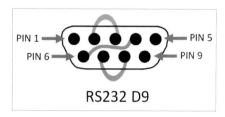

RS232 full loopback

Create the following `serialTest.py` script:

```python
#!/usr/bin/python3
#serialTest.py
import serial
import time

WAITTIME=1
serName="/dev/ttyAMA0"
ser = serial.Serial(serName)
print (ser.name)
print (ser)
if ser.isOpen():
  try:
    print("For Serial Loopback - connect P1-Pin8 and P1-Pin10")
    print("[Type Message and Press Enter to continue]")
    print("#:")
    command=input()
    ser.write(bytearray(command+"\r\n","ascii"))
    time.sleep(WAITTIME)
    out=""
    while ser.inWaiting() > 0:
      out += bytes.decode(ser.read(1))
    if out != "":
      print (">>" + out)
    else:
      print ("No data Received")
  except KeyboardInterrupt:
    ser.close()
#End
```

When a loopback is connected, you will observe that the message is echoed back to the screen (when removed, `No data Received` will be displayed):

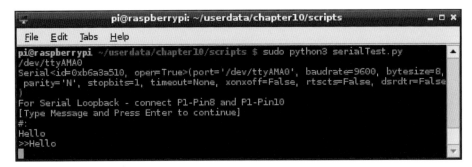

An RS232 loopback test on GPIO serial pins

If we require nondefault settings, they can be defined when the serial port is initialized (the pySerial documentation at `http://pyserial.sourceforge.net` provides full details of all the options), as shown in the following code:

```
ser = serial.Serial(port=serName, baudrate= 115200,
    timeout=1, parity=serial.PARITY_ODD,
    stopbits=serial.STOPBITS_TWO,
    bytesize=serial.SEVENBITS)
```

Controlling the Raspberry Pi over Bluetooth

Serial data can also be sent through Bluetooth by connecting a HC-05 Bluetooth module that supports the **Serial Port Profile** (**SPP**) to the GPIO serial RX/TX pins. This allows the serial connection to become wireless, which allows Android tablets or smartphones to be used to control things and read data from the Raspberry Pi.

The HC-05 Bluetooth module for the TLL serial

While it is possible to achieve a similar result using a USB Bluetooth dongle, additional configuration would be required depending on the particular dongle used. The TTL Bluetooth module provides a drop-in replacement for a physical cable, requiring very little additional configuration.

Getting ready

Ensure that the serial console has been disabled (see the previous *There's more...* section).

The module should be connected using the following pins:

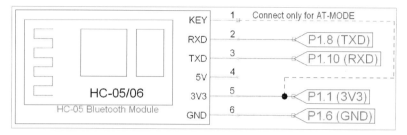

Connection to a Bluetooth module for the TLL serial

How to do it...

With the Bluetooth module configured and connected, we can pair the module with a laptop or smartphone to send and receive commands wirelessly. Bluetooth SPP Pro provides an easy way to use a serial connection over Bluetooth to control or monitor the Raspberry Pi for Android devices.

Alternatively, you may be able to set up a Bluetooth COM port on your PC/laptop and use it in the same way as the previous wired example:

1. When the device is connected initially, the LED flashes quickly to indicate that it is waiting to be paired. Enable Bluetooth on your device and select the **HC-05** device.

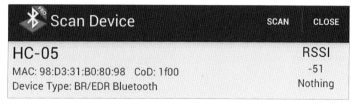

The HC-05 Bluetooth module viewable in Bluetooth SPP Pro

2. Click on the **Pair** button to begin the pairing process and enter the device **PIN** (the default is `1234`).

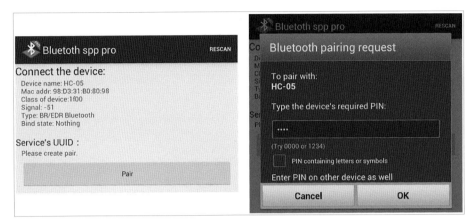

Pair the Bluetooth device with the PIN code (1234)

3. If the pairing was successful, you will be able to connect with the device and send and receive messages to and from the Raspberry Pi.

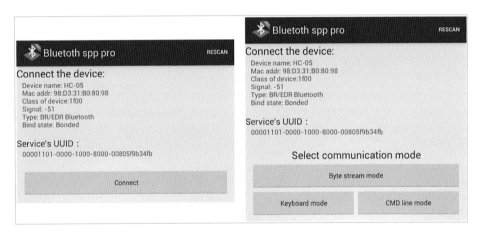

Connect to the device and select the control method

4. In **Keyboard mode**, you can define actions for each of the buttons to send suitable commands when pressed.

   For example, **Pin12 ON** can be set to send `gpio 12 on`, and **Pin12 OFF** can be set to send `gpio 12 off`.

5. Ensure that you set the end flag to `\r\n` via the menu options.

6. Ensure that `menuSerial.py` is set to use the GPIO serial connection:

   ```
   serName="/dev/ttyAMA0"
   ```

7. Run the `menuSerial.py` script (with the LEDs attached):

   ```
   sudo python3 menuSerial.py
   ```

8. Check that the Bluetooth serial app displays the `GPIO Serial Control` menu as shown in the following screenshot:

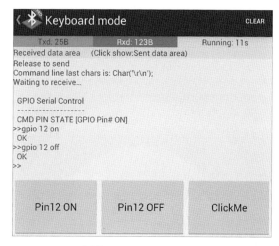

GPIO control over Bluetooth

We can see from the output in the following screenshot that the commands have been received and the LED connected to pin 12 has been switched on and off as required.

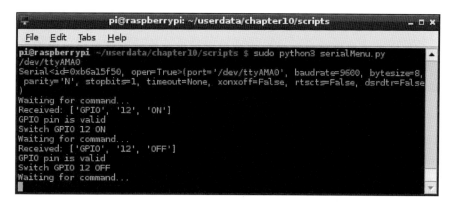

The Raspberry Pi receiving GPIO control over Bluetooth

How it works...

By default, the Bluetooth module is set up to act like a TTL serial slave device, so we can simply plug it in to the GPIO RX and TX pins. Once the module is paired with a device, it will transfer the serial communication over the Bluetooth connection. This allows us to send commands and receive data via Bluetooth and control the Raspberry Pi using a smart phone or PC.

This means you can attach a second module to another device (such as an Arduino) that has TTL serial pins and control it using the Raspberry Pi (either by pairing it with another TTL Bluetooth module or suitably configuring a USB Bluetooth dongle). If the module is set up as a master device, then you will need to reconfigure it to act as a slave (see the *There's more...* section).

There's more...

Now, let's understand how to configure the Bluetooth settings.

Configuring Bluetooth module settings

The Bluetooth module can be set in two different modes using the KEY pin.

In a normal operation, serial messages are sent over Bluetooth; however, if we need to change the settings of the Bluetooth module itself, we can do so by connecting the KEY pin to 3V3 and putting it into the AT mode.

The AT mode allows us to directly configure the module, allowing us to change the baud rate, the pairing code, the device name, or even set it up as a master/slave device.

You can use `miniterm`, which is part of pySerial, to send the required messages, as shown in the following code:

```
python3 -m serial.tools.miniterm
```

The miniterm program, when started, will prompt for the port to use:

```
Enter port name: /dev/ttyAMA0
```

You can send the following commands (you will need to do this quickly, or paste them, as the module will time out if there is a gap and respond with an error):

- `AT`: This command should respond with **OK**.
- `AT+UART?`: This command will report the current settings as `UART=<Param1>,<Param2>,<Param3>`. The output of this command will be **OK**.
- To change the current settings, use `AT+UART=<Param1>,<Param2>,<Param3>`, that is, `AT+UART=19200,0,0`.

<Param1> Baud Rate (bits/s)									
4800	9600	19200	38400	57600	115200	23400	460800	921600	1382400
<Param2> Stop Bit			0	1 Bit			1		2 Bits
<Param3> Parity Bit			0	None	1	Odd Parity	2		Even Parity

HC-05 AT mode AT+UART command parameters

For details on how to configure modules as paired master and slave devices (for example, between two Raspberry Pi devices), Zak Kemble has written an excellent guide. It is available at the following link:

```
http://blog.zakkemble.co.uk/getting-bluetooth-modules-talking-to-
each-other/
```

For additional documentation on the HC-05 module, visit the following link:

```
http://www.exp-tech.de/service/datasheet/HC-Serial-Bluetooth-
Products.pdf
```

Controlling USB devices

The **Universal Serial Bus** (**USB**) is used extensively by computers to provide additional peripherals and expansion through a common standard connection. We will use the Python library **PyUSB** to send custom commands to connected devices over USB.

The following example controls a USB toy missile launcher, which in turn allows it to be controlled by our Python control panel. We see that the same principle can be applied to other USB devices, such as a robotic arm, using similar techniques, and the controls can be activated using a sensor connected to the Raspberry Pi GPIO.

The USB Tenx Technology SAM missile launcher

Getting ready

We will need to install PyUSB for Python 3 using `pip-3.2` as follows:

```
sudo pip-3.2 install pyusb
```

You can test whether PyUSB has installed correctly by running the following:

```
python3
> import usb
> help (usb)
> exit()
```

This should allow you to view the package information if it was installed correctly.

How to do it...

We will create the following `missileControl.py` script, which will include two classes and a default `main()` function, to test it.

1. Import the required modules as follows:

```python
#!/usr/bin/python3
# missileControl.py
import time
import usb.core
```

2. Define the `SamMissile()` class, which provides the specific commands for the USB device, as follows:

```python
class SamMissile():
    idVendor=0x1130
    idProduct=0x0202
    idName="Tenx Technology SAM Missile"
    # Protocol control bytes
    bmRequestType=0x21
    bmRequest=0x09
    wValue=0x02
    wIndex=0x01
    # Protocol command bytes
    INITA    = [ord('U'), ord('S'), ord('B'), ord('C'),
                  0,  0,  4,  0]
    INITB    = [ord('U'), ord('S'), ord('B'), ord('C'),
                  0, 64,  2,  0]
    CMDFILL  = [ 8,  8,
```

```
                      0,   0,   0,   0,   0,   0,   0,   0,
                      0,   0,   0,   0,   0,   0,   0,   0,
                      0,   0,   0,   0,   0,   0,   0,   0,
                      0,   0,   0,   0,   0,   0,   0,   0,
                      0,   0,   0,   0,   0,   0,   0,   0,
                      0,   0,   0,   0,   0,   0,   0,   0,
                      0,   0,   0,   0,   0,   0,   0,   0]#48 zeros
STOP      = [ 0,   0,   0,   0,   0,   0]
LEFT      = [ 0,   1,   0,   0,   0,   0]
RIGHT     = [ 0,   0,   1,   0,   0,   0]
UP        = [ 0,   0,   0,   1,   0,   0]
DOWN      = [ 0,   0,   0,   0,   1,   0]
LEFTUP    = [ 0,   1,   0,   1,   0,   0]
RIGHTUP   = [ 0,   0,   1,   1,   0,   0]
LEFTDOWN  = [ 0,   1,   0,   0,   1,   0]
RIGHTDOWN = [ 0,   0,   1,   0,   1,   0]
FIRE      = [ 0,   0,   0,   0,   0,   1]
def __init__(self):
  self.dev = usb.core.find(idVendor=self.idVendor,
                           idProduct=self.idProduct)
def move(self,cmd,duration):
  print("Move:%s %d sec"% (cmd,duration))
  self.dev.ctrl_transfer(self.bmRequestType,
                         self.bmRequest,self.wValue,
                         self.wIndex, self.INITA)
  self.dev.ctrl_transfer(self.bmRequestType,
                         self.bmRequest,self.wValue,
                         self.wIndex, self.INITB)
  self.dev.ctrl_transfer(self.bmRequestType,
                         self.bmRequest, self.wValue,
                         self.wIndex, cmd+self.CMDFILL)
  time.sleep(duration)
  self.dev.ctrl_transfer(self.bmRequestType,
                         self.bmRequest, self.wValue,
                         self.wIndex, self.INITA)
  self.dev.ctrl_transfer(self.bmRequestType,
                         self.bmRequest, self.wValue,
                         self.wIndex, self.INITB)
  self.dev.ctrl_transfer(self.bmRequestType,
                     self.bmRequest, self.wValue,
                     self.wIndex, self.STOP+self.CMDFILL)
```

3. Define the `Missile()` class, which allows us to detect the USB device and provide command functions, as follows:

```python
class Missile():
  def __init__(self):
    print("Initialize Missiles")
    self.usbDevice=SamMissile()

    if self.usbDevice.dev is not None:
      print("Device Initialized:" +
            " %s" % self.usbDevice.idName)
      #Detach the kernel driver if active
      if self.usbDevice.dev.is_kernel_driver_active(0):
        print("Detaching kernel driver 0")
        self.usbDevice.dev.detach_kernel_driver(0)
      if self.usbDevice.dev.is_kernel_driver_active(1):
        print("Detaching kernel driver 1")
        self.usbDevice.dev.detach_kernel_driver(1)
      self.usbDevice.dev.set_configuration()
    else:
      raise Exception("Missile device not found")
  def __enter__(self):
    return self
  def left(self,duration=1):
    self.usbDevice.move(self.usbDevice.LEFT,duration)
  def right(self,duration=1):
    self.usbDevice.move(self.usbDevice.RIGHT,duration)
  def up(self,duration=1):
    self.usbDevice.move(self.usbDevice.UP,duration)
  def down(self,duration=1):
    self.usbDevice.move(self.usbDevice.DOWN,duration)
  def fire(self,duration=1):
    self.usbDevice.move(self.usbDevice.FIRE,duration)
  def stop(self,duration=1):
    self.usbDevice.move(self.usbDevice.STOP,duration)
  def __exit__(self, type, value, traceback):
    print("Exit")
```

4. Finally, create a `main()` function, which provides a quick test of our `missileControl.py` module if the file is run directly, as follows:

```python
def main():
  try:
    with Missile() as myMissile:
      myMissile.down()
      time.sleep(2)
```

```
        myMissile.up()
    except Exception as detail:
      print("Error: %s" % detail)


if __name__ == '__main__':
    main()
#End
```

When the script is run using the following command, you should see the missile launcher move downwards and then up again:

sudo python3 missileControl.py

To provide easy control of the device, create the following GUI:

The Missile Command GUI

Although simple commands have been used here, you could use a series of preset commands if desired.

Create the GUI for the `missileMenu.py` missile command:

```
#!/usr/bin/python3
#missileMenu.py
import tkinter as TK
import missileControl as MC

BTN_SIZE=10

def menuInit():
  btnLeft = TK.Button(root, text="Left",
                    command=sendLeft, width=BTN_SIZE)
  btnRight = TK.Button(root, text="Right",
                    command=sendRight, width=BTN_SIZE)
  btnUp = TK.Button(root, text="Up",
                    command=sendUp, width=BTN_SIZE)
  btnDown = TK.Button(root, text="Down",
                    command=sendDown, width=BTN_SIZE)
```

```
    btnFire = TK.Button(root, text="Fire",command=sendFire,
                        width=BTN_SIZE, bg="red")
    btnLeft.grid(row=2,column=0)
    btnRight.grid(row=2,column=2)
    btnUp.grid(row=1,column=1)
    btnDown.grid(row=3,column=1)
    btnFire.grid(row=2,column=1)

def sendLeft():
  print("Left")
  myMissile.left()

def sendRight():
  print("Right")
  myMissile.right()

def sendUp():
  print("Up")
  myMissile.up()

def sendDown():
  print("Down")
  myMissile.down()

def sendFire():
  print("Fire")
  myMissile.fire()


root = TK.Tk()
root.title("Missile Command")
prompt = "Select action"
label1 = TK.Label(root, text=prompt, width=len(prompt),
                  justify=TK.CENTER, bg='lightblue')
label1.grid(row=0,column=0,columnspan=3)
menuInit()
with MC.Missile() as myMissile:
  root.mainloop()
#End
```

How it works...

The control script consists of two classes: one called `Missile` which provides a common interface for the control, and another called `SamMissile` which provides all the specific details of the particular USB device being used.

In order to drive a USB device, we need a lot of information about the device, such as its USB identification, its protocol, and the control messages it requires to be controlled.

The USB ID for the Tenx Technology SAM missile device is determined by the vendor ID (`0x1130`) and the product ID (`0x0202`). This is the same identification information you would see within **Device Manager** in Windows. These IDs are usually registered with `www.usb.org`; therefore, each device should be unique. Again, you can use the `dmesg | grep usb` command to discover these.

We use the device IDs to find the USB device using `usb.core.find`; then, we can send messages using `ctrl_transfer()`.

The USB message has five parts:

- **Request type** (`0x21`): This defines the type of the message request, such as the message direction (Host to Device), its type (Vendor), and the recipient (Interface)
- **Request** (`0x09`): This is the set configuration
- **Value** (`0x02`): This is the configuration value
- **Index** (`0x01`): This is the command we want to send
- **Data**: This is the command we want to send (as described next)

The `SamMissile` device requires the following commands to move:

- It requires two initialization messages (`INITA` and `INITB`).
- It also requires the control message. This consists of the `CMD`, which includes one of the control bytes that has been set to `1` for the required component. The `CMD` is then added to `CMDFILL` to complete the message.

You will see that the other missile devices and the robot arm (see the following *There's more...* section) have similar message structures.

For each device, we created the `__init__()` and `move()` functions and defined values for each of the valid commands, which the `missile` class will use whenever the `left()`, `right()`, `up()`, `down()`, `fire()`, and `stop()` functions are called.

For the control GUI for our missile launcher, we create a small Tkinter window with five buttons, each of which will send a command to the missile device.

We import `missileControl` and create a `missile` object called `myMissile` that will be controlled by each of the buttons.

There's more...

The example only shows how to control one particular USB device; however, it is possible to extend this to support several types of missile devices and even other USB devices in general.

Controlling similar missile-type devices

There are several variants of USB missile-type devices, each with their own USB IDs and USB commands. We can add support for these other devices by defining their own classes to handle them.

Use `lsusb -vv` to determine the vendor and product ID that matches your device.

For `Chesen Electronics/Dream Link`:

```python
class ChesenMissile():
    idVendor=0x0a81
    idProduct=0x0701
    idName="Chesen Electronics/Dream Link"
    # Protocol control bytes
    bmRequestType=0x21
    bmRequest=0x09
    wValue=0x0200
    wIndex=0x00
    # Protocol command bytes
    DOWN    = [0x01]
    UP      = [0x02]
    LEFT    = [0x04]
    RIGHT   = [0x08]
    FIRE    = [0x10]
    STOP    = [0x20]
    def __init__(self):
        self.dev = usb.core.find(idVendor=self.idVendor,
                                 idProduct=self.idProduct)
    def move(self,cmd,duration):
        print("Move:%s"%cmd)
        self.dev.ctrl_transfer(self.bmRequestType,
                               self.bmRequest,
                               self.wValue, self.wIndex, cmd)
        time.sleep(duration)
        self.dev.ctrl_transfer(self.bmRequestType,
                               self.bmRequest, self.wValue,
                               self.wIndex, self.STOP)
```

For `Dream Cheeky Thunder`:

```
class ThunderMissile():
  idVendor=0x2123
  idProduct=0x1010
  idName="Dream Cheeky Thunder"
  # Protocol control bytes
  bmRequestType=0x21
  bmRequest=0x09
  wValue=0x00
  wIndex=0x00
  # Protocol command bytes
  CMDFILL = [0,0,0,0,0,0]
  DOWN    = [0x02,0x01]
  UP      = [0x02,0x02]
  LEFT    = [0x02,0x04]
  RIGHT   = [0x02,0x08]
  FIRE    = [0x02,0x10]
  STOP    = [0x02,0x20]
  def __init__(self):
    self.dev = usb.core.find(idVendor=self.idVendor,
                             idProduct=self.idProduct)
  def move(self,cmd,duration):
    print("Move:%s"%cmd)
    self.dev.ctrl_transfer(self.bmRequestType,
                           self.bmRequest, self.wValue,
                           self.wIndex, cmd+self.CMDFILL)
    time.sleep(duration)
    self.dev.ctrl_transfer(self.bmRequestType,
                           self.bmRequest, self.wValue,
                           self.wIndex, self.STOP+self.CMDFILL)
```

Finally, adjust the script to use the required class as follows:

```
class Missile():
  def __init__(self):
    print("Initialize Missiles")
    self.usbDevice = ThunderMissile()
```

Robot arm

Another device that can be controlled in a similar manner is the OWI Robotic Arm with a USB interface.

The OWI Robotic Arm with a USB interface (Image courtesy of Chris Stagg)

This has featured in *The MagPi* magazine several times, thanks to Stephen Richards' articles on Skutter; the USB control has been explained in detail in issue 3 at http://www.themagpi.com/issue/issue-3/article/skutter-write-a-program-for-usb-device.

The robotic arm can be controlled using the following class. Remember that you will also need to adjust the commands from UP, DOWN, and so on when calling the move() function, as shown in the following code:

```
class OwiArm():
  idVendor=0x1267
  idProduct=0x0000
  idName="Owi Robot Arm"
  # Protocol control bytes
  bmRequestType=0x40
  bmRequest=0x06
  wValue=0x0100
  wIndex=0x00
  # Protocol command bytes
  BASE_CCW   = [0x00,0x01,0x00]
  BASE_CW    = [0x00,0x02,0x00]
```

```
SHOLDER_UP   = [0x40,0x00,0x00]
SHOLDER_DWN  = [0x80,0x00,0x00]
ELBOW_UP     = [0x10,0x00,0x00]
ELBOW_DWN    = [0x20,0x00,0x00]
WRIST_UP     = [0x04,0x00,0x00]
WRIST_DOWN   = [0x08,0x00,0x00]
GRIP_OPEN    = [0x02,0x00,0x00]
GRIP_CLOSE   = [0x01,0x00,0x00]
LIGHT_ON     = [0x00,0x00,0x01]
LIGHT_OFF    = [0x00,0x00,0x00]
STOP         = [0x00,0x00,0x00]
```

Taking USB control further

The theory and method of control used for the USB missile device can be applied to very complex devices such as the Xbox 360's Kinect (a special 3D camera add-on for the Xbox game console) as well.

The company Adafruit's website has a very interesting tutorial written by Limor Fried (also known as Ladyada) on how to analyze and investigate USB commands; access it at `http://learn.adafruit.com/hacking-the-kinect`.

This is well worth a look if you intend to reverse engineer other USB items.

Hardware and Software List

In this chapter, we will cover:

- ▸ General component sources
- ▸ Hardware list
- ▸ Software list

Introduction

This book uses a wide range of hardware to demonstrate what can be achieved by combining hardware and software in various ways. To get the most out of this book, it is highly recommended that you experiment with some of the hardware projects. I feel it is particularly rewarding to observe physical results from your coding efforts, and this differentiates the Raspberry Pi for learning over a typical computer.

A common problem is finding the right components for a project while not spending a fortune on it. All the hardware used in this book focuses on using low cost items that can usually be purchased from a variety of suppliers, in most cases with only a few dollars.

To help you locate suitable items, this appendix will list each hardware item used in the chapters with links to where they can be obtained. The list is not exhaustive, and it is likely that the availability of the items (and prices) may vary over time, so whenever you purchase, ensure you search around for the best value. Where practical, enough detail has been provided in the chapters to allow you to source your own components and build your own modules.

This appendix also includes a full list of software and Python modules mentioned in the book, including the specific versions used. If the software used in the book is updated and improved, it is likely that some modules will lose backward compatibility. Therefore, if you find the latest version installed does not function as expected, it may be that you will need to install an older version (details on how to do this are provided in the *There's more...* section of the *Software list* recipe).

General component sources

Once you have completed some of the hardware-based recipes in this book, you may find that you want to experiment with other components. There are many places where you can get good value for components and add-on modules for general electronics, and also specifically for Raspberry Pi or other electronic-based hobbies. This list is not exhaustive, but is a selection of places I have ordered items from in the past and that offer good value for money.

General electronic component retailers

You will probably find that every retailer mentioned in the following list has localized sites for their own country, offers worldwide services or has local distribution services:

- Farnell/element14/Newark: http://www.newark.com
- RS Components: http://www.rs-components.com
- Amazon: http://www.amzon.com
- eBay: http://www.ebay.com
- Tandy UK: http://www.tandyonline.co.uk
- Maplin UK: http://www.maplin.co.uk

Makers, hobbyists, and Raspberry Pi specialists

There are many companies that specialize in selling modules and add-ons that can be used with computers and devices, such as Raspberry Pi, that are aimed at the hobbyist. Some of them are as follows:

- Adafruit Industries: http://www.adafruit.com
- SparkFun Electronics: http://www.sparkfun.com
- Mouser Electronics: http://www.mouser.com
- Banggood: http://www.banggood.com
- DealExtreme: http://dx.com
- Pimoroni: http://shop.pimoroni.com
- Pi Supply: http://www.pi-supply.com
- PiBorg: http://www.piborg.com

▶ Hobbyking: `http://www.hobbyking.com`

▶ ModMyPi: `http://www.modmypi.com`

▶ Quick2Wire: `http://quick2wire.com`

▶ GeekOnFire: `http://www.geekonfire.com`

▶ Ciseco: `http://shop.ciseco.co.uk`

You can also have a look at my own site at the following which specializes in educational kits and tutorials:

▶ Pi Hardware: `http://PiHardware.com`

Hardware list

A summary of the hardware used in the chapters of this book is mentioned in this section.

Chapter 1

This chapter describes the Raspberry Pi setup; the items mentioned include the following:

▶ Raspberry Pi and power supply

▶ An HDMI display and HDMI cable / analog TV and analog video cable

▶ Keyboard

▶ Mouse

▶ Network cable / Wi-Fi adaptor

Chapter 2-5

No additional hardware has been used in these chapters as they discuss purely software recipes.

Chapter 6

The components used in this chapter are available at most electronic component retailers (such as those listed previously in the *General electronic component retailers* section). They are also available as a complete kit from **Pi Hardware**. Where items are available from specific retailers, they are highlighted in the text.

The kit for controlling an LED includes the following equipment:

▶ 4x Dupont Female to Male Patch Wires (**Pimoroni** Jumper Jerky)

▶ A mini breadboard (170 tie-point) or a larger one (**Pimoroni**)

▶ An RGB LED (Common-Cathode) / 3 standard LEDs (ideally Red/Green/Blue)

▶ A breadboarding wire (solid core)

▶ 3x 470-ohm resistors

The kit for responding to a button includes the following equipment:

- 2x Dupont Female to Male Patch wires (**Pimoroni** Jumper Jerky)
- A mini breadboard (170 tie-point) or a larger one (**Pimoroni**)
- A push button to make switch and momentary switch (or a wire connection to make/break the circuit)
- A breadboarding wire (solid core)
- A 1K ohm resistor

The items used for the controlled shutdown button are as follows:

- 3x Dupont Female to Male Patch Wires (**Pimoroni** Jumper Jerky)
- A mini breadboard (170 tie-point) or larger (**Pimoroni**)
- A push button
- A normal LED (red)
- 2x 470-ohm resistors
- A breadboarding wire (solid core)

The additional items used in the *There's more...* section of the recipe *A controlled shutdown button* are as follows:

- A push button
- A 470-ohm resistor
- A pin header x2 pins with a jumper connector (or optionally a switch)
- A breadboarding wire (solid core)
- 2 x 4 pin headers

The items used for the GPIO keypad input are as follows:

- Breadboard: half-sized or larger (**Pimoroni**)
- 7x Dupont Female to Male Patch Wires (**Pimoroni** Jumper Jerky)
- 6x push buttons
- 6x 470-ohm resistors
- Alternatively a self-solder DPad Kit (**Pi Hardware**)

The items used for multiplexed color LEDs are as follows:

- 5x Common-Cathode RGB LEDs
- 3x 470-ohm resistors

- ▸ Vero-prototype board or large breadboard (**Tandy**)
- ▸ A self-solder RGB-LED kit (**Pi Hardware**)

Chapter 7

This chapter uses the following hardware:

- ▸ A PCF8591 chip or module (**DealExtreme** SKU: 150190 or **Quick2Wire** I2C Analogue Board Kit)
- ▸ Adafruit I2C Bidirectional logic-level translator (**Adafruit** ID: 757)

Chapter 8

This chapter uses the Raspberry Pi camera module; it is available from most makers, hobbyists, and Raspberry Pi specialists.

Chapter 9

Pi-Rover requires the following hardware or similar:

- ▸ A giant paper clip (76 mm / 3 inches) or caster wheel
- ▸ Motor and geared wheels (**ModMyPi** or **PiBorg**)
- ▸ Battery / power source
- ▸ Chassis: push nightlight
- ▸ Motor driver/controller: Darlington Array Module ULN2003 (**DealExtreme** SKU – 153945)
- ▸ Small cable ties or wire ties

The following list is also mentioned in the *There's more...* section:

- ▸ PicoBorg Motor Controller (**PiBorg** PicoBorg)
- ▸ Magician Robot Chassis (**Sparkfun** ID: 10825)
- ▸ 4-Motor Smart Car Chassis (**DealExtreme** SKU: 151803)
- ▸ 2-Wheel Smart Car Model (**DealExtreme** SKU: 151803)

The advanced motor control example uses the following item:

- ▸ The H-Bridge motor controller (**DealExtreme** SKU: 120542 or **GeekOnFire** SKU: A2011100407).

The Hex Pod Pi-Bug requires the following hardware or similar:

- Adafruit I2C 16-Channel 12-bit PWM/Servo Driver (**Adafruit** ID: 815)
- MG90S 9g Metal Gear Servos (**HobbyKing**)
- Giant paper clips x 3 (76mm/3inch)
- Light gauge wire/cable ties
- A small section of plywood or a fiberboard

The following hardware is used in the remaining sections to expand the available inputs/outputs, avoid obstacles, and determine the direction of the robot:

- MCP23017 I/O Expander (**Ciseco** SKU: K002)
- Micro switches
- HC-SR04 Ultrasonic sensor (**DealExtreme** SKU: 133696)
- The ultrasonic sensor uses a 2K ohm resistor and a 3K ohm resistor
- XLoBorg: MAG3110 Compass Module (**PiBorg** XLoBorg)
- Optionally x4 Female to Male Dupont wires can be used to connect with the XLoBorg (**Pimoroni** Jumper Jerky)

Chapter 10

This chapter uses the following hardware:

- Remote Controlled Mains Sockets (**Maplin/Amazon**)
- Relay Modules (**Banggood** 8-Way SKU075676)
- The alternative is to use the 433Mhz RF Transmitter/Receiver (**Banggood** SKU075671)
- LED 8x8 SPI Matrix Module MAX7219 (**Banggood** Self-solder kit SKU072955)
- RS-232 to USB Cable (**Amazon/general computer supplies**)
- RS-232 Null-Modem Cable/Adaptor (**Amazon/general computer supplies**)
- RS-232 TTL USB Console Cable (**Adafruit** ID: 70)
- HC-05 Bluetooth Master/Slave Module with PCB Backplate (**Banggood** SKU078642)
- USB Tenx Technology SAM Missile Launcher
- OWI Robotic Arm with USB Interface (**Maplin/Amazon**)

Software list

The book uses a range of software packages to extend the capabilities of the preinstalled software.

PC software utilities

In most cases, the latest version of the software available should be used (versions are listed just in case there is a compatibility issue in a later release). The list of software used is as follows:

▸ Notepad ++: `www.notepad-plus-plus.org` (Version 6.5.3)

▸ PuTTY: `www.putty.org` (Version 0.62)

▸ VNC Viewer: `www.realvnc.com` (Version 5.0.6)

▸ Xming: `www.straightrunning.com/XmingNotes` (Version 6.9.0.31 Public Domain Release)

▸ SD Formatter: `www.sdcard.org/downloads/formatter_4` (Version 4.0)

▸ RealTerm: `realterm.sourceforge.net` (Version 2.0.0.70)

Raspberry Pi packages

This section lists each of the packages used in the chapters in the book in the following format (versions are listed just in case there is a compatibility issue in a later release):

▸ Package name (version) `Supporting website`
`Install command`

Chapter 1

▸ This chapter describes the hardware setup, and so no additional packages are installed (except specific hardware drivers where necessary).

Chapter 2

▸ Tkinter (Version 3.2.3-1): `https://wiki.python.org/moin/TkInter`
`sudo apt-get install python3-tk`

Chapter 3

▸ Tkinter (Version 3.2.3-1): `https://wiki.python.org/moin/TkInter`
`sudo apt-get install python3-tk`

- pip-3.2 (Version 1.1-3): `http://www.pip-installer.org/en/latest`
  ```
  sudo apt-get install python3-pip
  ```

- libjpeg-dev (Version 8d-1): `http://libjpeg.sourceforge.net`
  ```
  sudo apt-get install libjpeg-dev
  ```

- Pillow (Version 2.1.0): `http://pillow.readthedocs.org/en/latest`
  ```
  sudo pip-3.2 install pillow
  ```

Chapter 4

- Tkinter (Version 3.2.3-1): `https://wiki.python.org/moin/TkInter`
  ```
  sudo apt-get install python3-tk
  ```

Chapter 5

- pip-3.2 (Version 1.1-3): `http://www.pip-installer.org/en/latest`
  ```
  sudo apt-get install python3-pip
  ```

- Pi3D (Version 1.5): `http://pi3d.github.io`
  ```
  sudo pip-3.2 install pi3d
  ```

Chapter 6

- RPi.GPIO is usually pre-installed on Raspbian (Version 0.5.4-1): `http://sourceforge.net/p/raspberry-gpio-python/wiki/BasicUsage`
  ```
  sudo apt-get install python3-rpi.gpio
  ```

- flite (Version 1.4-release-6): `http://www.festvox.org/flite`
  ```
  sudo apt-get install flite
  ```

- uInput (Version 0.10.1): `http://tjjr.fi/sw/python-uinput`
  Installation instructions are provided in *Chapter 6, Using Python to Drive Hardware*

- Fuze: `http://raspi.tv/2012/how-to-install-fuse-zx-spectrum-emulator-on-raspberry-pi`

Chapter 7

- i2c-tools (Version 3.1.0-2): `http://www.lm-sensors.org/wiki/I2CTools`
  ```
  sudo apt-get install i2c-tools
  ```

- pip-3.2 (Version 1.1-3): `http://www.pip-installer.org/en/latest`
  ```
  sudo apt-get install python3-pip
  ```

- python3-dev (Version 3.2.3-6): header files and static library for Python required for some software

```
sudo apt-get install python3-dev
```

- wiringpi2 (Version 1.0.10): http://wiringpi.com

```
sudo pip-3.2 install wiringpi2
```

Chapter 8

- picamera (Version 1.0-1): http://picamera.readthedocs.org/en/latest

```
sudo apt-get install python3-picamera
```

- flite (Version 1.4-release-6): http://www.festvox.org/flite

```
sudo apt-get install flite
```

- zbarcam and zbarimg (Version 0.10): http://zbar.sourceforge.net

```
sudo apt-get install zbar-tools
```

- pyqrcode (Version 0.10.1): http://pythonhosted.org/PyQRCode

```
pip-3.2 install pyqrcode
```

Chapter 9

- wiringpi2 (Version 1.0.10): http://wiringpi.com

```
sudo pip-3.2 install wiringpi2
```

Chapter 10

- RPi.GPIO is usually preinstalled on Raspbian (Version 0.5.4-1): http://sourceforge.net/p/raspberry-gpio-python/wiki/BasicUsage

```
sudo apt-get install python3-rpi.gpio
```

- Tkinter (Version 3.2.3-1): https://wiki.python.org/moin/TkInter

```
sudo apt-get install python3-tk
```

- wiringpi2 (Version 1.0.10): http://wiringpi.com

```
sudo pip-3.2 install wiringpi2
```

- minicom (Version 2.6.1-1): http://linux.die.net/man/1/minicom

```
sudo apt-get install minicom
```

- pyserial (Version 2.7): http://pyserial.sourceforge.net

```
sudo pip-3.2 install pyserial
```

- pyusb (Version 1.0.0b1): https://github.com/walac/pyusb

```
sudo pip-3.2 install pyusb
```

There's more...

The majority of the Raspberry Pi software packages used in the book have been installed and configured using `Apt-get` and `Pip`. Useful commands have been given for each in the following sections.

APT commands

Useful commands for APT (this is preinstalled by default on Raspbian) are listed as follows:

- ▶ Always update the package list to obtain the latest versions and programs before installing a package with the command `sudo apt-get update`
- ▶ Find software by searching for any packages that include the `<searchtext>` command in the package name or description using `sudo apt-cache search <seachtext>`
- ▶ Install software with a particular `<packagename>` using `sudo apt-get install <packagename>`
- ▶ Uninstall a particular software package using `sudo apt-get remove <packagename>`
- ▶ Display the currently installed version of a software package using `sudo apt-cache showpkg <packagename>`
- ▶ If you want to install a specific version of a software package, use `sudo apt-get install <package name>=<version>`

Details of additional commands are listed by running `sudo apt-get` and `sudo apt-cache`. Alternatively, they are listed by reading the manual pages using the `man` command, the `man apt-get` command, and the `man apt-cache` command.

Pip Python package manager commands

Useful commands for Pip (this is not usually preinstalled on Raspbian) are listed as follows:

- ▶ To install Pip or Python 3, use the command `sudo apt-get install python3-pip`
- ▶ Install a required package using `sudo pip-3.2 install <packagename>`
- ▶ Uninstall a particular package using `sudo pip-3.2 uninstall <packagename>`
- ▶ To find out the version of an installed package, use `pip-3.2 freeze | grep <packagename>`
- ▶ Install a specific package version using `sudo pip-3.2 install <packagename>==<version>`

For example, to check the version of Pi3D installed on your system, use `pip-3.2 freeze | grep pi3d`.

To replace the installed version of Pi3D with Version 1.6a, use `sudo pip-3.2 uninstall pi3d` and `sudo pip-3.2 install pi3d==1.6a`.

Index

Thank you for buying
Raspberry Pi Cookbook for Python Programmers

About Packt Publishing

Packt, pronounced 'packed', published its first book "*Mastering phpMyAdmin for Effective MySQL Management*" in April 2004 and subsequently continued to specialize in publishing highly focused books on specific technologies and solutions.

Our books and publications share the experiences of your fellow IT professionals in adapting and customizing today's systems, applications, and frameworks. Our solution based books give you the knowledge and power to customize the software and technologies you're using to get the job done. Packt books are more specific and less general than the IT books you have seen in the past. Our unique business model allows us to bring you more focused information, giving you more of what you need to know, and less of what you don't.

Packt is a modern, yet unique publishing company, which focuses on producing quality, cutting-edge books for communities of developers, administrators, and newbies alike. For more information, please visit our website: www.packtpub.com.

Writing for Packt

We welcome all inquiries from people who are interested in authoring. Book proposals should be sent to author@packtpub.com. If your book idea is still at an early stage and you would like to discuss it first before writing a formal book proposal, contact us; one of our commissioning editors will get in touch with you.

We're not just looking for published authors; if you have strong technical skills but no writing experience, our experienced editors can help you develop a writing career, or simply get some additional reward for your expertise.

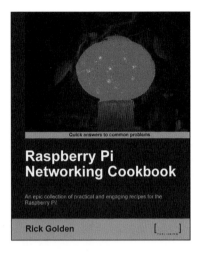

Raspberry Pi Networking Cookbook

ISBN: 978-1-84969-460-5   Paperback: 204 pages

An epic collection of practical and engaging recipes for the Raspberry Pi!

1. Learn how to install, administer, and maintain your Raspberry Pi.

2. Create a network fileserver for sharing documents, music, and videos.

3. Host a web portal, collaboration wiki, or even your own wireless access point.

4. Connect to your desktop remotely, with minimum hassle.

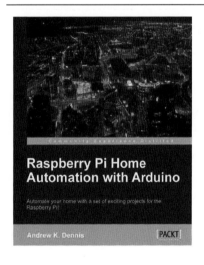

Raspberry Pi Home Automation with Arduino

ISBN: 978-1-84969-586-2   Paperback: 176 pages

Automate your home with a set of exciting projects for the Raspberry Pi!

1. Learn how to dynamically adjust your living environment with detailed step-by-step examples.

2. Discover how you can utilize the combined power of the Raspberry Pi and Arduino for your own projects.

3. Revolutionize the way you interact with your home on a daily basis.

Please check **www.PacktPub.com** for information on our titles

PUBLISHING

Instant Raspberry Pi Gaming

ISBN: 978-1-78328-323-1   Paperback: 60 pages

Your guide to gaming on the Raspberry Pi, from classic arcade games to modern 3D adventures

1. Learn something new in an Instant! A short, fast, focused guide delivering immediate results.

2. Play classic and modern video games on your new Raspberry Pi computer.

3. Learn how to use the Raspberry Pi app store.

4. Written in an easy-to-follow, step-by-step manner that will have you gaming in no time.

Raspberry Pi Super Cluster

ISBN: 978-1-78328-619-5   Paperback: 126 pages

Build your own parallel-computing cluster using Raspberry Pi in the comfort of your home

1. Learn about parallel computing by building your own system using Raspberry Pi.

2. Build a two-node parallel computing cluster.

3. Integrate Raspberry Pi with Hadoop to build your own super cluster.

Please check **www.PacktPub.com** for information on our titles